THE
WORDHO

THE
WORDHORD
Daily Life in Old English

Hana Videen

Princeton University Press
Princeton and Oxford

Published in the United States and Canada by Princeton University Press
41 William Street, Princeton, New Jersey 08540
press.princeton.edu

First edition published in Great Britain by Profile Books Ltd 2021.
Princeton University Press edition 2022
First Princeton University Press paperback edition 2023

All Rights Reserved
Paper ISBN 978-0-691-23718-3
Cloth ISBN 978-0-691-23274-4
ISBN (e-book) 978-0-691-23275-1
Library of Congress Control Number 2021948163

Text Design: Crow Books
Illustrations by Joanna Lisowiec

Cover illustration: Joanna Lisowiec
Cover design: Samantha Johnson

This book has been composed in Alegreya, Junicode, Historical and
GLC -1584 Rinceau Normal.

Printed in the United States of America

For Mum and Dad, who unlocked my first words,
and for *mīne mōdlufe* Ryan

CONTENTS

I

The Language You Thought You Knew

Ye Olde English?

WANDER DOWN A SMALL alley off London's Fleet Street and you'll find a pub with a crooked, creaky charm. Its black and white sign says 'Rebuilt 1667', the year after the Great Fire gutted England's largest city. Go inside for a pint in its wood-panelled dining room, where literary greats like Samuel Johnson, Charles Dickens and Mark Twain ate their fill. This may not be London's oldest pub, but it sure looks the part, with atmospheric vaulted cellars that supposedly date back to medieval times. And if you harbour any doubts concerning the pub's antiquity, its name sets you straight: 'Ye Olde Cheshire Cheese'.

It's nearly impossible to spend time in London without seeing a number of traditional 'ye olde' English pubs: 'Ye Olde Mitre', 'Ye Olde Watling' and the curiously named 'Ye Olde Cock Tavern' are just a few. It may seem that these places are real relics, or at least their names themselves are written in an ancient language – but they are not. 'Ye olde' is in fact a pseudo-archaic term; no one ever said 'ye olde' except in imitation of an imagined speech of the distant past.

But that's not to say it has no roots in the past. Once there was a letter called *thorn* that made a th sound. It looked like this: þ. Over the centuries, þ was written increasingly like the letter y with some scribes using them interchangeably. Early printers even substituted y for þ, so the word 'þe' (the) ended up looking like 'ye'. Eventually þ fell out of use, but people continued using 'ye' to abbreviate the word 'the' in print during the fifteenth and sixteenth centuries and in handwriting until the nineteenth century. English speakers' memory of the origin of 'ye' faded over time, until people began reading the word anew, pronouncing it wrong, and eventually creating the habit in English of saying 'ye' to sound old.

So if Old English is not 'ye olde' English, what is it and how far back must we go to find it? More than sixty years before the rebuilding of Ye Olde Cheshire Cheese, William Shakespeare wrote this monologue for his tragic hero Hamlet:

> Who calls me villain, breaks my pate across,
> Plucks off my beard and blows it in my face,
> Tweaks me by the nose, gives me the lie i' th' throat
> As deep as to the lungs? Who does me this?
> Hah, 'swounds, I should take it; for it cannot be
> But I am pigeon-liver'd and lack gall
> To make oppression bitter, or ere this
> I should 'a' fatted all the region kites
> With this slave's offal.

The phrasing and vocabulary are unfamiliar, but the English is not 'Old'. Hamlet's speech, written by Shakespeare around 1600, is in Early Modern English, the English used from the end of the Middle Ages in the late fifteenth century until the mid to late seventeenth century. The phrase 'gives me the lie in the throat as deep as to the lungs' sounds strange, although forcibly shoving unpleasant words down someone's throat is a familiar concept. We still use the words 'villain' and 'slave', but they are no longer common insults, and it's more likely you'll hear 'chicken-shit' or even 'lily-livered' rather than 'pigeon-livered'. People no longer curse with ''swounds', short for 'God's wounds' (although you may spot 'zounds' in a comic book), but in the sixteenth century using God's name in vain like this was considered particularly foul-mouthed. Other Shakespearean oaths included ''slid' (God's lid, i.e. eyelid) and 'God's bodykins' (God's dear body), the origin of the mild, antiquated oath 'odd's bodkins'.

Hamlet's monologue is unlike anything you'd hear in modern English today, but a fluent English speaker can probably get the gist of it. Much of the vocabulary can be found in a modern dictionary, even if some words are now used infrequently. Shakespeare employs unfamiliar syntax, or word order ('who does me this' rather than 'who does this to me'), but overall the passage makes sense grammatically, even to us today.

Compared to Shakespeare's Early Modern English, Geoffrey Chaucer's *Canterbury Tales* is significantly more difficult to read:

> Lordynges, herkneth, if yow leste.
> Ye woot youre foreward, and I it yow recorde.
> If even-song and morwe-song accorde,
> Lat se now who shal telle the firste tale.
> As evere mote I drynke wyn or ale,
> Whoso be rebel to my juggement
> Shal paye for al that by the wey is spent.
> Now draweth cut, er that we ferrer twynne;
> He which that hath the shorteste shal bigynne.

Written in the late 1380s to 1390s, over 200 years before *Hamlet*, Chaucer's writing has more strange spellings and unfamiliar words than Shakespeare's. But the grammar is familiar enough that you may understand the passage better just from reading it aloud. The publican Harry Bailly is speaking to his travelling companions, reminding them that the night before they had accepted his invitation to take part in a storytelling contest. Anyone who argues with him, warns Harry, must pay for all the wine and ale he consumes throughout their journey. He orders everyone to draw straws, and the person with the shortest will tell the first tale: 'he which that hath the shorteste shal bigynne'.

Chaucer's English may look ancient but it is not 'Old'. Chaucer wrote in Middle English, the English used from the first half of the twelfth century until sometime during the fifteenth. Some linguists suggest an end date of 1400–1450 based on fundamental changes in the pronunciation of vowels (the Great Vowel Shift). Others give a later end date, closer to 1500, by which time the impact of the printing press had really taken hold in England. The advent of printing in England was in 1476, when William Caxton set up his own press in London. Printing, as opposed to writing by hand, meant that far more books were available, with a much wider circulation, which in turn led to greater standardisation in spelling and pronunciation.

Some of the words that Chaucer uses, like 'juggement' and 'paye', may sound completely 'English', but they, along with many other French loanwords, had only entered the language relatively recently. The Normans defeated the English in the Battle of Hastings in 1066, and this Norman Conquest would add many new words to the English language. Throughout the late eleventh and early twelfth centuries, under the influence of the new French-speaking ruling class, English changed bit by bit until it became 'Middle English'. French introduced words like 'juggement' and 'paye', and shaped the way Chaucer and his contemporaries spoke and wrote; slowly, the words that they replaced were forgotten.

But these forgotten words, the language that the English would have spoken in the Battle of Hastings – this, finally, is Old English. 'Juggement' and 'paye' replaced words like **dōm** (judgement) and **gieldan** (pay, pronounced YE-ELL-dahn). These older words still persist in our current language, like ghosts from the past, in 'doom' and 'yield'. They are just two words among many that survived the Norman invasion, the Great Vowel Shift, the revolutions of grammar, and Shakespearean reinvention, to crop up in the language we speak today.

The oldest English

How much Old English is around to read today? In all texts that survive (not including duplicate manuscripts) there are only around 3.5 million Old English words, which, as the linguist David Crystal points out, is only 'the equivalent of about 30 medium-sized novels'. Most early medieval English manuscripts that survive were written primarily or completely in Latin. Only 200 manuscripts contain any Old English at all, the earliest dating from around 700 CE. Most surviving literature dates from after the reign of King Alfred (849–99), the period between 900 and 1100. King Alfred feared for the decline in learning in his kingdom following the Viking raids of the late eighth and ninth centuries. During the 870s he promoted education and rebuilt an intellectual community by inviting monks and scholars from abroad to bring their knowledge to his court. King Alfred encouraged literature to be translated into and recorded in Old English rather than Latin, since books written in the vernacular would be accessible to more readers.

The most famous Old English text, the poem *Beowulf*, was copied down around 1000 CE. Because most people couldn't read or write, stories were passed down orally for many years, so despite the date of the manuscript it was most likely composed centuries earlier. If other manuscripts containing the 3,182-line poem existed, they have not survived the test of time. The one extant copy was very nearly lost in the Ashburnham House library fire in 1731. Fortunately, the (slightly singed) manuscript was among those rescued and now resides in London's British Library – you can go see it for free in the Treasures Gallery, where it is usually on display.

The first lines of *Beowulf* are:

HƿÆT ƿE GARDE
na ingear dagum . þeod cyninga
þrym gefrunon huða æþelingas ellen
fremedon . . .

Unlike Shakespearean English, unlike even Chaucer's English, this text defies interpretation by a modern reader. Modern editions of the poem usually add capitalisation, punctuation and line breaks to make it easier to read:

Hwæt, we Gar-Dena   in geardagum,
þeodcyninga   þrym gefrunon,
hu ða æþelingas   ellen fremedon.

Still, it's not obvious how it should be read aloud, let alone what it means. Guesswork is hopeless. Even a rough pronunciation guide for these lines is unlikely to help:

HWAT way GAR-den-ah in YAY-ar-da-gum THAY-odd KUEN-ing-ga
THRUEM yeh-FROO-non HOO tha ATH-el-ing-gas EL-len FREM-eh-don

At least that might clarify the sound of some of the Old English letters that no longer appear in modern English: æ (ash), ð (eth) and þ (thorn). But it's obviously not enough. A word-for-word translation is:

So we Spear-Danes in days gone by great kings glory heard of how those noble men brave deeds performed.

It doesn't make much sense grammatically to us. But for those speaking it, word order wasn't essential. Unlike Middle and modern, Old English uses inflection (word endings) rather than syntax to indicate meaning. When we say 'the cat chased the dog' it means something different from 'the dog chased the cat', even though the spelling and form of the words are identical. The syntax (subject-verb-object) tells you who is chasing and who is being chased. In Old English (as in Latin) you have to look at the word endings (*-um*, *-a*, *-as*, etc.) to get the meaning. Armed with this knowledge, if we were to translate these lines using modern syntax, we'd get something like:

> So! We have heard about the glory of the Spear-Danes' great kings in
> days gone by, how those noble men performed brave deeds.

This not only makes sense, it has the stirring sound of an epic about to begin. Each time a translator tackles *Beowulf* they must balance how true they are to the text with how easily their translation is understood by modern readers, and on top of that every writer has their own literary style, their own unique voice. Reading a new translation of the poem can sometimes feel like reading a new poem.

It took us many steps to reach an understanding of these lines, and it would be the same with most other Old English texts, whether poems or land charters, sermons or medical remedies. Old English is the language you think you know until you actually hear or see it. It may as well be a foreign language to English speakers today and, as with any foreign language, we learn Old English with study, practice and ideally a good teacher.

This book is not like a language primer so much as an old photo album. Old English words are familiar but also strange, like seeing pictures of your parents as children. There's something recognisable in their smiles. But before digging into the more recent family history, let's skip back a few more generations.

From ᚠᚨᚦᚠᚱᚨ to *englisc*

What was spoken on the island that we now call Great Britain before the language that we now call Old English? The first peoples in Britain included the Picts, the Scoti and the Britons. Relatively little is known about the language of the Picts. The Scoti and Britons spoke languages from which Irish, Scots-Gaelic, Welsh, Cornish and Breton derive.

In 410 CE Emperor Honorius of Rome ordered the Britons to see to their own defences. The Roman military forces were pulling out to deal with conflicts closer to home, leaving the Britons to defend themselves or hire mercenaries from other parts of Europe to protect them. Settlement by immigrants from Northern Europe (Saxons, Angles, Frisians, Jutes) lasted for about a century. The settlers' homelands may have become less fertile due to flooding or over-farming. We don't know for sure why so many people decided to make the move, and scholars are divided on whether that settlement was peaceful or aggressive.

Regardless of why or how the settlers came to Britain, they brought with them their own distinct tongues. Because these peoples came from modern-day Netherlands, northern Germany and Denmark, the language of their descendants – Old English – may be easier to learn if you know modern Dutch, German or Danish. Because we lack written records from this time, it's impossible to say with certainty how similar or different the various Germanic tongues were. The newcomers made homes for themselves in all regions of Britain apart from the western and northern highlands, speaking languages that would eventually become the oldest of Englishes. The 'Old English period' is usually said to commence sometime around 550 CE, at the very beginning of the European Middle Ages.

The Old English period lasted for about six centuries; historians tend to give the year 1150 as its end date, although linguistic change is, of course, far more gradual. Old English changed slowly over that time, influenced by other languages. After the arrival of Christian missionaries from Rome in the late sixth century, Latin, the language of the Christian Church, was also spoken among the more learned. In the ninth century, with the arrival of Scandinavian raiders (Vikings) and settlers came yet another language, Old Norse. But Old Norse and Old English are modern names for those medieval languages. People in the ninth century didn't think their speech was 'Old'; it was simply *englisc* (ENG-glish).

The Roman missionaries also brought their alphabet to Britain, the writing system familiar to English speakers today. Before the arrival of the Latin or Roman alphabet people wrote in runes. Runic inscriptions appear on jewellery, tools and weapons in Northern Europe from as early as the second century CE. Most runic inscriptions in Britain are from the eighth and ninth centuries; the latest ones are thought to be from the late tenth or early eleventh century.

Why people continued using runes after the Roman alphabet came to town remains a bit of a mystery. Old English *rūn* actually means 'whisper', 'mystery', 'secret', or 'speech not meant to be overheard'. Because of the word's association with secrecy, some scholars think that runes must have originated as a script for magic spells. Other scholars believe that whatever they may have been used for later on, runes were created for more practical, ordinary purposes, administration and commerce rather than magic and religious rituals. The straight, angular lines of runes are certainly easier to carve on wood and stone than the curving letters of the Latin alphabet.

Children learning their ABCs are often taught to associate a word with each letter, a mnemonic device to recall the sound it makes ('a' is for apple, 'b' is for bear . . .). While you may grow up associating the letter 'a' with 'apple', 'a' has neither the pronunciation nor the meaning of 'apple'. 'A' is called 'ay', and 'ay' doesn't mean anything; it's only a sound. Runes, however, have names with meanings. The rune ᚫ is called *æsc* (pronounced ASH), and Old English *æsc* means 'ash tree'. Perhaps their dual purpose is why runes persisted for so many centuries. The letter 'w' only represents a sound in the Latin alphabet; the rune ᚹ (**wynn**) does that as well as communicating the concept of joy.

The following chart shows the runic alphabet of early medieval England: the transliteration for each rune (how it's written in the Latin alphabet), the sound it makes, its name in Old English and its meaning. The runes are composed of vertical and angled lines, designed to show up better against the horizontal grain of the wood. The first six runes of the alphabet are:

ᚠᚢᚦᚩᚱᚳ
fuþorc

We don't know what the runic alphabet was called in the early medieval period, but in the nineteenth century scholars gave it the name 'fuþorc' or 'futhark'. Similarly, we get 'alphabet' from combining the first two letters of the Greek alphabet: *alpha* α and *beta* β. Below are the runes, with question marks to indicate scholarly guesses.

Rune	Transliteration	Pronunciation	Name	Meaning(s)
ᚠ	f	**f**an / se**v**en	*feoh*	cattle, wealth
ᚢ	u	m**u**d / p**oo**l	*ūr*	aurochs?
ᚦ	þ, th	**th**in	*þorn*	thorn
ᚩ	o	**c**orn / **t**oe	*ōs*	mouth, god
ᚱ	r	**r**at	*rād*	journey, riding
ᚳ	c	**c**ave / **ch**ip	*cēn*	torch, flame
ᚷ	g	**g**ate / **y**ellow	*gyfu*	gift
ᚹ	w	**w**et	*wynn*	joy
ᚻ	h	**h**at	*hægl*	hail
ᚾ	n	**n**eck	*nȳd*	need, affliction
ᛁ	i	**p**in / s**ee**	*īs*	ice

Rune	Transliteration	Pronunciation	Name	Meaning(s)
ᛡ	j	**y**ellow	gēr	year, a year's harvest
ᛁ	ï	p**i**n? / s**ee**?	ēoh, īh	yew
ᛈ	p	**p**ot	peorð	?
ᛉ	x	ta**x**	eolhx	a kind of sedge grass
ᛋ	s	**s**et / depo**s**it	sigel	sun
ᛏ	t	**t**all	tīr	the god Týr, glory?
ᛒ	b	**b**ill	beorc	birch
ᛖ	e	b**e**d / s**ay**	eh	horse
ᛗ	m	**m**ilk	man	man, person
ᛚ	l	**l**ate	lagu	water, sea
ᛝ	ng	si**ng**	ing	the hero Ing
ᛟ	œ	s**ay**? / b**e**d? / c**or**n?	ēðel	homeland, estate
ᛞ	d	**d**og	dæg	day
ᚫ	a	c**a**r	āc	oak
ᚨ	æ	c**a**t	æsc	ash tree
ᚣ	y	T**ue**sday	ȳr	bow? horn?

Runes ᛡ and ᛠ are combinations of more than one vowel sound, something we don't have in the alphabet we use today. Old English also has letter combinations that are pronounced differently from what you might expect in modern English: 'sc' is usually pronounced like **sh**ip and 'cg' like bri**dg**e.

Although most surviving Old English texts are from the tenth century, 400 years or so after the introduction of Latin letters, runes still pop up now and again, and you'll come across them throughout this book. One place they appear is in a poem known as *Elene*. (Most Old English texts were untitled, so the titles we use today were invented by scholars long after the medieval period.) We do not know when *Elene* was originally composed, but the manuscript that contains it is from the latter half of the tenth century.

> . . . ᚳ . *drusende þeah he in medo healle maðmas þege*
> *æplede gold* . ᚣ . *gnornode* . ᚾ . *gefera, nearu sorge dreah enge*
> *rune þær him* . ᛖ . *fore milpaðas mæt modig þrægde wirum ge*
> *wlenced* . ᚹ . *is geswiðrad gomen æfter gearum geogoð is gecyrred*
> *ald onmedla* . ᚢ . *wæs geara geogoð hades glæm nu synt geardagas*
> *æfter fyrst mearce forð gewitene lif wynne geliden swa*
> . ᛚ . *toglideð flodas gefysde* . ᚠ . *æghwam bið læne under lyfte* . . .

This passage describes a man troubled by anxiety, like a torch or flame (ᚳ) that fails. The warrior's own horn (ᚣ) grieves for him, the companion in need (ᚾ), who travels the milestone-marked paths on his proud horse (ᛖ). The poet speaks more broadly about the nature of time: over the years, joy (ᚹ) diminishes and youth fades, a radiance that was once ours (ᚢ). (ᚢ *ūr* usually means 'ox' or 'aurochs', but as this doesn't fit the context, translators have interpreted the rune as *ūre*, 'ours'.) In a mood that is quintessentially Old English, the poet comments on the fleeting nature of life's joys, which depart the way the sea (ᛚ) withdraws;

wealth (ᚠ) is transient under the heavens. The interspersed runes represent actual words in the text of the poem: ᚳ is *cēn* (torch), ᚣ is *ȳr* (horn), and so on. But these eight runes also spell the name of the poet, Cynewulf: ᚳ ᚣ ᚾ ᛖ ᚹ ᚢ ᛚ ᚠ. This sort of runic 'signature' is highly unusual, and Cynewulf is one of only a handful of Old English poets whose name is known. Most Old English texts have no known author.

Manuscripts from the eleventh century onwards rarely include runes apart from ᚦ (*þorn*) and ᚹ (*wynn*), which continued to indicate th and w sounds long after their other meanings were forgotten. Today Renaissance fairs and London pubs still unwittingly retain ᚦ with their 'ye olde' signs, continuing to misinterpret the letter þ. It seems that letters, as well as words, the building blocks of language, are repurposed again and again.

Unlocking the *wordhord*

I have chosen the words in this book for many reasons. Some are familiar, some strange, and some so completely tied to early medieval life that they really can't be translated. Understanding a language is not just about knowing words and grammar: each language tells you something about the people who speak it, their culture, dreams and daily life, how they see the world and their place within it. Old English is no different. The Old English words I've collected for this book will give you a glimpse of life in early medieval England, and hopefully provide some insight into the language you use today. My interest in history comes first from an obsession with words, and this book's approach to the past is thus guided by words, not historical events or individual people.

English is constantly changing, taking in fresh words for contemporary concepts and forgetting words that have outlived their purpose. Every decade has new words for new concepts: 'feminist' (1850s), 'nine-to-five' (1900s), 'genome' (1920s), 'cybercrime' (1990s), 'selfie' (2000s). Each new invention is quickly followed by a new word to describe it: 'light bulb' (1884), 'television' (1900), 'smartphone' (1980). The June 2019 update to the *Oxford English Dictionary* included new entries like 'gamification', 'spit take', 'schmoozefest' and 'twattery', and noted five additional meanings of the word 'stupid'. Today's newly coined words reflect contemporary concerns.

Some words, like Old English **word** (word), have remained completely unchanged, perhaps showing how certain ideas and concepts endure. We have always needed a word for 'word'. While some words have persisted across centuries, others have slipped into obscurity. Archaic words like 'nithing' (coward, villain, outlaw) used to be commonplace but have become rarities. In Old English a **nīþing** is a villain, someone who commits a vile action. If you use the word 'nithing' today you will sound a bit like a time traveller, or at the very least old-fashioned. It's found in texts that describe or harken back to medieval times, whether in the form of fiction, history or epic verse. Obsolete words have been deemed no longer useful or acceptable for contemporary speech. Although Old English **friþ** (peace) appears in many different texts and compound words, modern English 'frith' (peace, protection, security) is obsolete.

Some Old English words are so strange that, even in translation, they seem to confirm that the past is a foreign country: the word **gafol-fisc** (tax-fish), for example. Other words may still resonate with us, even in their obsolescence, words like **ūht-cearu** (pre-dawn anxiety) or **ān-genga** (one who walks alone), perfect single words for the worries that keep you awake in the wee hours of the morning, or your introverted colleague who enjoys long, solitary walks.

One obsolete word that continues to resonate with me in this way is **wordhord**. A 'word-hoard' is exactly what it sounds like: a hoard or store of words. *Wordhord* appears only seven times in extant Old English literature, most often alongside the verb **on-lūcan** (to unlock). Christ, in the guise of a sailor, unlocks his *wordhord*:

> Again the Guardian of the way underlined his word-hoard (*wordhord onleac*). The man over the gangway spoke boldly.

The warrior Beowulf unlocks his *wordhord* when addressing King Hrothgar's watchman:

> The most senior answered him, the leader of the band, underlined his word-hoard (*wordhord onleac*).

Even the personification of Wisdom has a *wordhord* to unlock:

> Then Wisdom underlined her word-hoard (*wordhord onleac*) again, sang her own truths and spoke thus.

We know from our own language that a hoard's contents are always valuable, if not to everyone then certainly to the hoarder. Hoards are often associated with physical treasure (perhaps gold bullion hidden by pirates on a desert island or gemstones guarded by a fearsome dragon), but words are their own kind of treasure. And, like other kinds of treasures, these ones are revealed on special occasions, when the hoard is 'unlocked'. *Wordhord* brings to mind libraries big and small, notebooks full of scribbled pages, quotes underlined to be remembered later, and precious letters stored in boxes.

But what did *wordhord* mean in Old English? In the Middle Ages, poetry was shared primarily through speaking and singing rather than writing, and in songs instead of books. If you're reciting hundreds or even thousands of lines of poetry, you need to have a well-stocked 'hoard' of words to draw upon. A *wordhord* wasn't a physical object like a dictionary, or even a library, but a metaphor for the collection of words and phrases a poet memorised and drew upon for their craft.

This book is a *wordhord* of sorts, a hoard of words collected, treasured and shared. It was inspired by **hord-wynn** (hoard-joy), the joy that comes from hoarding. As I gathered words like gems, I realised that they weren't just funny, strange and beautiful, but that together they told a story about people's lives more than a millennium ago.

What can words tell us about those people? Words can tell us about the things people do every day, the things closest to their hearts. Words that have endured reveal what has remained significant over time. Forgotten words tell us about things now foreign to the modern world, ideas or concepts we've lost. Words reflect changes in society, showing how people view the world around them and make sense of the cosmos beyond them. The following chapters unlock a *wordhord* that explores all of these topics, taking you on a journey through Old English, from our basic needs to our loftiest pursuits. Language and our understanding of it affect the way we see our world. The secret histories of words, the stories behind words we read, write and speak every day, not only teach us about the past; they enrich our present.

This book will share the journeys of words through time, some of which have taken many twists and turns over the centuries. One such word is **hāl** (whole, hale, sound). In Old English, *hāl* appears in a common **grēting-word** (greeting-word, salutation), the phrase **wes hāl** (be well). *Hāl* is the root of modern words like hale, whole, wholesome, wholesale, holy, holiday, hallow, Halloween, healer and healthy. By the thirteenth century 'wæs hail' had narrowed semantically from a standard greeting to a greeting you make when offering someone an alcoholic beverage. Over time 'wesseyl' or 'wassail' took on the meaning of the drink itself, especially a hot, spiced alcohol served at Yuletide. By the 1600s 'wassailing' referred to the revelry and carousing during which one partook of the wassail. Today English speakers still sing 'Here we come a-wassailing' at Christmas without knowing what it once meant to *wes hāl*.

Though the phrase *wes hāl* is perfectly sound, it doesn't seem quite the right *grēting-word* to start our word journey. I choose instead a *grēting-word* that requires no translation because something like this word exists everywhere, a simple sound that demands your attention. That word is *ēalā* (pronounced AY-ah-la), not far off from 'oh!', 'hey!', 'eh!', or 'oi!'.

Ēalā, dear reader! Enter. The *wordhord* is unlocked.

First *wordhord*

(Old English spans several centuries, and there are variations to its pronunciation across this period, not to mention differences in dialect. My pronunciations thus reflect only one version of Old English. The pronunciations of each word are given in two styles: a simpler but slightly less precise one, and one that uses the International Phonetic Alphabet.)

ān-genga, noun (AHN-YENG-ga / ˈaːn-ˌjɛŋ-ga): Solitary walker, lone wanderer.

æsc, noun (ASH / ˈæʃ): Ash, ash tree; name of the Æ-rune ᚠ.

dōm, noun (DOAM / ˈdoːm): Judgement.

ēalā, interjection (AY-ah-la / ˈeːa-laː): Oh!

englisc, noun (ENG-glish / ˈɛŋ-glɪʃ): English, the English language.

friþ, noun (FRITH / ˈfrɪθ): Peace.

gafol-fisc, noun (GA-voll-FISH / ˈga-vɔl-ˌfɪʃ): Fish paid as tax or tribute.

gieldan, verb (YE-ELL-dahn / ˈjɪɛl-dan): To yield, pay.

grēting-word, noun (GRAY-ting-WORD / 'greː-tɪŋ-ˌwɔrd): Word of greeting, salutation.

hāl, adjective (HALL / 'haːl): Whole, hale, sound, safe, secure.

hord-wynn, noun (HORD-WUEN / 'hɔrd-ˌwyn): Delightful treasure (hoard-joy).

nīþing, noun (NEETH-ing / 'niːθ-ɪŋ): Villain, one who commits a vile action.

on-lūcan, verb (on-LOO-kahn / ɔn-'luː-kan): To unlock, open, disclose.

rūn, noun (ROON / 'ruːn): Mystery, secret; speech not meant to be overheard, a whisper.

ūht-cearu, noun (OO'HT-CHEH-ah-ruh / 'uːxt-ˌtʃɛa-rʌ): Care that comes in the early morning.

wes hāl, phrase (wess HALL / wɛs 'haːl): 'Be well' or 'be healthy' (a greeting).

word, noun (WORD / 'wɔrd): Word; saying, maxim; tale, story; report, tidings; command, order; message, announcement; promise, oath; speech, language.

wordhord, noun (WORD-HORD / 'wɔrd-ˌhɔrd): Hoard or trove of words (word-hoard).

wynn, noun (WUEN / 'wyn): Joy, delight; something that causes pleasure; name of the W-rune ᚹ.

2

Eating and Drinking

Sweeter than bee-bread

SOME OF THIS *wordhord*'s gems sparkle with familiarity and have remained much the same for a thousand years. Perhaps you can guess what kinds of foods *æg*, **butere** and **meolc** are. Other words are trickier until you know how they're pronounced, like **cȳse** (CHUE-zuh) and **hunig** (HUN-ih). We use the word 'bread' now instead of **hlāf**, but we still use *hlāf*'s descendant 'loaf'.

In early medieval England, the go-to meal for most people would have been *hlāf* and something to eat with it (*butere* perhaps, or a dense, crumbly *cȳse*). The *hlāf* would not resemble modern sandwich bread in any way, not even a crusty rustic loaf. Wheat was quite expensive; it didn't flourish in England's climate and could only be grown in the south. Most people satisfied their hunger with cheaper, hardier grains like rye, barley and oats, or legumes like peas. Even the people wealthy enough to afford wheat flour would probably have mixed it with rye to bulk it out. Rye and barley don't allow for as much rise as wheat, so the bread would have been flat and dense. Whatever rise the bread had would have been achieved with barm (yeast left over from brewing ale) or a sourdough starter (flour and water combined with wild yeast, from either the air or flour).

We take it for granted now, but access to an **ofen** (oven) was rare in early medieval England. Given how much it cost to build an *ofen* and supply it with fuel, a community like a monastery or a village might have one to share, but there certainly would not have been one in each house. Most people would have baked their *hlāf* on a bakestone (a flat stone over a fire or raised hearth) with an inverted pot on top, or on an iron griddle, or even in the embers of a dying cookfire. (Remember to dust the ashes off your bread before eating.) Baking flatbread on a griddle or bakestone would have been the norm in England from the fifth century to the thirteenth or fourteenth century, and even later in some regions. In the early centuries of the Old English period, most of the baking and cooking seems to have taken place in the same room as the sleeping and eating. The **heorþ** (hearth) was so central to a dwelling that the word could stand in metonymically for 'home' or 'household' (although the alliterative expression 'hearth and home' didn't appear until the nineteenth century).

A common word for the male head of a household was **hlāford**, derived from *hlāf* + **weard** (keeper, guardian), from which we get 'lord'. Like today's 'breadwinner', the bread-guardian ensured his followers had enough to eat. The female head of a household was the **hlǣfdige** (bread-maker, pronounced H'LAV-dih-yuh), from whose humble origins we get today's far more refined-sounding 'lady'. While bread-guardian and bread-maker have indelibly marked our language, the **hlāf-ǣta** (bread-eater) has left less of a trace – perhaps understandably, since they were a dependant, a lowly member of the household who relied on the *hlāford*'s provisions. If *hlāf* was the most common word for bread in Old English, then another was **cycel** (little cake, pronounced KUE-chell). We usually think of cakes as sugary desserts, but a 'cake' was originally a small, flat sort of bread, rounded in shape, usually hard on both sides from being turned part-way through baking. The *cycel* was so ubiquitous that from this word we get modern

English 'cook' and 'kitchen'. 'Bread' was present in Old English, but this ***brēad*** was of such importance that (at least linguistically) it sometimes stood in for 'food'.

Thanks to this broader definition, ***bēo-brēad*** (bee-*brēad*) is not the delicious honeyed loaf you might imagine, but a word meaning 'bee-food'. The *Bosworth-Toller Anglo-Saxon Dictionary* (1898) defines *bēo-brēad* as 'the pollen of flowers collected by bees and mixed with honey for the food of the larvæ'. *Bēo-brēad*, according to *Bosworth-Toller*, is 'quite distinct' from honeycomb or beeswax, with the caveat that sometimes it *could* be honeycomb due to someone's 'deficient knowledge of natural history'. Meanwhile, the University of Toronto's *Dictionary of Old English: A to I* (2018) says that *bēo-brēad* is 'honeycomb with honey'. Abbot Ælfric of Eynsham, a prolific English writer of the late tenth and early eleventh centuries, says in one of his homilies that *bēo-brēad* is honeycomb and beeswax together – although in this instance it feels more like pushing a metaphor. After his resurrection, says Ælfric, Christ consumed roasted fish and 'honey's bee-*brēad*' (*hunies beobread*): the roasted fish represents his suffering and the bee-*brēad* his sweet divinity:

> Bee-*brēad* (*beobread*) is of two things: wax (*weaxe*) and honey (*hunie*). Christ is of two substances: divinity with no beginning and humanity with a beginning. He became for us at his passion a roasted fish and at his resurrection bee-*brēad* of honey (*hunies beobread*).

This occurs in the Gospel of Luke, when Christ requests food after his resurrection. In the Old English translation of Luke, Christ's disciples offer him fish and *bēo-brēad*, but the original Latin is *favum mellis*, which is usually translated as 'honeycomb'.

An Old English psalm describes the word of God as *swetran ðonne hunig oððe beobread* (sweeter than honey or bee-*brēad*). *Bēo-brēad* could be honeycomb here, but the original Latin version of the psalm refers only to *mel* (honey). *Bēo-brēad* was added to *hunig* in the Old English translation. Is *bēo-brēad* simply another word for honey, or did the translator think the phrase 'honey or honeycomb' sounded better than 'honey' on its own?

Another theory is that *bēo-brēad* is the viscous, white, glandular secretion of worker bees that is a bee superfood. Immature larvae consume this highly nutritious substance for the first two or three days of their maturation, but only the queen bee gets to consume it throughout her entire life cycle. The substance has been called 'royal jelly' since the early nineteenth century, perhaps because it's food for the queen, and the main reason for the queen's longevity compared to other bees. While worker bees only live for a few weeks over the summer, queen bees can survive several years. Royal jelly is also consumed by humans around the world. Research has shown it has medicinal properties for humans as well as bees: antioxidant, anti-tumour, anti-inflammatory and anti-ageing. When Christ is offered royal jelly to eat, he is presented with the best of the food, not mere honey or honeycomb but *bēo-brēad*, a food valued for its healing properties as well as its sweetness.

Whether it is honeycomb or royal jelly or something else entirely, *bēo-brēad* appears in a remedy for **smēga-wyrm** in *Bald's Leechbook* (tenth century). A leechbook is an Old English medical text, often containing advice on diagnosis and treatment as well as recipes for herbal-, animal- and mineral-based medications. A literal translation of *smēga-wyrm* is 'burrowing worm', indicating how this particular parasite penetrates the skin and works its way into the body. The remedy instructs the patient to consume new cheese, wheat bread and *bēo-brēad* – simple enough as long as you know what *bēo-brēad* is. (The next step is, however, slightly more complex: burn a man's skull to ashes and then apply it topically using a pipe.)

Another food word that appears to relate to bees is **bēon-broþ**. Indeed, the word has been translated as 'bee-broth', possibly another name for **medu** (mead), an alcoholic drink made from fermented honey. To me, a reference to mead as 'bee-broth' seems far too poetic in a remedy for an inflamed liver. The remedy instructs the patient to take an emetic and then drink nothing but *bēon-broþ* for a week. It is possible that the leechbook is recommending an alcohol-only diet for a liver-sick patient, but it seems far more likely that *bēon-broþ* is really **bēan-broþ** (bean broth), a warming, protein-rich food that's easy to consume. **Brīw**, a pottage or thick paste made from grains, meal or beans, would have been a dietary staple, and the word appears most frequently in leechbooks. *Bēon-broþ* may be an alternative spelling that appears to turn a simple *brīw* into something boozier.

Although *hunig* was fermented to make *medu*, it was primarily used as a food sweetener. Sugar was not an option; there is not even a word for 'sugar' in Old English because it was virtually unknown in Western Europe. Sugar was occasionally used medicinally in parts of Europe, but it does not appear in any English medical texts of the time. The word 'sugar' did not enter English until the thirteenth century, via French from Arabic *sukkar*. While stereotypical depictions of medieval peasants often have blackened, rotten teeth, archaeological evidence shows tooth decay to be far less of a problem than in later centuries, probably due to the lack of sugar.

Undern-food and morning-drink

Most people in England in the early medieval period were peasants, growing what they needed to eat and eating most of what they grew. If you were rich you might be able to import spices and consume greater quantities of meat, the main meats being chicken and pork. The word 'chicken' hasn't changed much from Old English *cicen* (CHIH-chen); both words can refer to either the animal or the meat. 'Pork', however, didn't enter English until later (Middle English 'pork', 'porke' or 'porc'), with the influence of French. Old English *swīn* (pig, swine) refers to the animal as well as the meat, but with the influence of the Normans came words like 'pork' and 'beef' that were used to indicate the meat specifically. When the animal was still on the farm it had a humble English name, but once it got to the table French provided a loftier label.

While modern English 'meat' does come from the Old English word *mete*, the latter would have included beans, bread, cheese, fruit, or really any kind of food. In Middle English 'mete' still referred generally to food or a meal, but it was used in compounds to indicate specific types of foods: 'flesh-mete' (meat), 'whit-mete' (dairy products, like milk, cheese, butter and eggs), 'est-mete' (delicacies or 'dainty' food), and so on. Around 1300 'mete' alone sometimes meant animal flesh, and by the Early Modern period Shakespeare was using 'meat' in both the general and specific senses. In *Coriolanus* 'the grace 'fore meat' is the prayer before a meal, but in *The Comedy of Errors* Dromio of Syracusa says the meat wants basting, expressing concern that it will make Antipholus choleric. (It was once believed that dry, overdone meat would cause an excess of the humour called choler, which made people hot-tempered.) The original definition of 'meat' as simply food is now considered archaic, though you can still find it in places like *Lallans*, the journal of the Scots Language Society whose mission is 'tae forder an uphaud the Scots leid'. Food-'meat' took a litigious turn in 2019, when Missouri law actually censored the more general 'meat' definition, threatening with criminal sanctions those companies who sold vegan, plant-based meat substitutes as 'meat'.

'Meat' is an example of semantic narrowing, the process of a word acquiring a less general, more specialised meaning over time. Most languages undergo semantic narrowing, usually because a particular definition for a word begins to be used more frequently than others. In the case of 'meat', people must have used the word specifically for animal flesh more and more frequently until a point in time when 'meat' sounded strange when used for any other sense. So although the word **morgen-mete** (**morgen** 'morning' + *mete*), or 'morning-meat', looks like bacon and sausages, a more accurate translation is 'morning-food', or what we'd call 'breakfast'.

Bacon in Old English is not *morgen-mete* but **spic** (SPITCH), a word related to 'speck', a prosciutto-like meat from northern Italy. The earliest citation of this Italian speck in English is relatively recent (1981), but 'speck' entered the English vocabulary via Dutch as early as 1633. Over the centuries it has always had the definition of 'fatty meat': mostly pork but sometimes whale or even hippopotamus bacon. Old English *spic* fell out of use during the later Middle Ages, replaced by Middle English 'lard' and 'bacoun'. While today a larder is a cupboard or room for storing food in general, it was once intended specifically for meat storage.

The intriguing compound **offrung-spic** (offering-bacon or sacrifice-bacon) is an example of a hapax legomenon (or just hapax), a word that appears only once in extant literature. The one occurrence of *offrung-spic* is in an Old English translation of the Second Book of Maccabees, in which King Antiochus of Greece takes pleasure in persecuting his Jewish subjects, trying to force them to renounce their faith. Jewish faith forbids the faithful from eating pork, so mandatory bacon consumption was apparently a favourite method of torture. The fact that this pork is intended as a sacrificial offering to pagan idols makes the torture that much worse for the faithful. Eleazar, an elderly Jewish teacher of law, refuses to eat (or even pretend to eat) the king's pork, especially not *offrung-spic*, and is flogged to death for his steadfast faith and resolve. Afterwards, the old teacher is celebrated by the Jews as a holy man and martyr. In any case, *offrung-spic* is clearly an undesirable option for *morgen-mete*.

Another 'breakfast' word is **undern-mete** (*undern*-food). Like *morgen*, **undern** is morning, and according to *Bosworth-Toller* it is specifically nine o'clock in the morning. Nine o'clock seems rather late for breakfast. Did it really take hard-working peasants that long to get out of bed in the morning? Probably not. We have limited information about how lay people lived in early medieval England but, given the amount of work to be done each day, they would have wanted to get an early start, as soon as there was enough light to see by. There is more information about how people of religious vocations lived, the monks and nuns, since rules were written to guide them in the use of their time. Monks were expected to get up in the wee hours of the morning (two or three o'clock) for prayers. They might have a bit more sleep after that, but there were more prayers at first light. As a monk or nun you could expect one or two meals a day, depending on the time of year. In the summer you might have dinner, the main meal, shortly after midday and a second, smaller meal after evening prayers. During the winter, fewer hours of daylight gave you less time to do all your work, so you could expect a single meal served a bit later in the afternoon and perhaps a light snack or glass of wine before bedtime.

Clearly, breakfast was not a full-English, eggs-and-sausage affair at this point in history, so why is there an Old English word for a 9 a.m. meal? *Undern-mete*, in fact, occurs in only a handful of places – it's certainly not common. The places where the word appears are not necessarily in the context of early medieval England. One such occurrence is in *Orosius*, the earliest world history in English, written *c*.900 and based on an earlier history in Latin. *Orosius* describes the famous Battle of Thermopylae in 480 BCE, when King Leonidas of Sparta tried to stop the invasion of Greece by King Xerxes of Persia. The tension mounts on the morning of the battle, when King Leonidas bids his officers, 'Let us now enjoy this breakfast (*undern-mete*) as we should if we are to end up in hell for supper!' Here *undern-mete* is used in retelling a story from a distant time and place. Neither does the word reflect the reality of life in medieval England when it's used to retell scripture. In the Bible, Old English *undern-mete* is used to translate Latin *prandium* (dinner, the main meal of the day). In a parable from the Gospel of Matthew, a king invites all his friends to his son's wedding feast but soon discovers that everyone has better things to do. 'I have prepared my breakfast!' the king proclaims, or in Old English, *undern-mete min geiarwad! Undern-mete* also appears in the Book of Daniel in a reference to Habakkuk, a man whom an angel carried to Babylon by his hair so that he could give a proper meal to Daniel in the lions' den. (Never face lions on an empty stomach.) In the Latin Vulgate Bible the word *prandium* (dinner) is used, but the Old English translation says, 'Habakkuk could in one moment go so far and carry with him his breakfast (*undern-mete*)'.

The truth is that time was far less exact than a dictionary definition of 'nine in the morning' implies. The word 'hour' didn't appear in English until the thirteenth century (Middle English 'ure'). Common time words in Old English include **tīd** (from which we get 'Yuletide' and 'Shrovetide') and **stund**. Although *tīd* and *stund* are usually translated as 'time' or 'hour', they really refer to a time *when a thing happens* (time for dinner, time for bed), not an exact time of day (five o'clock, two forty-five). For most people, knowing approximately when the sun would rise and set would have been sufficient.

There was more of a need for precision in the monastery, since monks had to pray at regular intervals throughout the day. The monastic hours were governed by sunlight and darkness: matins (or lauds) was at dawn, prime at sunrise, sext at midday, vespers at sunset and compline when complete darkness finally arrived. Terce (between prime and sext) and none (between sext and vespers) were based on the schedule for the changing of the guard in ancient Rome. The Latin names for the monastic hours endured, and an evening prayer service in the Catholic Church is still called vespers.

Terce was the third hour of the day, which is how *Bosworth-Toller* defines *undern*, an hour roughly halfway between prime (sunrise) and sext (midday). If the sun rises at six, reaching its zenith at twelve noon, terce (or *undern*) would be approximately nine in the morning. But because the sun rises and sets at different times throughout the year, terce and *undern* could not be as specific as 'nine in the morning'. A more accurate translation of *undern* is thus 'between sunrise and midday' or simply 'morning'.

Etymologically, *undern* has to do with an 'interim', 'inner time', or 'in-between time'. During the early medieval period this interim was between sunrise and midday, but that changed over time, gradually shifting to later in the day. An eleventh-century guidebook for priests instructs that if you're fasting, do not be 'he who fasts and saves his *undern-mete* until evening', deceitfully 'giving up' food that you intend to eat later. Here *undern-mete* may simply refer to the earlier meal of the day, which would have been midday dinner. By the fourteenth century, Middle English 'undern' referred to midday (between sunrise and sunset), while in the fifteenth century it could be afternoon (between midday and sunset) or even evening (between sunset and complete darkness). In the nineteenth century, modern English 'undern' wasn't even a time but the *meal* consumed at that time. Over the course of a millennium, 'undern' went from meaning 'morning' to 'afternoon snack'.

While *undern* survived (albeit as a changing entity) for centuries, the word **morgen-drenc** did not. *Morgen-drenc* (morning-drink) appears only a couple times in Old English in leechbooks. With only a few contexts from which to infer a definition, *morgen-drenc* is tricky to define. It appears to be a drink consumed in the morning with special (perhaps even magical) healing properties. To me this is an excellent description of coffee, but England didn't get its first coffee-house until 1651, so the scribe must have had something else in mind.

According to a leechbook called the *Lacnunga* (or *Recipes*), a king named Arestolobius, who was particularly knowledgeable in medicine, could make a *godne morgendrænc*, or 'good morning-drink'. His drink could cure almost anything: headache, giddiness, brain fever, lung disease, jaundice, tinnitus, unhealthy faecal discharge, not to mention 'every temptation of the Devil'. To make a good *morgen-drenc*, the *Lacnunga* says, you must combine a variety of plants (dill, mint, celandine, betony, sage, wormwood, etc.) and spices (such as cumin and ginger) in a cup of cold wine. Puzzlingly, although the remedy is called a morning-drink, the *Lacnunga* specifies that the patient should consume it at night. Is it a morning-drink because it has the greatest effect the morning after taking it? Are you meant to brew it in the morning? Unfortunately, as is the case with many rare and short-lived words, we can only guess.

Skinking cow-warm milk

In early medieval England cattle were essential to maintaining a good food supply. Not only did they provide milk and meat, they performed essential physical labour. Fields could be ploughed faster with cattle, enabling farmers to grow crops on a larger scale. Cattle were so important to the economy that linguistically they were equated with riches. The primary definition of *feoh* (the F-rune ᚠ, pronounced FEH-oh), is 'cattle', but *feoh* also means 'money' or 'wealth'.

Feoh, the first rune in futhark, appears in *The Rune Poem*, a sort of Old English alphabet song:

> ᚠ *byþ frofur   fira gehwylcum.*
> *Feoh* is a comfort to all men.

Either 'cattle' or 'wealth' suits this context. Today the word 'wealth' might conjure up thoughts of big houses and fancy cars rather than cows, but the word 'fee' (which only dropped its bovine connotations sometime in the sixteenth century) still bears the comforting promise of money.

The resemblance of Old English *cū* (cow) to Scots 'coo' is no coincidence. The kingdom of Northumbria, which lay partly in south-eastern Scotland, spoke Old English. This was pretty much the only English-speaking area of Scotland until the thirteenth century; the rest of the land spoke Gaelic. By the end of the Middle Ages, the Middle English of Northumbria had diverged significantly from that in the southern part of the kingdom, becoming what we now call Early Scots. Some Old English words that changed in modern English have remained much the same in modern Scots.

Old English has a wealth (or *feoh*) of cow-related words, ranging from anatomy – *cū-ēage* (cow's eye), *cū-horn* (cow's horn), *cū-tægel* (cow's tail) – to useful by-products – *cū-meoluc* (cow's milk), *cūe mesa* (cow's dung), *cū-micge* (cow's urine, used in medical remedies). A *cū-cealf* (calf) lives in a *cū-bȳre* (cowshed), watched over by a *cū-hyrde* (cowherd). From *cū-meoluc* you can make *cū-butere* (cow's butter), or you can drink it straight after milking when it's still *cū-wearm* (cow-warm).

How warm is 'cow-warm' milk? Milk comes out of a cow at around 38.3°C (101°F), a temperature that a medieval farmer would neither know nor need to know. Do you know the temperature of milk straight from the fridge? It should be no more than 5°C (41°F), just cold enough to slow the growth of psychotropic bacteria. You don't need to measure the temperature of the milk you're drinking to know whether it came straight from the fridge or if it has been sitting out for a while. You know this instinctually from years of drinking 'fridge-cold' milk. Similarly, with years of experience drinking 'cow-warm' milk, you would probably be able to tell if the milk was warm enough to be straight from the udder.

The phrase 'cow-warm milk' sounds rather poetic, evoking green pastures and industrious milkmaids, but *cū-wearm* appears only in prosaic, practical contexts like this medical remedy:

> *Gehæt scenc fulne <u>cuwearmre</u> meolce.*
> Heat a cupful of <u>cow-warm</u> milk.

The words for 'heat' (*gehæt*), 'full' (*fulne*), 'cow-warm' (*cuwearmre*) and 'milk' (*meolce*) look or at least sound vaguely familiar, but what about *scenc* (pronounced SHENCH)? The verb **scencan** means 'to pour out liquor for drinking' or 'to give to drink', actions for which a **scenc** (cup) is required. The Middle English verb 'shench' or 'shenk' survived into the fifteenth century and is related to the now obsolete Scots word 'skink', which also means 'to pour out liquor for drinking'. Though unfamiliar to most English speakers, the word still pops up in contemporary Scottish literature. Don Paterson, born in Dundee, refers to someone who 'skinks' rum into cups for drinking in his poem 'Nil Nil' (1993).

Whether you prefer milk *cū-wearm* or fridge-cold, you can skink it into a *scenc*, thinking of a time when wealth was measured in cows.

Having a bite

Someone who is 'going for a bite' generally does not wish to be gnawed upon by a hungry or overly aggressive dog. They merely want a snack. However, when Middle English 'snack' made its first appearance around 1400, its primary definition was 'a snap, a bite, especially that of a dog'. Around 350 years later, 'snack' finally acquired the definition 'a mere bite or morsel of food', as opposed to a regular-sized meal.

In Old English a bite or morsel of food is a ***snǣd***. ***Sin-snǣd***, like *offrung-spic*, is a hapax, and the fact that there is only one context from which to infer its meaning makes it especially difficult to translate. *Sin-snǣd*'s one occurrence is in the poem *Beowulf*, when the frightening creature called Grendel murders a sleeping warrior in King Hrothgar's mead-hall:

> He tore eagerly, bit the body, drank streams of blood, swallowed *synsnædum*.

The prefix ***sin-*** (or *syn-*) has two potential meanings – 'everlasting' or 'big' – so is a *sin-snǣd* an 'ever-morsel' or a 'big-bite'? A 'big bite' could last a long time, theoretically, so perhaps a *sin-snǣd* could also be an 'ever-morsel'. But the one occurrence of *sin-snǣd* in Old English is in no way an 'everlasting' bite. Grendel devours his victim in no time at all, chomping off huge morsels of human flesh – definitely 'big bites', certainly *not* 'ever-morsels'.

Cheese week?

Moving on from man-flesh, a much tastier *snǣd* to swallow is *cȳse* (cheese), and what better time for it than ***cȳswuce***? If *cȳse* is cheese and **wuce** is week, then the meaning of *cȳswuce* (pronounced CHUEZ-WUCH-uh) must be obvious.

In Old English religious texts, the word *cȳswuce*, which looks a lot like 'cheese week', refers to the week following the last Sunday before Lent, a forty-day period of fasting for Christians. The first day of Lent, Ash Wednesday, changes its date each year but falls sometime in February or March. On this day of penitence, the faithful receive ashes on their foreheads. It has been suggested that 'cheese week' would have been the last week that cheese was allowed before Lent – a somewhat random specification given that cheese was just one among many foods to be avoided. The day before Ash Wednesday is Shrove Tuesday, also known today as Pancake Day or Mardi Gras (Fat Tuesday). Shrove Tuesday is the last chance for Christians to use up the fatty foods in their pantries before their forty-day fast. So is *cȳswuce* a week specially designated as the time to eat all your cheese? After all, in Slavic countries there is the Orthodox Christian tradition of Maslenitsa, or Cheesefare Week. During Maslenitsa, the last week before Lent, meat is forbidden, but cheese, milk, eggs and other dairy products are still allowed.

But there are a few problems with *cȳswuce* meaning 'cheese week'. It is true that medieval Christians were permitted to consume cheese on the Monday and Tuesday before Lent, but according to an Old English sermon, *cȳswuce* is actually the first four days of Lent, beginning on Ash Wednesday. Why would these four days be called 'cheese week' if it's when Christians *weren't* allowed to eat cheese?

It helps if we know that the first four days of Lent (Wednesday through Saturday) were known in Middle English as 'clensing daies' (cleansing days). They were a time for Christians to cleanse and purify themselves for the holy fast. What if, instead of *cȳse* 'cheese' + *wuce* 'week', *cȳswuce* were **cīs** + *wuce*? Old English *cīs* (pronounced CHEES) is an adjective meaning 'fastidious' or 'choosy in one's diet', so rather than a time for cheese consumption, *cȳswuce* would be a time for fastidious eating, fasting and purification. As there was no dictionary or standardised system of spelling words in medieval England, people tended to spell them however they pronounced them. You might spell a word differently due to your local dialect, so *cȳswuce* isn't necessarily an error. Of course, there's still the problem of a four-day 'week', but 'choosy week' makes a lot more sense than 'cheese week'. And really, if cheese had been limited to only four days of the year, that would have been a sorry situation indeed.

Trial by bite

Cheese may not have a place in a Lenten homily or sermon, but it does belong in a code of law. How do you tell whether someone is telling the truth? With a *snǣd* of bread and cheese, of course!

Cor-snǣd is one of four ordeals referred to in Old English law books to determine an accused person's guilt or innocence. The noun **ge-cor** means 'choice' or 'decision', so a literal translation of *cor-snǣd* is 'decision-bite'. To be cleared of a crime, you needed family or friends who would vouch for you. Ideally you'd ask family or friends to take oaths on your behalf, testifying to your impeccable character. Character witnesses would either make amends with your accuser or carry on the feud for your sake. But if you lacked witnesses, or their petitions didn't work, you might have to face an ordeal like one of the following:

1 *Boiling water.* Suspend a stone in a vessel of boiling water (wrist-deep or elbow-deep, depending on the required severity). The accused must lift out the stone with one hand. Afterwards, the accused's hand must be bound and left otherwise untreated. Unwrap the hand after three days; if it is infected, the accused is guilty.

2   *Hot iron.* Heat an iron ball. The accused must carry the hot ball a pre-measured distance. Depending on the required severity of the ordeal, a one-pound ball must be carried a distance of three feet, or a three-pound ball a distance of nine feet. Afterwards, bind the accused's hand and wait three days. If the hand is infected, the accused is guilty.

3   *Cold water.* First, a priest must exorcise and consecrate a pit of water. Then tie the hands of the accused below their knees and lower them into the water. If the accused sinks to a depth of 1.5 ells (about two to three feet), they are innocent. If the accused floats, it means the sanctified water is rejecting them for their sins, thus proving their guilt.

4   *Cor-snǣd.* The accused must place an ounce of bread and cheese in their mouth. If they can easily swallow it, they are innocent. If they choke or have difficulty swallowing, they are guilty.

For the first two ordeals, you have to hope your immune system kicks in quickly and effectively, and that there's no nasty bacteria on the bandage. For the cold-water ordeal, you have to defy physics and somehow have a body mass denser than water (perhaps by hiding some rocks in your pockets). But the ordeal of chewing and swallowing some food? How could you *not* pass such an easy test?

Sarah Larratt Keefer, a scholar of medieval literature, posits a gag reflex theory based on the fact that the bread and cheese would have been quite different in early medieval England from what we eat today. The ordeal bread would most likely have been made from barley, a high-protein, glutinous grain that can really dry out your mouth, making it harder to swallow. English barley was less refined and harder to chew than barley from the Mediterranean, so much so that it was referred to as *horse mete*, 'food for horses'. Not only would barley bread have been unpalatable, it may have contained toxins that cause throat and stomach inflammation and vomiting. The cheese would not have been prepared with today's food safety standards and may have contained salmonella. The symptoms of salmonella don't kick in for twelve to seventy-two hours on average, but then the law books do not specify the period of time the accused must wait after eating to be cleared of guilt. Did you have to wait a day to be in the clear? I would guess that God's judgement was supposed to be made sooner rather than later and not require a three-day test period. In any case, Keefer argues that someone undergoing the *cor-snæd* ordeal would have been forced to eat food that was not only 'unpalatable to a very considerable degree' but potentially toxic.

The medieval literature scholar John Niles is sceptical of Keefer's theory, saying that in medieval England, 'barley bread and cheese would probably have been routine fare in a humble household'. Food of any kind would likely be welcome to the person undergoing the ordeal, who would have endured fasting over the three days prior. As Niles points out, 'an empty stomach is the best sauce'. Barley was grown for feeding animals as well as humans; it wasn't as tasty as wheat, but it was easier to grow. The cheese would have been heavily salted, dense and crumbly, similar to Cheshire cheese – probably not seen as potentially toxic since people ate it all the time. Niles is more on board with Keefer's explanation of *cor-snæd* as a psychological ordeal. When you're nervous, your throat constricts and your mouth becomes dry. During an ordeal, you are bound to feel nervous, whether guilty or innocent. You may even experience nausea or an upset stomach as you would in any high-stakes examination.

According to the eleventh-century law codes, the *cor-snæd* ordeal is intended for a 'friendless altar-servant', a priest or cleric of limited power with no kinsmen to support his oath. Being 'friendless' had far worse implications than feeling lonely. A friendless cleric, with no one to vouch for him, would have had to take his chances with *cor-snǣd*, and the outcome of this 'decision-bite' would be seen as God's own judgement. The fear of perjuring himself before God (a sure way to end up in hell) may have been enough to make a priest confess to a crime. The bread was most likely symbolic; during Mass, after all, bread could represent or even be transformed into the body of Christ. Today, when a person swears with their hand on the Bible, they do not necessarily believe that a lie will bring God's wrath upon them, but the Bible (like the bread) is a symbol that signifies the seriousness of their oath.

There is arguably one secular, rather spontaneous example of *cor-snǣd* in 1053. Godwin, Earl of Wessex, denied his own treachery to King Edward the Confessor at a royal banquet, saying, 'God forbid that I should swallow this morsel, if I am conscious of any thing which might tend, either to [your brother's] danger or your disadvantage.' According to the twelfth-century chronicle of William of Malmesbury, 'On saying this, [Godwin] was choked with the piece he had put into his mouth, and closed his eyes in death.'

Whatever the effectiveness of *cor-snǣd*, it's best to face any trial with a clear conscience, a clear throat and a strong stomach.

Second *wordhord*

ǣg, noun (AIE / 'æj): Egg.

bēan-broþ, noun (BAY-ahn-BROTH / 'beːan-ˌbrɔθ): Bean broth.

bēo-brēad, noun (BAY-oh-BRAY-ad / 'beːɔ-ˌbreːad): Royal jelly (bee-food), the glandular secretion of worker bees used to feed larvae; (in some contexts) honeycomb.

bēon-broþ, noun (BAY-on-BROTH / 'beːɔn-ˌbrɔθ): Definition uncertain: possibly a drink made from honey or mead (bee-broth), but more likely an alternate spelling of *bēan-broþ*.

brēad, noun (BRAY-ad / 'breːad): Bread (not as common as *hlāf*); food.

brīw, noun (BREE-ew / 'briːw): Paste or pottage made mainly from grain or meal.

butere, noun (BUH-teh-ruh / 'bʌ-tɛ-rə): Butter.

cicen, noun (CHIH-chen / 't͡ʃɪ-t͡ʃɛn): Chicken, chick.

cīs, adjective (CHEES / 't͡ʃiːs): Fastidious, squeamish (in eating).

cor-snǣd, noun (KOR-SNAD / 'kɔr-ˌsnæːd): Trial morsel (decision-bite); consecrated piece of bread or cheese to be swallowed in trial by ordeal.

cū, noun (KOO / 'kuː): Cow.

cū-butere, noun (KOO-BUH-teh-ruh / 'kuː-ˌbʌ-tɛ-rə): Cow's butter, butter made from cow's milk.

cū-bȳre, noun (KOO-BUE-ruh / 'kuː-ˌbyː-rə): Cow byre, cowshed.

cū-cealf, noun (KOO-CHEH-alf / 'kuː-ˌt͡ʃɛalf): Cow's calf.

cū-ēage, noun (KOO-AY-ah-yuh / 'kuː-ˌeːa-jə): Cow's eye.

cūe mesa, noun (KOO-eh-MEH-za / 'kuː-ɛ-ˌmɛ-za): Cow's dung.

cū-horn, noun (KOO-HORN / 'kuː-ˌhɔrn): Cow's horn.

cū-hyrde, noun (KOO-HUER-duh / 'kuː-ˌhyr-də): Cowherd, person in charge of cows.

cū-meoluc, noun (KOO-MEH-o-luk / 'kuː-ˌmɛɔ-lʌk): Cow's milk.

cū-micge, noun (KOO-MIDG-uh / 'kuː-ˌmɪ-d͡ʒə): Cow's urine.

cū-tǣgel, noun (KOO-TA-yell / 'kuː-ˌtæ-jɛl): Cow's tail.

cū-wearm, adjective (KOO-WEH-arm / 'kuː-ˌwɛarm): Warm from the cow (cow-warm).

cycel, noun (KUE-chell / 'ky-t͡ʃɛl): Little cake (not sweet).

cȳse, noun (CHUE-zuh / 't͡ʃyː-zə): Cheese.

cȳswuce, noun (CHUEZ-WUCH-uh / 't͡ʃyːz-ˌwʌ-t͡ʃə): Definition uncertain: possibly a time for fasting and purification at the beginning of Lent.

feoh, noun (FEH-oh / 'fɛɔx): Cattle, livestock; property, wealth, money; value, price, fee; name of the F-rune ᚠ.

ge-cor, noun (yeh-KOR / jɛ-ˈkɔr): Choice, decision.

heorþ, noun (HEH-orth / ˈhɛɔrθ): Hearth, fireplace; home, household.

hlāf, noun (H'LAWF / ˈhlaːf): Bread, loaf.

hlāf-ǣta, noun (H'LAW-VAT-ah / ˈhlaː-ˌvæ-ta): Dependant (bread-eater).

hlāford, noun (H'LAW-vord / ˈhlaː-vɔrd): Lord, male head of a household (bread-guardian).

hlǣfdige, noun (H'LAV-dih-yuh / ˈhlæːv-dɪ-jə): Lady, female head of a household (bread-maker).

hunig, noun (HUN-ih / ˈhʌ-nɪj): Honey.

medu, noun (MEH-duh / ˈmɛ-dʌ): Mead, alcoholic drink made from honey.

meolc, noun (MEH-olk / ˈmɛɔlk): Milk.

mete, noun (MEH-tuh / ˈmɛ-tə): Food.

morgen, noun (MOR-gen / ˈmɔr-gɛn): Morning.

morgen-drenc, noun (MOR-gen-DRENCH / ˈmɔr-gɛn-ˌdrɛntʃ): 'Morning-drink', some sort of healing drink or potion.

morgen-mete, noun (MOR-gen-MEH-tuh / ˈmɔr-gɛn-ˌmɛ-tə): Breakfast (morning-food).

ofen, noun (OV-en / ˈɔ-vɛn): Oven.

offrung-spic, noun (OFF-frung-SPITCH / ˈɔf-frʌŋ-ˌspɪtʃ): 'Offering-bacon', bacon offered to idols.

scenc, noun (SHENCH / ˈʃɛntʃ): Cup.

scencan, verb (SHEN-khan / ˈʃɛn-kan): To pour out liquor for drinking; to give to drink.

sin-, prefix (SIN / ˈsɪn): Ever, everlasting; (in some cases) big.

sin-snǣd, noun (SIN-SNAD / ˈsɪn-ˌsnæd): Huge morsel, big bite.

smēga-wyrm, noun (SMAY-ga-WUERM / ˈsmeː-ga-ˌwyrm): Penetrating worm that makes its way into the flesh.

snǣd, noun (SNAD / ˈsnæd): Morsel, bit, bite, slice, cut.

spic, noun (SPITCH / ˈspɪtʃ): Bacon, the fatty meat of swine.

stund, noun (STUND / ˈstʌnd): Time, hour; the time appointed for a particular action.

swīn, noun (SWEEN / ˈswiːn): Pig, swine.

tīd, noun (TEED / ˈtiːd): Time, hour; period of time.

undern, noun (UN-dern / ˈʌn-dɛrn): The time between sunrise and midday, morning.

undern-mete, noun (UN-dern-MEH-tuh / ˈʌn-dɛrn-ˌmɛ-tə): Food eaten at *undern* (in the morning), breakfast.

wuce, noun (WUCH-uh / ˈwʌ-t͡ʃə): Week.

3

Passing the Time

Morning cares

IN ADDITION TO *morgen-mete* and *morgen-drenc*, Old English has another useful morning compound: **morgen-colla**, meaning 'morning-dread' or 'morning-rage'. This hapax's single appearance is in the poem *Judith*, which retells the story of an Old Testament heroine who beheads an enemy general and sexual predator to save her people. This general, Holofernes, forces Judith to come to bed with him, but he is so drunk that he passes out immediately. This gives Judith the opportunity to cut Holofernes' head from his shoulders and place it in her maidservant's satchel for safekeeping. The next day the battle isn't going well for Holofernes' side; his senior officers are informed of their enemies' stout swordplay and the terrifying news that they are losing. This atmosphere of fear, the soldiers' dread of dying in battle, is described as *morgen-colla*. What a useful word for describing that feeling when you wake up on the wrong side of the bed. 'Nothing is going right this morning #MorgencollaMondays.' (Remember that no matter how bad your day is going, if your head is still attached, you're one up on Holofernes.)

Morgen-mete and *morgen-drenc* may have seemed perplexing: after all, it doesn't seem likely that breakfast was even a thing in early medieval England, and the so-called 'morning-drink' was meant to be consumed at night. But even the definition of ***morgen*** itself is far from straightforward.

Somewhat confusingly, the word *morgen* (pronounced MOR-gen) can either mean 'morning' or 'tomorrow morning'. You may be able to figure it out by context; if someone says they're riding a horse 'in the morning' and it's already morning, you'd figure the ride is occurring the *following* morning, or tomorrow morning. Otherwise they could just say ***nū*** (now).

Sometimes the preposition ***tō*** precedes *morgen* to mean 'tomorrow morning'. By the thirteenth century, people were using 'to morewe' to designate a time of day on the following day, tomorrow noon or tomorrow evening, for instance. The pronunciation of g changed in Middle English: Old English ***folgian*** (to follow) became 'folwen', ***fugel*** (bird, fowl) became 'fouel', *morgen* became 'morewe'. The preposition *to* appears in other Old English temporal words to indicate a duration of time or a specific point in time. If something happens on *this* specific day, it happens ***tō dæge*** (today).

Gyrstan doesn't look very familiar at first glance, but when g precedes y in Old English, it is palatalised or softened. That means *gyrstan* is actually pronounced YUER-stahn, not far off from the 'yester' of yesterday. For 'yesterday' in Old English you could say *gyrstan*, *dæg gyrstan*, or the form most familiar to modern English speakers, ***gyrstan-dæg***. *Morgen, to morgen, to dæge, gyrstan-dæg* ... aside from some minor changes in pronunciation and spelling, we've kept using these words for over a millennium.

Sometimes a busy day seems to fly by, and in Old English 'day' does sort of have wings. ***Dæg*** (day, pronounced DAIE), when represented with the D-rune, looks like a butterfly, with two wing-like appendages joined together: ᛗ. The rune appears in a verse that celebrates the divine gift of light:

<u>Day</u> (ᛗ), dear to men, is sent by the Lord, the Creator's celebrated light, mirth and hope for the blessed and the wretched, a benefit to all.

ᛗ (*dæg*) here could refer simply to the time that the sun brightens the sky, but perhaps it is also the duration of a person's life. The time when someone is alive, their 'day', is also worth celebrating.

The *dæg* is youngest at *ūht*. *Ūht* is just past night's end, the time right before daybreak. It is followed by **dæg-rēd** (day-red), when the day reddens with the first light of dawn, or **dæg-rima** (day-rim or day-border), the narrow space of time between night and day, when the sun just peeps over the horizon. *Dæg-rēd* and *dæg-rima* are followed by **ǣr-morgen** (daybreak), which is followed by *morgen* itself.

Great things happen at *ūht*, such as Christ's Harrowing of Hell. Although not all Christians are familiar with the Harrowing of Hell today, it was a popular theme of medieval art and literature. This is an episode that occurs after Christ's crucifixion but before his resurrection. Christ makes a quick journey down to hell in order to rescue the souls of good people who had the misfortune of dying before he did, people who would theoretically have been good Christians if Christianity had actually existed during their lifetimes. Before ascending to heaven, Christ 'harrows' hell, jailbreaking many worthy souls, such as the preacher who baptised him, John the Baptist.

Christ's descent into the world of the dead is alluded to a couple of times in scripture, but these instances depend on interpretation. The First Epistle of Peter says that the gospel was 'preached also to the dead', and the Epistle of Paul to the Ephesians says that before Christ ascended to heaven, he 'descended first into the lower parts of the earth'. A harrow is a heavy tool with iron teeth that is dragged across ploughed land to break apart and pulverise the soil, rooting up weeds or spreading seeds. The word 'harwe' doesn't appear until Middle English, but it may be related to Old English **hergian**

Christ's Harrowing of Hell

(to ravage, pillage, lay waste). (Remember how g changed its sound? *Hergian* became 'harwen' in Middle English.) The term 'Harrowing of Hell' may not have existed in early medieval England, but the story itself appears in Old English texts like this one:

> The Lord himself overcame death and made the Devil flee. The prophets of the ancient days had said he would do so. It all happened at *ūht*, before *dæg-rēd*. A din resounded, loud from the heavens, when he destroyed and demolished the gates of hell.

Christ feels no anxiety on his *ūht*-time adventure, but it's not uncommon to lie awake before dawn, your mind racing with unhelpful thoughts. The worry that plagues you during those moments before daybreak is *ūht-cearu* (*ūht*-care, pronounced OO'HT-CHEH-ah-ruh). At least, that might be what it is; it's a hapax, so there's only one example to provide context. In one of the very few Old English poems that addresses what we might call 'romance', *ūht-cearu* torments the female narrator of a poem known as *The Wife's Lament*. The woman has been abandoned by her husband, although she doesn't know whether he is to blame or to pity. Did he go away wilfully, or did people force him to leave? Either way, she dwells upon her loss with pain and sorrow. No matter what your cares may be, *ūht* is a time for ruminating on the troubling things in life that you cannot change.

Thank god it's Frigg's day

Time is so important to humans that we've named the days of the week after gods – or sometimes after celestial bodies that have themselves been named after gods. In many Romance languages (French, Spanish, etc.), the days of the week derive from the Latin names of Roman gods and goddesses. Because the Angles, Saxons, Jutes and Frisians were pagans with their *own* pantheon, Old English days of the week get their names from Germanic and Norse deities. For the most part, the English used 'equivalent' deities to the ones the Romans had already chosen for their day names.

Deity (Roman)	Deity (Northern European)	Day (Old English)	Day (modern English)
Sol	Sól or Sunna	*sunnandæg*	Sunday
Luna	Máni	*mōnandæg*	Monday
Mars	Týr or Tīw	*tīwesdæg*	Tuesday
Mercury	Woden or Odin	*wōdnesdæg*	Wednesday
Jupiter or Jove	Þūr or Thor	*þūresdæg*	Thursday
Venus	Frigg	*frigdæg*	Friday
Saturn	(no equivalent)	*sæterndæg*	Saturday

Sunnandæg (Sunday) literally means 'sun day'. In Northern Europe, the sun goddess was called Sól or Sunna, and both **sōl** and **sunna** mean sun in Old English. Sól rides in a chariot drawn by two horses. She is so hot that her horses require special cooling devices, bellows tucked under the animals' shoulders to blow air on them. Sól's brother is Máni, the moon god. (In Roman mythology, the genders of the sun and moon deities are reversed: the god Sol and the goddess Luna.) **Mōnandæg** (Monday) is Máni's day, literally 'moon day' since **mōna** means moon.

The Romans named Tuesday after Mars, their god of war and agriculture. Mars is destructive by nature, but he represents military strength as a means of achieving peace (and the conditions for grow-ing crops). His Northern European counterpart is Týr or Tīw, a god of war, law and heroic glory, considered by many to be the bravest of all the gods. Norse myth tells of the gods trying to secure Fenrir, a giant wolf symbolic of the apocalypse. Fenrir refuses to cooperate unless one of the gods sticks an arm in his mouth as security for his freedom. Týr bravely (unwisely?) volunteers, even though he knows the gods have no intention of setting the wolf free. Týr loses his arm, but at least he gets his own day of the week: *tīwesdæg*. He even has his own rune, the T-rune ↑. *The Rune Poem* says:

> Týr (↑) is one of the signs. Lords would do well to keep it in good faith.
> Across the mists of night, it is always in motion. It never fails.

Here Týr may represent heroic glory, which lords would do well to believe in. Although glory can be elusive at times, and some fail to attain it, glory itself never fails.

Wōdnesdæg (Wednesday) and *þūresdæg* (Thursday) are named after two of the most popular gods: Woden and Thor. Woden (or Odin), All-Father of the Norse pantheon, was considered the closest equivalent to the Roman god Mercury, for whom Wednesday was named in Latin. They aren't a perfect match. Woden presides over wisdom, war, death and magic, while Mercury is associated with commerce and luck, but both are gods of poetry and divination. Each god is known for his eloquence, his exceptional speed and a penchant for long-distance travel. This travel includes journeys to the lands of the dead: Mercury guides souls to the underworld and Odin rules over Valhalla, a home in the afterlife for those slain in combat. The Romans associated Jupiter (or Jove) with Thursday, and his closest match in the Norse pantheon was fellow sky-and-thunder god Thor. Thor, whose day is *þūresdæg* in Old English, wields a magic hammer called Mjolnir, which is what makes the sound of thunder.

Frigdæg (Friday) is named for the Norse fertility goddess Frigg, a devoted wife and loving mother. She has perhaps less in common with her Roman counterpart than the other weekday deities. Originally, the Roman goddess Venus presided over agriculture and the earth's fertility, but as people came to associate her more with Aphrodite, the Greek goddess of love, she increasingly represented sex, beauty and desire. Frigg too is a fertility goddess, but she has more in common with the earlier agricultural Venus than the later love goddess.

The Romans named Saturday after their god Saturn, and the name endured in the Old English word **sæterndæg**, for want of a good Northern European equivalent. Saturn was Jupiter's father. Since Jupiter was equated with Thor, logic dictates that Saturn be paired with Thor's father, Woden. But Woden was already paired with Mercury (see *wōdnesdæg*). Saturn, the Roman god of agriculture, was associated with abundance, wealth, renewal, liberation and time. During Saturnalia, the Roman festival held annually in Saturn's honour, all work and business came to a halt. Saturnalia was originally just one day, but later it was extended to seven. For the duration of the festival the rules of normal life were to be ignored; for instance, slaves could (allegedly) do or say what they liked without fear of consequence. It seems appropriate that Saturn's day is still associated by many with freedom from work.

Loud March and three-milkings month

Winter is **cealdost** (most cold) of the seasons. The word hasn't changed for 1,000 years, although *winter* used to be more than just a season. Since it was the harshest, deadliest season, *winter* was also a unit for measuring time. If you could survive a winter, you could survive a year, so why not just count your age in winters?

In early medieval England, *winter* began on 7 November, *wintres dæg* (winter's day). The *Menologium*, a poem that describes the year's seasons and feast days in chronological order, says that *wintres dæg* overthrows sun-bright autumn like an invading army, troops of ice and snow. The name for November itself is similarly fierce: **blōt-mōnaþ**, which means 'sacrifice-month'. Bede, a monk and historian of the late seventh and early eighth centuries, explains that November's name is a reference to the time when pagan Saxons would sacrifice animals to their gods, supposedly an annual event prior to their conversion to Christianity. It's quite possible, however, that Bede is making a bigger deal of pagan customs than they were for the sake of his *Ecclesiastical History* (*c.*731) – the more barbaric the heathens are, the better! It may have been that slaughtering extra livestock in November was simply the economical thing to do. It's significantly harder to feed cattle during the winter, so it is logical to cut back on the number of mouths to feed, as well as stocking up on meat for winter provisions.

The concept of months comes from observing the phases of the moon, so it makes sense that *mōna* (moon) and **mōnaþ** (month, pronounced MO-nath) share an etymological origin. Month names in Old English (like *blōt-mōnaþ*) are often *mōnaþ* compounds, but some of these have alternative names. December is **midwinter-mōnaþ** (midwinter-month) and **gēol-mōnaþ** (Yule-month), but it's also **ǣrra gēola** (first Yule). January is called **æfterra gēola** (second Yule). The system of beginning the year on 1 January comes from ancient Rome, but the preferred start date for medieval Christians was 25 December, Christmas Day.

A rather puzzling *mōnaþ* compound is **sol-mōnaþ** (February). *Sōl* with a long o means sun (see *sunnandæg*), but **sol** with a short o means 'mire' or 'muddy place'. *Sol* as an adjective means 'filthy' or 'dirty'. So is February 'sun-month' or 'dirty-month'? February 7 was the first day of spring, and spring is the season that is **hrīmigost** (frostiest) and cold for the longest. Why would such a dismal time of year be named 'sun-month'? The medieval literature scholar Kazutomo Karasawa points out that in Old Norse, *sólmánuðr* is the third month of summer, and that is definitely not February. Is February 'dirty-month' or 'mire-month' because of the heavy precipitation? Or did whoever came up with the name simply think 'mud-month' was a good description of their least favourite month? The etymology of *sol-mōnaþ* remains uncertain, although experience tells us that mud seems more likely than sun.

The Old English word for spring, **lencten**, also refers to the Lenten fast, which was formalised by the Church in 325 CE. But *lencten* meant 'spring' before it meant 'Lent'. Cognates of *lencten* in other Germanic languages (Old Dutch *lentin*, Old High German *lenzin*, etc.) just mean 'spring'; it is only in English that the word acquired an ecclesiastical definition. The *Oxford English Dictionary* says that this word for spring may derive from a Germanic root word for 'long', since spring coincides with the lengthening of days. While *spring* is a word in Old English, it doesn't refer to a season. Old English *spring* can mean a source of water; a springing or rising; or, in a medical context, an ulcer, sore or pustule. A pustule *does* spring up from your skin, I suppose, but such an image really does detract from a word that in modern English is a beautiful season. The earliest recorded example of 'spring' meaning 'the season between winter and summer' doesn't appear until the fourteenth century in Middle English.

Bede claims that **hrēþ-mōnaþ** (March) gets its name from a pagan goddess called Hreda. We know very little about non-Christian religions in medieval Britain: our main source of knowledge is two letters of Pope Gregory the Great (*c.*540–604 CE), transcribed by Bede into his *Ecclesiastical History* well over a century later. These accounts are inspired by paganism as depicted in the Bible and descriptions of the ancient world rather than the reality of life in early medieval Britain. As with *blōt-mōnaþ*, Bede supposes *hrēþ-mōnaþ* was a time when certain sacrifices were made by the pagan Saxons (which begs the question: why would November be 'sacrifice-month' if sacrifices occur at other times of the year?). That *hrēþ-mōnaþ* is named for a pagan goddess about whom there is no mention elsewhere is highly suspect. It's more likely that the name comes from **hrēþ** (glory, victory). This name works in the context of Christianity since Christ triumphed over death in the month of March.

Another name for March was **hlȳda**, possibly related to **hlūd** (loud). Was this due to the clamour of wind and storms in March? March continued to be called 'Lide', a variant of *hlȳda*, as recently as the seventeenth century. According to the *Menologium*, March arrives 'adorned with rime, passing through middle-earth with hail-showers'. It is both **rēðe** (fierce) and **hēa-līc** (proud).

March might have fierce weather, but the adjective 'proud' seems an odd choice of words. Why would March be proud? Perhaps because it was the **swyðost** (greatest) of the months, as is claimed by Byrhtferth, schoolmaster of Ramsey Abbey during the late tenth and early eleventh centuries. Kazutomo Karasawa suggests a few reasons for March's import in his edition of the *Menologium*. March was when God's spirit came to humankind and when Christ's birth was announced to the Virgin Mary (the annunciation) as well as the resurrection. The spring equinox was 21 March, a key date for determining the date of Easter, one of the most important holidays on the Christian calendar. If all that wasn't enough, March is the month during which God created the world. Bede's explanation has to do with the spring equinox, the creation of the sun and stars, the division of light and dark into two equal parts, and the date of a full moon. But not everyone agreed. Some people argued for the first day being on 21 March, others on 25 March. To be honest, when I try to follow their various explanations my head feels on the verge of imploding, and I begin to question the very meaning of time. Regardless, March certainly has enough going for it to be *swyðost*.

Proud March is followed by **ēaster-mōnaþ** (April), literally 'Easter-month' (although Easter can fall in either March or April). Then comes **þrimilce-mōnaþ** (May), the peculiarly named 'three-milkings-month'.

Supposedly *þrimilce-mōnaþ* gets its name due to the land's fertility at that time, for cows have plenty of grass to eat and thus require three milkings a day. That's a lot of *cū-wearm meolc*! May 7 was the first day of **sumer** (summer), the season both hottest and **sunwlitegost** (most beautiful with sunshine).

June was known as **midsumer-mōnaþ** (midsummer-month) or **sēremōnaþ**, which may have meant 'dry-month' (as opposed to *sol-mōnaþ*, February's 'mud-month'). July was **mǣd-mōnaþ** (meadow-month), perhaps a reference to the time of year when cattle could graze in the meadows. These summer months were also called **līða**: June **ǣrra līða** (first *līða*) and July **æftera lȳða** (second *līða*). Bede connects *līða* to the words **līðe** (gentle, soft) and **līðan** (to travel, sail), saying that this time of year was 'amiable and navigable', with pleasant winds and easy travel by boat.

August was **wēod-mōnaþ** (weed-month), a time of agricultural abundance, with plenty of work to do in the fields. **Hlāf-mæsse** (bread-Mass) was a harvest festival at the very end of the summer on 1 August. On *hlāf-mæsse* (later known as Lammas Day), priests blessed loaves of bread made from the first harvested grain of the year. August 7 marked the beginning of **hærfest** (harvest, autumn). Although August was the beginning of *hærfest*, September was the month known as **hærfest-mōnaþ** (harvest-month).

Another name for September was **hālig-mōnaþ** (holy month). According to Bede, *hālig-mōnaþ* was when the pagans used to make sacrifices to their gods. (See *blōt-mōnaþ* and *hrēþ-mōnaþ* – the man was obsessed.) But September could just as well be a 'holy month' for Christians. Although there is no mention of it in the Bible, tradition says that Mary, the mother of Christ, was born on 8 September, exactly nine months after her Immaculate Conception. Often confused with the virgin birth of Jesus, the Immaculate Conception actually refers to *Mary's* conception in the womb of her mother, which rendered her free of original sin from the first moment of her existence. In the

Western Church, the Immaculate Conception has been celebrated on 8 December since the eighth century. So as the birth-month of the holy Virgin Mary, September has reason enough to be called *hālig-mōnaþ*.

Finally, there was **winter-fylleþ** (October), which literally means 'winter-full-moon'. Bede's explanation (rather predictably) goes back to pagans. Although in Bede's time *wintres dæg* was in November, the pagans supposedly recognised October's full moon as the beginning of winter. How likely this is to be true is anyone's guess: everything written about early British pagans is by non-pagans, often centuries after the fact. And we're not so different from Bede, attributing the unexplainable to pagan religion. 'Winter-full-moon' month is also the month of our Halloween, a festival that some speculate has roots in ancient pagan harvest festivals.

In an eye-twinkle

In Old English there is **tīma** (time) but also **un-tīma** (wrong or improper time).

In a homily for Ash Wednesday, Ælfric of Eynsham shares a series of anecdotes about people who have disobeyed the rules of fasting, abstinence and penitence. In one story, a man insists on having sex with his wife on Ash Wednesday, refusing to receive blessed ashes from the Church. He is out riding later that same week when he is attacked by hounds, and while attempting to fend them off he accidentally impales himself on his own spear. In another cautionary tale, a man ignores the rules of fasting and has a snack during Mass. The moment the first bite passes his lips he falls into a faint, spitting up blood. (He survives, but only barely.)

Each of these men exemplifies the consequences of doing something (which in other circumstances would be acceptable) at the wrong time.

The word *un-tīma* is in the third story, in which a man decides to drink as much booze as he wants during Lent. The bishop refuses to bless his cup, but the fool has a drink anyway and then steps outside. The homily says:

> By chance, people were baiting a boar outside, and the boar ran towards him, throwing him so he lost his life. And so he paid for <u>that untimely drink</u> (ðone untiman drenc). During holy Lent or on appointed fasting days, every man who eats or drinks <u>at an improper time</u> (*on untiman*) should know truly that his soul must pay dearly for it, even if the body lives on unharmed.

Never do something at its 'un-time', the time when it is forbidden. Whether you impale yourself on your own spear or simply burn in hell, the consequences won't be pretty. Although we continue to use the adverb 'untimely' today, after the Middle Ages the noun 'un-time' met its untimely end.

It takes a good, long **hwīl** (while) to consider all the time-related words in Old English. *Hwīl*, an interval or period of time of a loosely specified duration, appears in many compounds. **Earfoþ-hwīl** is a time of hardship or tribulation, **orleg-hwīl** a time of battle, **gryre-hwīl** a time of terror, **þræc-hwīl** a time of suffering, **langung-hwīl** a time of longing or weariness, and **sige-hwīl** a time of victory. **Rōt-hwīl** looks like it should be the time it takes for something to rot, but it's actually a time for refreshment; **rōt** means glad or cheerful. Leisure time is **ǣmet-hwīl**, which you should take care not to confuse with an **ǣmett-hyll** (ant hill). The *ǣmet* in *ǣmet-hwīl* derives from **ǣmta** (leisure), and the *ǣmett* in *ǣmett-hyll* means 'ant'. It's a funny coincidence that the words are so similar, ants being characterised as hard-working and industrious, with no *ǣmet-hwīl* to speak of.

Some *hwīl*-compounds are trickier to define. Take **wræc-hwīl**, for instance, the literal translation of which is 'exile-time' or 'misery-time'. It appears in a poem that describes what happens to souls after death:

> Then after their <u>time of exile</u> (*wræc-hwile*), the blessed will be clothed
> in their own works and deeds.

When you die, you can't hide behind fancy garments or wealth; your only 'clothes' are the actions you took during your life. These actions determine your status in the afterlife. But before you die, you spend time living on earth – *this* is what the poet means by *wræc-hwīl*. Was life in early medieval England so terrible that it was considered a time of misery? Perhaps we are meant to think of life on earth as a time of exile from God, to whom we'll return after death. It may seem strange to think of life as *wræc-hwīl*, a time of exile or misery, but for people living in difficult times, it might make things easier to believe that the good life is still to come.

And one day ***ge-sceap-hwīl*** will come, 'the time appointed by fate for dying'. The primary definition of ***ge-sceap*** is 'creation', but it can also mean 'fate' or 'destiny'. Your *ge-sceap* (pronounced yeh-SHEH-op) is 'shaped', whether it's by God, by fate, or by the decisions you freely make. Although *Beowulf* was recorded in a Christian England, the heroes of the poem live in a pagan past, and sometimes the poet seems to be trying to reconcile this pagan past with a Christian present. A term like *ge-sceap-hwīl* conveniently works in both contexts. It appears near the beginning of the poem at the ship-burial-style funeral of King Scyld:

> Then Scyld, strong and vigorous, departed at the <u>fated time</u> (*ge-scæp-*
> *hwile*), going into the lord's protection.

Scyld is a pagan king undergoing pagan funeral rites, but the 'lord' offering protection is presumably the Christian God. But is Scyld's *ge-sceap-hwīl* determined by God or by fate? Even the strong and vigorous must always be prepared for death; you never know when your *ge-sceap-hwīl* may be.

Along with specific moments in time, *hwīl* can refer to a duration of time. **Be-prīwan** (to wink) combines with *hwīl* to make **prēowt-hwīl**, 'the time it takes to wink', or 'in the blink of an eye'. Another way to say this is **ēagan bryhtm** (eye's twinkle), which appears in a passage about the short and fleeting nature of earthly life. Imagine you're feasting and drinking with your buddies in a nice warm mead-hall. It's winter outside, but inside you're protected from the snow and wind. A sparrow flies in the door at one end of the mead-hall and departs at the other. For that brief time, the sparrow is untroubled by the inclement weather outside, but that time is only *ēagan bryhtm*, an eye-twinkle. The same is true of life's pleasures and earthly comforts, luxuries that only last for a blink of an eye. *Feoh* – wealth and property – is only useful until you die, which is a very short time relative to eternity.

A conventional way to begin a story in modern English is 'Once upon a time . . .'. The phrase removes you from the present so you can enter a different life, in a non-specific past or an imaginary time. *Beowulf*, the most famous story in Old English, begins similarly:

So, we Spear-Danes <u>in days gone by</u> (*in geardagum*) . . .

The phrase 'once upon a time' didn't appear until the fourteenth century, when you begin to find examples in literature, like 'ones on a tyme' in Chaucer's *Canterbury Tales*. But before 'once upon a time' there was Old English **gēar-dagas**. Literally translating to 'year-days', *gēar-dagas* (pronounced YAY-ar-DA-gahs) are the days of one's life, the old days, former times. There is still an echo of the word in modern English, in the phrase 'days of yore'. Long ago in a faraway land . . . *in geardagum* . . . this is how a story works its way into the reader or listener's imagination.

Third *wordhord*

æftera līða, noun (AV-teh-rah LEE-tha / ˈæv-tɛ-ra ˈliː-θa): July (second *līða*).

æfterra gēola, noun (AV-teh-rah YAY-o-la / ˈæv-tɛ-ra ˈjeːɔ-la): January (second Yule).

ǣmet-hwīl, noun (AM-et-HWEEL / ˈæː-mɛt-ˌhwiːl): Leisure time; idleness.

ǣmett-hyll, noun (AM-et-HUELL / ˈæː-mɛt-ˌhyl): Ant hill.

ǣmta, noun (AM-ta / ˈæːm-ta): Leisure; freedom or opportunity (to do something).

ǣr-morgen, noun (AER-MOR-gen / ˈæːr-ˌmɔr-gɛn): Early morning, daybreak.

ǣrra gēola, noun (AE-ra-YAY-o-la / ˈæː-ra ˈjeːɔ-la): December (first Yule).

ǣrra līða, noun (AE-ra-LEE-tha / ˈæː-ra ˈliː-θa): June (first *līða*).

be-prīwan, verb (beh-PREE-wahn / bɛ-ˈpriː-wan): To wink.

blōt-mōnaþ, noun (BLOAT-MO-nath / ˈbloːt-ˌmoː-naθ): November (sacrifice-month).

cealdost, adjective (superlative) (CHEH-al-dost / ˈt͡ʃeal-dɔst): Coldest.

dæg, noun (DAIE / ˈdæj): Day; person's lifetime; name of the D-rune ᛗ.

dæg-rēd, noun (DAIE-RAID / ˈdæj-ˌreːd): Dawn, daybreak, early morning.

dæg-rima, noun (DAIE-RIM-ah / ˈdæj-ˌrɪ-ma): Daybreak, morning.

ēagan bryhtm, noun (AY-ah-gahn BRUE-h'tm / ˈeːa-gan ˈbryx-təm): Moment, eye's twinkle.

earfoþ-hwīl, noun (EH-ar-voth-HWEEL / ˈɛar-vɔθ-ˌhwiːl): Time of hardship.

ēaster-mōnaþ, noun (AY-ah-ster-MO-nath / ˈeːa-stɛr-ˌmoː-naθ): April (Easter-month).

folgian, verb (FOL-yih-ahn / ˈfɔl-jɪ-an): To follow.

frigdæg, noun (FRIH-DAIE / ˈfrɪj-ˌdæj): Friday (Frigg's day).

fugel, noun (FUH-yell / ˈfʌ-jɛl): Bird.

gēar-dagas, plural noun (YAY-ar-DA-gahs / ˈjeːar-ˌda-gas): Days (of one's life), lifetime; days of old, former times.

gēol-mōnaþ, noun (YAY-ol-MO-nath / ˈjeːɔl-ˌmoː-naθ): December (Yule-month).

ge-sceap, noun (yeh-SHEH-op / jɛ-ˈʃɛap): Creation, created being or thing, creature; fate, destiny; form, shape.

ge-sceap-hwīl, noun (yeh-SHEH-op-HWEEL / jɛ-ˈʃɛap-ˌhwiːl): Time for dying (as determined by fate).

gryre-hwīl, noun (GRUE-ruh-HWEEL / ˈgry-rə-ˌhwiːl): Time of terror.

gyrstan-dæg, noun/adverb (YUER-stahn-DAIE / ˈjyr-stan-ˌdæj): Yesterday.

hālig-mōnaþ, noun (HA-lih-MO-nath / ˈhaː-lɪj-ˌmoː-naθ): September (holy month).

hærfest, noun (HAER-vest / ˈhær-vɛst): Harvest, autumn.

hærfest-mōnaþ, noun (HAER-vest-MO-nath / ˈhær-vɛst-ˌmoː-naθ): September (harvest-month).

hēa-līc, adjective (HAY-ah-leech / ˈheːa-liːt͡ʃ): High, elevated, lofty, proud, noble, deep, profound.

hergian, verb (HER-yih-ahn / ˈhɛr-jɪ-an): To ravage, spoil, pillage; to lay waste.

hlāf-mæsse, noun (HLAWV-MASS-uh / ˈhlaːv-ˌmæs-sə): 'Bread-Mass' or Lammas Day (1 August).

hlūd, adjective (HLOOD / ˈhluːd): Loud, sonorous.

hlȳda, noun (HLUE-dah / ˈhlyː-da): March.

hrēþ, noun (HRAITH / ˈhreːθ): Glory, victory.

hrēþ-mōnaþ, noun (HRAITH-MO-nath / ˈhreːθ-ˌmoː-naθ): March.

hrīmigost, adjective (superlative) (HREE-mi-gost / ˈhriː-mɪ-gɔst): Frostiest.

hwīl, noun (HWEEL / ˈhwiːl): Indefinite or loosely specified duration of time; interval, period.

langung-hwīl, noun (LAHNG-gung-HWEEL / ˈlaŋ-gʌŋ-ˌhwiːl): Time of longing or weariness.

lencten, noun (LENK-ten / ˈlɛnk-tɛn): Spring, Lent.

līða, noun (LEE-tha / ˈliː-θa): June and July.

līðan, verb (LEE-than / ˈliː-θan): To go (generally by sea), sail.

līðe, adjective (LEE-thuh / ˈliː-θə): Soft, gentle, mild, serene.

mǣd-mōnaþ, noun (MAD-MO-nath / ˈmæːd-ˌmoː-naθ): July.

midsumer-mōnaþ, noun (MID-sum-er-MO-nath / ˈmɪd-sʌ-mɛr-ˌmoː-naθ): June (midsummer-month).

midwinter-mōnaþ, noun (MID-win-ter-MO-nath / ˈmɪd-wɪn-tɛr-ˌmoː-naθ): December (midwinter-month).

mōna, noun (MO-na / ˈmoː-na): Moon.

mōnandæg, noun (MO-nahn-DAIE / ˈmoː-nan-ˌdæj): Monday (moon-day).

mōnaþ, noun (MO-nath / ˈmoː-naθ): Month.

morgen, noun (MOR-gen / ˈmɔr-gɛn): Morning; morning of the next day, tomorrow.

morgen-colla, noun (MOR-gen-KOLL-ah / ˈmɔr-gɛn-ˌkɔl-la): 'Morning-dread', 'morning-rage'.

nū, adverb (NOO / ˈnuː): Now.

orleg-hwīl, noun (OR-ley-HWEEL / ˈɔr-lɛj-ˌhwiːl): Time of battle or war.

prēowt-hwīl, noun (PRAY-owt-HWEEL / ˈpreːɔwt-ˌhwiːl): Time taken to close and open the eye, twinkling of an eye.

rēðe, adjective (RAY-thuh / ˈreː-θə): Fierce, cruel, savage, wild.

rōt, adjective (ROAT / ˈroːt): Glad, cheerful.

rōt-hwīl, noun (ROAT-HWEEL / ˈroːt-ˌhwiːl): Refreshing time.

sæterndæg, noun (SAT-ern-DAIE / ˈsæ-tɛrn-ˌdæj): Saturday (Saturn's day).

sēremōnaþ, noun (SAY-reh-MO-nath / ˈseː-rɛ-ˌmoː-naθ): June.

sige-hwīl, noun (SI-yuh-HWEEL / ˈsɪ-jə-ˌhwiːl): Time of victory, hour of victory.

sol, noun/adjective (SOLL / ˈsɔl): Mire, miry place; filthy, dirty.

sōl, noun (SOAL / ˈsoːl): Sun.

sol-mōnaþ, noun (SOLL-MO-nath / ˈsɔl-ˌmoː-naθ): February.

spring, noun (SPRING / ˈsprɪŋ): Source of water; springing, rising; ulcer, sore, pustule; flux; squirting, sprinkling.

sumer, noun (SUM-er / ˈsʌ-mɛr): Summer.

sunna, noun (SUH-na / ˈsʌ-na): Sun.

sunnandæg, noun (SUH-nahn-DAIE / ˈsʌ-nan-ˌdæj): Sunday (sun-day).

sunwlitigost, adjective (superlative) (SUN-WLI-ti-gost / ˈsʌn-ˌwlɪ-tɪ-gɔst): Most beautiful with sunshine.

swyðost, adjective (superlative) (SWUE-thost / ˈswy-θɔst): Greatest, strongest.

tīma, noun (TEE-ma / ˈtiː-ma): Time, hour.

tīwesdæg, noun (TEE-wez-DAIE / ˈtiː-wɛz-ˌdæj): Tuesday (Tīw's or Týr's day).

tō dæge, noun with preposition (toh DAIE-yuh / toː ˈdæ-jə): Today.

þræc-hwīl, noun (THRACK-HWEEL / ˈθræk-ˌhwiːl): Time of suffering, hard time.

þrimilce-mōnaþ, noun (THRI-mill-chuh-MO-nath / ˈθrɪ-mɪl-t͡ʃə-ˌmoː-naθ): May (three-milkings-month).

þūresdæg, noun (THOO-rez-DAIE / ˈθuː-rɛz-ˌdæj): Thursday (Thor's day).

ūht, noun (OO'HT / ˈuːxt): Time just before daybreak.

un-tīma, noun (UN-TEE-ma / ˈʌn-ˌtiː-ma): Wrong or improper time; bad time.

wēod-mōnaþ, noun (WAY-odd-MO-nath / ˈweːɔd-ˌmoː-naθ): August (weed-month).

winter, noun (WIN-ter / ˈwɪn-tɛr): Winter; year.

winter-fylleþ, noun (WIN-ter-FUELL-eth / ˈwɪn-tɛr-ˌfyl-lɛθ): October.

wōdnesdæg, noun (WOAD-nez-DAIE / ˈwoːd-nɛz-ˌdæj): Wednesday (Woden's day).

wræc-hwīl, noun (WRACK-HWEEL / ˈwræk-ˌhwiːl): Period of misery or exile.

4

Learning and Working

From wasp's eggs to lapis lazuli

THE ONLY REASON WE still have stories from *geardagum*, from way back in the early medieval period, is because of the onerous work performed by scribes. Every letter, flourish and illustration in every book was painstakingly drawn by hand, and before you even got to writing, you needed materials and tools to write with. The word 'manuscript' comes from Latin *manus* (hand) + *scriptus* (written); it is a book written by hand. Movable type was invented around 1040 CE by the Chinese artisan Bi Sheng, but Europe didn't get its first commercial-use printing machine until the Gutenberg press around 1450. The first printing press in England was set up by William Caxton at Westminster Abbey in 1476; some scholars use this event to signify the end of the Middle Ages. So all medieval books in Europe are manuscripts.

Writing a **bōc** (book) today may seem a laborious endeavour, but it's nothing compared to medieval book-making. Acquiring pages alone was incredibly time-consuming and required significant resources. Manuscript pages were made of animal skin, either vellum (from a calf) or parchment (from a sheep or goat). In Old English, parchment and vellum were called **bōc-fell**, literally 'book-skin'. There was no shortage of sheep in early medieval England, but there were times when even adequate sheepskin was difficult to obtain. Good-quality *bōc-fell* came from 'harvesting' the animals, not making do with the remains of fatalities. During the periods of rampant Viking attacks farming was frequently disrupted, meaning fewer sheep and fewer skins. Because of this, not a lot of book-making was happening in England during the second half of the ninth century.

But assuming you do have plenty of sheep, how do you make *bōc-fell*? The steps went something like this:

1   Peel the skin off of the animal carcass, a process called flaying: in Old English, **be-flēan** (to flay).

2   Moisten the flayed skin and then soak it in a solution of lime. (If you're short on lime, some rotting vegetable matter should do the trick.) This loosens the hairs and fatty tissues so they will come off the skin easily.

3   Soak the hair-free skin a second time and then stretch it out on a frame. Make sure the skin is pulled taut, or you will end up with leather, not parchment.

4   Scrape the taut skin with a half-moon-shaped knife, evening out the surface.

5   Rub the skin with a powder of pumice, bone or chalk. This process, called 'pouncing', makes the surface more matte, removing the grease and whitening the parchment.

After these steps you will need to cut the *bōc-fell* to the correct size and shape. You might choose to rule the pages, making it easier to write in a straight line, by lightly scoring the sheets with a fine, round-tipped

Animal skin is pretty sturdy, far more resilient than paper, but occasionally a repair is required. Here a hole in the *bōc-fell* has been stitched shut.

tool called a stylus or the back of a knife. If you lived during the late tenth century, you might have done your ruling with lead.

The writing process itself required a ***feþer*** (FEH-ther, same as modern English 'feather') or ***wrīting-feþer*** (pen, literally 'writing-feather') and ink. (*Wrīting* was pronounced a little differently – WREE-ting – but its spelling hasn't changed at all.) If you want to make a quill pen, the feathers of a goose or swan work quite well, especially the flight feathers on the outer edge of the wing. Those feathers have the longest hollow sections, which serve as barrels for holding ink. Feathers curve a bit differently depending on which side of the bird they're from: left-wing feathers are best for right-handed people, while right-wing feathers are more comfortable for lefties. Cut the feather to a suitable length (eight or nine inches) and scrape the waxy outer layer away from the tip. Trim the tip and use a long hook to remove the membrane that supplies the bird's wing with blood. Don't forget to cut a small slit right at the tip of the pen, or the ink won't reach the *bōc-fell*.

Ink was made from many different materials: minerals like lapis lazuli (blue) and cinnabar (red), plant matter like woad (dark blue) and madder (pink), animal matter like sea molluscs (purple) and squid ink (dark brown or black). Common black ink was called **blæc**, or **bēam-telg** (tree-dye), reflecting its origin, an oak tree, or **āc** in Old English. (*Āc* is also the name of the A-rune ᚪ.) Modern English 'acorn' comes from *āc*, since it's the tree's **corn**, its seed or fruit. But acorns are not the only thing that comes from an oak tree. Oak gall wasps lay their eggs on the branches, leaves and roots of oak trees. The eggs develop inside round galls, which can be harvested from the tree and used for ink-making. If you smash the galls and soak them in rainwater for a few days, the water will gradually turn brown. The addition of copperas, or ferrous sulfate, will darken the brown until exposure to the air turns it a deep black. And there you have it: *bēam-telg*, 'tree-dye'. To get your ink to stick to the *bōc-fell* you need to add an adhesive like glair. If you beat an egg white until a froth forms on the surface, the clear liquid below the froth is glair. Egg yolk and gum arabic also make good adhesives.

Although black was the most common colour for writing (as it still is today), red-orange ink was the base pigment for illustrations. Red-orange was used to outline illustrations before adding all the other colours on top. Illustrations in medieval manuscripts are often called 'miniatures', which is rather confusing; after all, some are large, full-page images. But the name has nothing to do with an illustration's size. The word 'miniature' comes from the base ink used in illustrations, because the red-orange pigment is made from a mineral called minium.

Miniature isn't the only manuscript-related word that comes from a mineral name. Rubrica, an iron-based mineral, produces a red ink, a useful colour for highlighting headings and instructions in a manuscript. The word 'rubric' initially referred to anything written in red ink, most often a direction in a liturgical book, but eventually it came to mean a set of rules or established custom, regardless of the colour it came in.

Acquiring the necessary materials for luxurious, illustrated books was challenging. Medieval manuscripts are well known for having bright colours and gold leaf, burnished metal that makes a book glow when reflecting candlelight, but these manuscripts are exceptional. The use of certain inks was very costly indeed. For instance, minerals like orpiment (for yellow ink) and mercury (red) were not available in England and had to be imported at great expense. Deep-blue ink was more precious than gold, since it was made from lapis lazuli, a mineral imported from the Mediterranean, mined in modern-day Afghanistan. (Woad, which could be found locally, and indigo, imported from the Mediterranean, produced cheaper blues.) Even less costly pigments could be difficult to acquire. Organic matter was only available during certain seasons. Some pigments took months to produce, even when the materials could be sourced locally. White lead required a month at minimum, and some types of verdigris (green) needed as long as half a year.

Although medieval scribes were probably unaware of them, there were some major downsides to using certain pigments. Vermilion, made from lead or mercury, was toxic; inhaling it or touching it could cause nausea, vomiting, diarrhoea and migraine, and long-term exposure might result in irreversible damage to the nervous system. Orpiment contains arsenic; inhaling it irritates the mucus membranes and touching it too frequently causes skin ulcers. In the long term, your choice of yellow ink could even poison you to death.

Crafting with lore-servants

Until the later medieval period, only monastic houses had the resources, workforce and demand for manuscripts. In the early Middle Ages, a scribe would most likely be a *munuc* (monk) or a *nunne* (nun), a man or woman of the Church. Monastic houses needed manuscripts because it was through the written word that faith and knowledge could be preserved and passed down over the centuries.

In early medieval England there were monastic houses for both men and women, including double monasteries – two separate communities that shared a church and facilities. Most seventh-century women's houses were founded by queens and aristocratic women or were at least established at their request. During this period women were encouraged to form their own houses and could hold leadership positions like that of abbess. Upon entering a monastic house, both women and men could receive an education in history and grammar as well as scripture. An educated *nunne* or *munuc* might even travel to the Continent to teach Christianity.

A school in Old English has the pleasingly literal name of *leornung-hūs* (learning-house). A *leornung-mann* (learning-person) is a student. A younger student might be called a *leornung-cild* or a *leornung-cniht*. Modern English 'child' comes directly from Old English *cild* (pronounced CHILLD), while *cniht* (K'NIH'T) has given us 'knight'. The two are very far apart in our understanding now, so why did Old English give a small child a great warrior's name?

Today, knights are seen as highly accomplished and distinguished individuals. In the Middle Ages, a knight was a warrior of noble birth raised to an honourable rank by the king or queen. After the Crusades, a king or queen could grant knighthood simply to recognise personal merit or to reward services rendered to the Crown or country. Today, artists, scientists, athletes and philanthropists have all been honoured with knighthoods.

But in Old English *cniht* was not a badge of honour. A *cniht* was simply a boy. There was nothing special about a *cniht*, who could even be a boy employed as a servant or attendant. In fact, servitude, or low stature, never stopped being a connotation of 'knight', and it is this idea that allowed the word to be elevated from its seemingly lowly origins: noble knights of old and modern knights are all people who *serve* in some way. That *leornung-cniht* is a word in Old English implies that even a humble, lowly child could receive some sort of education.

Somewhere between a *cild* and a *cniht* is a **cnapa** (of possible relation to **cnafa**, which became 'knave'). We might translate *cild*, *cniht* and *cnapa* as 'boy' or 'youth', but the exact ages are unclear. What we do know is that children of any age can develop a reputation for being naughty. In Middle English a 'knape' could be a boy or male youth, a servant or attendant, a fellow or a rogue. A glossary of Yorkshire dialect compiled in 1855 shows that 'knap' retained the meaning of 'rogue' well into the modern period: 'A Knap, a person not strictly honest in dealing or appropriation.' While *cniht* rose through the ranks almost thanks to its lowly origins, it seems like *cnapa* only became more mired in trouble. Perhaps there's a reason there was no *leornung-cnapa*.

Whether you're a *leornung-cild* or a *leornung-cniht*, you need to have a good teacher, which is **lārēow** in Old English. *Lārēow*, rather unexpectedly, comes from the words **lār** (lore, teaching, instruction, knowledge) and **þēow** (servant, enslaved person). The term 'lore-servant' might sound a bit disrespectful. Were early medieval teachers actually enslaved? Probably not. They were servants of knowledge and learning, not of people. Saints, similarly, were called *þēow*, even though they were the holiest of human beings. Much respected and venerated, saints were the servants of God.

Leornung can refer to learning, study, reading or meditation, things you might gain from your *lārēow*. Learning itself is a 'craft' in Old English, for **cræft** is a wonderfully versatile word; it can mean 'power', 'strength', 'art', 'skill', 'trade', 'cunning', 'knowledge' or 'virtue'. **Leornung-cræft** (learning-craft) is thus 'education' or 'erudition'. 'Craft' survives in modern English, but unfortunately we have lost some compound words like **tungol-cræft** (star-craft), so much lovelier than 'astronomy'. Arts and crafts today includes woodworking, sewing, basket-weaving and scrap-booking, but *cræft* refers to an even more diverse collection of arts. **Wōþ** (pronounced WOATH) means voice, song or speech, and **meter** is metre or versification, so both **wōþ-cræft** and **meter-cræft** are the art of poetry or song. **Stæf** refers to a letter or written character, and so **stæf-cræft** (letter-craft) is grammar. *Stæf* also means 'staff' or 'stick'; a letter is called *stæf* because runes used to be carved into sticks of wood or staves.

Each of the above crafts is a **weorold-cræft** (world-craft), a secular art rather than a spiritual one. A poem known as *The Gifts of Men* lists the many skills bestowed by God upon human beings. The poem says that wise thoughts and worldly skills (*wise geþohtas ond woruldcræftas*) won't all go to a single person because such an individual would become overly proud and arrogant. It is God's effort to minimise the number of insufferable know-it-alls.

An Old English prayer says, 'May the beauty of world-craft (*woruldcræfta*) and every work bless you, gracious Father!' The prayer continues, asking literally every aspect of God's creation to bless him, from the heavens and angels to the clear water and stars, from the sun and moon to frost and snow. Every animal, both wild and tame, is asked to praise God. In this prayer, *weorold-cræft* refers not to any old secular art but to the grandest craft of all, the art of world-making. God is the master world-smith, who literally crafted the world.

Earthling, how do you do your work?

When the world-smith crafted the world, he did not craft its inhabitants equally. Free men in early medieval England broadly fell into two tiers: *eorl* (nobleman, warrior) and *ceorl* (peasant). Members of the unfree were called *þēow* or *þrǽl* (pronounced THRAL), both of which mean 'enslaved person'. Today when we're 'enthralled' by something, it means we are held captive by it, captivated and, in a sense, enslaved.

Given that it was mainly monks and nuns, people of the Church, who could write at the time, it is a challenge to learn about what secular careers would have been available to a young *ceorl*. We have no tenth-century payslips to consult.

Ælfric of Eynsham's *Colloquy*, a language exercise for students learning Latin, gives us some idea of what jobs were common in the early Middle Ages. Old English glosses, or translations, are supplied between the lines of Latin to assist the students. Ælfric's *Colloquy* is one of those dialogues a language teacher might give you to practise with a partner in order to learn new vocabulary. Just like the language exercises of today, the Latin dialogue doesn't sound like a conversation people would actually have in real life. The dialogue is an interrogation of average, everyday men about the importance of their occupations. Who ultimately is the most useful? Some of the possible candidates include a monk, a shepherd, a huntsman, a fisherman, a merchant, a baker and an 'earth-ling'.

In the *Colloquy* the teacher asks (in the Old English gloss), 'What do you say, *yrþlingc*? How do you do your work?'

Latin: *Quid dicit tu arator? Quomodo exerces opus tuum?*
Old English: *Hwæt sægest þu yrþlingc? Hu begæst þu weorc þin?*

Irþling (or *yrþlingc*, as it is spelled here) sounds exactly like modern English 'earthling' – but rather than being an extraterrestrial's name for humankind, the word refers to a ploughman or farmer, someone who works the earth. The *irþling* in the dialogue says that he must go out at daybreak each day, and that out of fear for his lord, he never dares to 'skulk at home', no matter how harsh the winter weather might be. Every day he must drive the oxen to the field and plough an acre of land or more. He also must water and feed the oxen and clean the dung out of their manger. He exclaims: *Hig, hig, micel gedeorf ys hyt!* (Oh, oh, it is a lot of work!) At one point the teacher asks which *weorold-cræft* is most important. The answer given is agriculture; everyone needs to eat, and it is the craft of the *irþling* that keeps everyone fed.

Although it sounds like 'earth', **irþ** is actually the Old English word for ploughing or tilling. The suffix *-ling* turns the noun *irþ* into a word meaning 'a person or thing belonging to or concerned with *irþ*', making 'ploughing' into 'ploughman'. *Irþling* became obsolete after the Middle Ages, although it was used by historians in the eighteenth and nineteenth centuries to refer specifically to these early medieval farmers. It may sound the same, but modern English 'earthling' has no connection to Old English *irþling*. The first recorded use of 'earthling' was in the late sixteenth century, a word meaning someone who lives on earth as opposed to in heaven: 'Wee (of all earthlings) are Gods vtmost subiects', wrote the playwright, poet and pamphleteer Thomas Nashe in 1593. 'Earthling' did not take on the definition of a person who lives on or comes from the earth as opposed to another planet until the mid nineteenth century. The *Fayetteville Observer*, an American newspaper, made the observation in 1858: 'The last time the great comet was seen by us earthlings is said to be three hundred years ago', referring to the Great Comet of 1556.

Although they never seem to be given the label of *irþling*, women were actively involved in farm work in early medieval England. The historians Debby Banham and Rosamund Faith note that although historical sources (as usual) centre the experiences of men, that is no reason to doubt the 'vital role' played by women in the rural economy. Even though August is called 'weed-month' (*wēod-mōnaþ*), and a **wēod-hōc** (hoe, 'weed-hook') is listed among a farmer's tools, very little is said about weeds or weeding in Old English. Banham and Faith suggest that this is because weeding, 'being a tedious job that was never definitively finished', was women's work. They say that the association of a particular kind of work with women could possibly explain why weeding is absent from 'even those written sources that do concern themselves with farming (which were undoubtedly produced by men)'.

If *irþling* was one of the most important occupations, many other secular professions are known to have been practised by women. Cloth-making could be quite lucrative, as well as weaving and embroidery. The word **sēamestre** is the feminine form of 'tailor' (like modern English 'seamstress'), and the surname Webster comes from the feminine form of the word for 'weaver' – **webbestre**. A less glamorous yet essential job for women was grinding grain to make flour, along with kneading dough and baking bread. Debby Banham suggests that while people may have considered the production of flour to be a lower-status activity, the same might not have been true for the actual making of bread. Banham gives the example of a riddle in which a lord's daughter kneads bread. Remember that *hlǣfdige* (woman, literally 'bread-maker') became the modern English word 'lady'. The feminine form of the word for 'baker' – **bæcestre** – gives us another familiar surname: Baxter.

If a lady is the 'bread-maker', the lord is (if you remember from Chapter 2) the 'bread-guardian' – *hlāford*, the *weard* of the *hlāf*. There are a variety of *weard* jobs in Old English (*weard* being the predecessor of modern English 'warden'), including **brycg-weard** (bridge-keeper), *dūru-weard* (door-keeper) and *bāt-weard* (boat-keeper, the commander of a ship). A *stig-weard* is someone who controls the domestic affairs of the household, especially matters of the table. From *stig-weard* we get the word 'steward', but *stig* gives us 'sty'. How did a 'sty-keeper' end up being a steward? Old English *stig* is not what we normally think of when we hear the word 'sty'. A *stig* was a wooden enclosure that was connected to a house, like a hall, so *stig-weard* really means 'hall-keeper'. It wasn't until the Middle English period in the thirteenth century that 'sty' came to mean an enclosure for keeping swine, a pigsty. By the end of the fourteenth century, 'sty' took on a more negative connotation: it was an 'abode of bestial lust' or a place frequented by the morally degraded. Hell was called a 'stynkyng stye'. From around the year 1600, 'sty' was used to describe a dwelling or sleeping place so wretched and filthy that it was no better than a pigsty.

There have been many types of *weard* and *cræft* jobs to consider thus far, but the historian Richard Britnell warns that medieval names for specific occupations can be 'misleading in the degree of rigidity and continuity they suggest'. A person could have more than one skill or occupation. Throughout the Middle Ages, the most successful towns (and on a smaller scale, households) would have been supported by income from a variety of industries: farming, trade and a variety of crafts. Although the teacher in Ælfric's *Colloquy* may consider the *irþling* to be the most important of occupations, all the *woruldcræftas*, those of both men and women, were precious.

Ale-poets and laughter-smiths

Old English **wyrhta** means 'worker', 'labourer' or 'maker', and the word appears in modern English as 'wright'. Some wrights were named for the material with which they worked: a **leðer-wyrhta** works with leather and a **stān-wyrhta** works with stone. Other wrights are named for the things they make, a **scip-wyrhta** (ship-maker) or **sealm-wyrhta** (psalm-maker) for instance. If your surname is Wainwright, perhaps one of your ancestors made carts and carriages as a **wægn-wyrhta** (wagon-maker). But perhaps the most familiar modern wright works with something much less material: a playwright.

A **scop** is a poet, someone who can **scippan** (shape, create). In Old English texts, God is often called **scippend** (creator), since he is the shaper of the world. An **ealu-sceop** (ale-poet) is a different kind of 'shaper', and its definition depends on which dictionary you're using. The Toronto *Dictionary of Old English* says that an *ealu-sceop* is 'one who recites poetry in the presence of those drinking' (a common enough occurrence in early medieval England), but *Bosworth-Toller* claims that *ealu-sceop* means 'brewer'. Personally, I love the latter explanation; certainly craft-beer connoisseurs would agree that the creation of IPAs and stouts is an art like poetry. *Ealu-sceop*, however, appears in two eleventh-century law codes for men of the Church, which warn that a priest should not be a musician, entertainer or *ealu-sceop* – and the definition of someone who recites poetry at drinking parties does fit this context better. Besides, monks brewed beer throughout the Middle Ages, so it seems unlikely that an ecclesiastical law code would forbid a priest to make ale.

One common profession has a name that has never changed, now one of the more familiar English surnames: **smiþ** (smith). **Smiþ-cræft** (smith-craft) is the art of working in metals or wood. An **iren-smiþ** works with iron, a **gold-smiþ** with gold, and a **mæstling-smiþ** with brass, but not all smiths are so easily explained. What, for example, is a **hleahtor-smiþ** (laughter-smith)?

According to the medieval literature scholar Eric Stanley, the laughter found in Old English texts is generally not indicative of pleasure or mirth. On the contrary, laughter often appears in negative contexts. The lamentations of the damned, the torments of hell – these are accompanied by devils' peals of laughter. Upon falling from God's grace, the angels need not laugh loudly. When Satan's messenger visits the Garden of Eden to deceive Adam and Eve, he laughs at his triumph. Examples of this kind of negative laughter are far from uncommon in Old English, particularly in religious texts. Stanley highlights the potential for wordplay, since the words **hleahtor** (laughter) and **leahter** (sin) are very similar. Perhaps that makes it seem more natural to align mirth and malice.

The hapax *hleahtor-smiþ* certainly appears in a mirthless context, a poem that tells the story of Passover, a Jewish holiday commemorating the time when God sent a deadly spirit that passed over the homes of the Israelites. According to the Book of Exodus, the Israelites were told to smear lamb's blood on their doors so the deadly spirit would know to pass over their homes. Since the Egyptians were not warned to do this, the deadly spirit killed the first-born son in each of their households. It is at this point in the Old English narrative that the poet says:

> A destroyer went far and wide, a hateful tyrant. The land choked on the corpses of the dead. The people set out. There was weeping far and wide, little worldly joy. The hands of the <u>laughter-smiths</u> (*hleahtorsmiðum*) were restrained.

Though you might not guess it from the solemn context, according to the Toronto *Dictionary of Old English* a *hleahtor-smiþ* is in fact a minstrel or entertainer, someone who causes laughter or mirth. This detail about silent minstrels is an addition of the Old English poet, for, as Stanley says, Old English poetry excels at depicting 'misery in rich variation'. The phrase 'weeping far and wide' was not enough on its own to describe the Egyptians' great sorrow.

Bench-sitters, backbiters and gold-givers

Hopefully, such sorrow does not apply to your place of work. What qualities might you desire in a boss or co-worker? No matter what line of work you're in, it's nice to be around people who are **wīs** (wise), **blīþe** (happy, kind) and **sib-sum** (friendly, peaceable). But chances are you'll have to work with someone who is just too **dysig** (pronounced DUE-zih). *Dysig* sounds somewhat like, and is in fact related to, modern English 'dizzy', but a *dysig* colleague is not one who suffers from vertigo. *Dysig* means 'foolish' or 'stupid'. According to a timeless Old English adage, *Hit byð dysig þæt man speca ær þone he þænce* (it is foolish for a man to speak before he thinks). By the end of the thirteenth century, this word had pretty much lost its association with stupidity, having acquired the more familiar definition of 'giddy' or 'having a sensation of whirling or vertigo'.

Maybe your co-workers aren't *dysig*, but there may be one or two who refuse to pull their own weight. Should you call such a person a **benc-sittend** (bench-sitter)? *Benc-sittend* sounds like a person who sits around idly. ('You're such a bench-sitter, why don't you do something useful!') In modern English, when someone is 'on the bench' they are either presiding over a courtroom or waiting on the sidelines during a sports match. *Benc-sittend* appears only twice in extant Old English literature, so we don't have a lot of context to go by, but the word seems to describe a guest or hall-retainer, literally 'one who sits on a bench'. In both instances the bench-sitters are in the process of consuming alcohol, but that could be a mere coincidence.

Benc-sittend appears in a tenth-century poem called *The Fortunes of Men*, which lists numerous potential outcomes for a person's life. It's not the most uplifting inventory, with such options as going blind, dying in battle or being consumed by birds of prey while hanging from a gallows. About halfway through the poem, the tone changes

– not *everyone* will live a life of misery. A person might become a clever craftsman, a talented musician or a popular drinking companion:

> One shall please a company of men, gladden the <u>bench-sitters</u> (*bencsittendum*) at their beers; there will be great mirth among the drinkers.

There's something heart-warming about the belief that God ordains certain individuals to be skilful at gladdening the mead-hall bench-sitters. The work of a laughter-smith or ale-poet is truly a worthy calling.

So a *benc-sittend* is simply someone who sits happily on a bench, drinking, perhaps being entertained, without any negative connotations. If you want a word to describe your lazy co-workers, the adjective **bæftan-sittende** (back-sitting) is a better choice. (Even in Old English there's a word that literally means 'sitting on one's arse'.)

Far worse than an office 'back-sitter', however, is a 'backbiter'. The word 'backbiting' has been around since at least the twelfth century. As one Middle English text says, 'bacbiteres' (backbiters) are those who 'biteð bi hinden bac oðre' (bite behind the backs of others), people who slander others behind their backs. A 'bacbiter' is no better than a serpent, which 'stingeth al stille' (strikes in secret). The Old English word that preceded 'bacbiter' was **bæc-slitol**. This hapax appears in an eleventh-century homily by Wulfstan, Archbishop of York, about how to live a Christian life. Wulfstan warns, *Se ðe wære bæcslitol, weorðe se wærsagol* (he who is a backbiter, let him be wary of what he says). *Slitol* comes from the verb **slītan** (to bite or tear), which usually describes the way a wild animal rips apart prey with its teeth. Somewhere along the way, the malicious traitors of the English-speaking world moved from teeth to knives as their weapon of choice; a more common word these days is 'back-stabber'. Back-stabber has only been around since 1906, when it appeared in the *Westminster Gazette* right before a general election. (Perhaps it's not a surprise that the word's debut describes a politician who failed to keep his promises.)

But hopefully there are no backbiters in your office, only *blīþe* and *sib-sum* colleagues. When it comes to bosses, though, you should always hope for a gold-giver. Both **gold-gifa** (gold-giver) and **bēah-gifa** (ring-giver) are words for a generous leader who distributes wealth among his followers in return for their service. The word *gifa* looks similar to modern English 'giver', but it's pronounced YIV-ah, not GIV-ah. In Old English, when g is followed by the vowels i, e or y, it usually has a y (consonant) sound, like 'yes' and 'yellow'. This pronunciation was maintained in Middle English, although the spelling changed to 'yēvere'.

Beowulf is an exemplary *gold-gifa*, equipping his men with helms and strong swords and rewarding them with treasure. But his men do not hold up their side of the bargain when Beowulf engages a dragon in mortal combat. The one faithful warrior of the lot, Wiglaf, reminds his cowardly colleagues of their obligation to their king. He says:

> I remember that time when we drank mead, when we made promises in the beer-hall to our lord . . . Now the day has come when our lord needs the strength of brave warriors. Let's go help the war-chief against the fierce fire-terror!

Wiglaf proclaims his desire to fight alongside Beowulf, immersing himself in the dragon's fiery breath rather than leaving his *gold-gifa* to perish alone.

Ideally, your boss won't ask you to join them on any dragon quests, but if they do, keep in mind that if you want your legacy to be remembered in a 1,000-year-old poem, you should probably go with your *gold-gifa*.

Tax-fish

The very existence of a word can tell you something about the people who use it. In the UK a 'cuppa' almost always refers to tea, but there's no particular reason why the colloquial shortening of 'cup of' couldn't mean coffee. Would Americans have started using the baseball term 'touch base' in business and politics if the sport were not a national pastime? Modern English lacks a word that means 'tax-fish', but *gafol-fisc* is a word (and thus a concept) in Old English.

Old English **gafol** is not the modern English 'gavel' of courthouses; it means 'tax' or 'rent'. ('Gavel', originally an American word for a hammer or mallet, has only been around since the nineteenth century and is etymologically unrelated.) **Gafol-fisc** (tax-fish) is not a common word in surviving Old English texts. In fact, it appears in only one text, albeit one that was copied into more than thirty different extant manuscripts. So *gafol-fisc* is a hapax but one that is relatively well-disseminated.

Gafol-fisc appears in an eleventh-century charter, in which King Cnut grants among other things a large quantity of fish to the Abbey of Bury St Edmunds. The abbey was established in the tenth century to guard the relics of St Edmund. King Cnut was concerned about his soul going to the right place in the afterlife, so he made generous donations to churches and monastic houses to obtain prayers for his soul. These gifts could come in the form of land, protection, relics, food and tax exemptions. According to the charter, King Cnut gave the Abbey of Bury St Edmunds 'my <u>tax-fish</u> that comes to me from the maritime district' (*min <u>gouelfisch</u> ðe me arist be selonde*). By giving to the abbey, the king was giving to St Edmund himself, who could intercede with God in his favour. We don't know the precise quantity of *gafol-fisc*, but the charter does note that Cnut's wife, Queen Ælfgyfu, threw in 4,000 eels for good measure.

In early medieval England, anyone who owned land was entitled to a portion of the goods produced on it. For the most part, taxes and rent were collected in goods and services rather than coins. Old English *feorm* refers specifically to food-rents, like King Cnut's *gafol-fisc*. During the late seventh and early eighth centuries, the law code of King Ine of Wessex states that the following should be paid for every ten hides of land (supposedly the amount of land needed to support ten families): 10 vats of honey, 300 loaves of bread, 42 measures of ale, 2 cows, 10 geese, 20 hens, 10 cheeses, a measure of butter, 5 salmon, 100 eels and 20 pounds of fodder. Monetary taxation became more common in later centuries, but the system of *feorm* seems to have lasted beyond the Norman Conquest; in these later centuries a manor might have to support the king and his retinue for up to twenty-four hours, and that's a lot of eating.

Depending on what was grown or produced in a certain region, farmers paid their taxes in different kinds of goods, some of which are identified by Old English words: **ealu-gafol** (ale-tax), **gafol-bere** (tax-barley), **gafol-wydu** (tax-wood or tax-lumber), **mete-gafol** (food-tax), **gafol-hwitel** (tax-blankets, 'whittle' being an obsolete word for a cloak or blanket), and **gafol-tȳning** (tax-fencing, the material needed for building fences). A **gafol-swān** was someone who rented a herd of swine from a lord and paid him back with a specified number of butchered swine. A **gafol-heord** was a swarm of bees that could be rented from one's lord, with the rental fee paid in honey. This tax paid in honey was called **hunig-gafol** (honey-tax).

Gafol-heord is another hapax, appearing only in *Rectitudines*, a manual for managing an estate. The manual was probably compiled at Bath Abbey or implemented somewhere in that area. It states that a beekeeper who keeps a *gafol-heord* (rental swarm) should pay at least five sesters of honey in rent. It's uncertain exactly how much a sester is, but it could be a liquid measure of around 700 to 950 ml (24–32 oz).

If that's accurate, the beekeeper could be expected to pay as much as 4.5 litres of honey. If you think about it, all human-tended honeycombs are rental swarms. The beekeeper is the 'landlord' of the bees, who pay their 'rent' in honey.

Fourth *wordhord*

āc, noun (AHK / 'aːk): Oak, oak tree; name of the A-rune ᚪ.

bāt-weard, noun (BAHT-WEH-ard / 'baːt-ˌwɛard): Commander of a ship.

bæcestre, noun (BACK-es-truh / 'bæ-kɛs-trə): Baker; (specifically) female baker.

bæc-slitol, noun (BACK-SLIT-ol / 'bæk-ˌslɪ-tɔl): Backbiter, someone who maligns another behind their back.

bæftan-sittende, adjective (BAV-tahn-SIT-ten-duh / 'bæv-tan-ˌsɪt-tɛn-də): Idle (back-sitting).

bēah-gifa, noun (BAY-ah-YIV-ah / 'beːax-ˌji-va): Ring-giver, giver of treasure or wealth.

bēam-telg, noun (BAY-ahm-TELG / 'beːam-ˌtɛlg): Ink (tree-dye).

be-flēan, verb (beh-FLAY-ahn / bɛ-'fleː-an): To flay, skin (an animal).

benc-sittend, noun (BENCH-SIT-tend / 'bɛntʃ-ˌsɪt-tɛnd): 'Bench-sitter', someone who sits on a bench (perhaps a guest or retainer).

blæc, noun (BLACK / 'blæk): Ink (especially black ink).

blīþe, adjective (BLEE-thuh / 'bliː-θə): Happy, joyful; gentle, kind, gracious.

bōc, noun (BOAK / 'boːk): Book.

bōc-fell, noun (BOAK-FELL / 'boːk-ˌfɛl): Parchment, vellum (book-skin).

brycg-weard, noun (BRUEDG-WEH-ard / 'brydʒ-ˌwɛard): Bridge-keeper.

ceorl, noun (CHEH-orl / 'tʃɛɔrl): Man (general term without reference to a particular social class); peasant; member of the lowest class of free men.

cild, noun (CHILLD / ˈt͡ʃɪld): Child, infant.

cnafa, noun (Kʼ NAH-va / ˈkna-va): Boy or youth.

cnapa, noun (Kʼ NAH-pa / ˈkna-pa): Boy or youth, older than a *cild* but younger than a *cniht*; servant.

cniht, noun (Kʼ NIHˈT / ˈknɪxt): Male youth, older than a *cnapa*; servant.

corn, noun (KORN / ˈkɔrn): Grain, cereal plants grown as crops; seed, berry or fruit of a plant.

cræft, noun (KRAFT / ˈkræft): Power, strength; art, skill, craft, trade; cunning, knowledge.

dūru-weard, noun (DOO-ruh-WEH-ard / ˈduː-rʌ-ˌwɛard): Door-keeper.

dysig, adjective (DUE-zih / ˈdy-zɪj): Foolish, stupid.

ealu-gafol, noun (EH-al-luh-GA-voll / ˈɛa-lʌ-ˌga-vɔl): Ale paid as tax or tribute.

ealu-sceop, noun (EH-al-luh-SHEH-op / ˈɛa-lʌ-ˌʃɛɔp): 'Ale-poet', someone who recites poetry in the presence of those drinking.

eorl, noun (EH-orl / ˈɛɔrl): Nobleman, warrior.

feorm, noun (FEH-orm / ˈfɛɔrm): Food-rent, a fixed contribution of provisions given to a person or institution as a levy.

feþer, noun (FEH-ther / ˈfɛ-θɛr): Feather, quill, pen.

gafol, noun (GA-voll / ˈga-vɔl): Tax, tribute, rent.

gafol-bere, noun (GA-voll-BEH-ruh / ˈga-vɔl-ˌbɛ-rə): Barley paid as tax or tribute.

gafol-fisc, noun (GA-voll-FISH / ˈga-vɔl-ˌfiʃ): Fish paid as tax or tribute.

gafol-heord, noun (GA-voll-HEH-ord / ˈga-vɔl-ˌhɛɔrd): Rented swarm of bees that is paid for in honey.

gafol-hwītel, noun (GA-voll-HWEE-tell / ˈga-vɔl-ˌhwiː-tɛl): Blankets or cloth paid as tax or tribute.

gafol-swān, noun (GA-voll-SWAN / ˈga-vɔl-ˌswaːn): Tax-paying

swineherd, someone who rents a herd of swine on condition of
paying a certain number of swine (butchered) as rent.

gafol-tȳning, noun (GA-voll-TUE-ning / ˈga-vɔl-ˌtyː-nɪŋ): Fence
materials paid as tax or tribute.

gafol-wudu, noun (GA-voll-WUD-uh / ˈga-vɔl-ˌwʌ-dʌ): Wood or lumber
paid as tax or tribute.

gifa, noun (YIV-ah / ˈjɪ-va): Giver, bestower.

gold-gifa, noun (GOLD-YIV-ah / ˈgɔld-ˌjɪ-va): Gold-giver, giver of gold
or wealth, a generous lord or king.

gold-smiþ, noun (GOLD-SMITH / ˈgɔld-ˌsmɪθ): Goldsmith.

hleahtor, noun (HLEH-ah-h'tor / ˈhlɛax-tɔr): Laughter.

hleahtor-smiþ, noun (HLEH-ah-h'tor-SMITH / ˈhlɛax-tɔr-ˌsmɪθ):
Entertainer, minstrel (laughter-smith).

hunig-gafol, noun (HUN-ih-GA-voll / ˈhʌ-nɪj-ˌga-vɔl): Honey paid as
tax or tribute.

iren-smiþ, noun (IH-ren-SMITH / ˈɪ-rɛn-ˌsmɪθ): Blacksmith
(iron-smith).

irþ, noun (IRTH / ˈɪrθ): Ploughing, tilling; ploughed land.

irþling, noun (IRTH-ling / ˈɪrθ-lɪŋ): Ploughman, farmer.

lār, noun (LAR / ˈlaːr): Lore, teaching, instruction, learning,
knowledge.

lārēow, noun (LA-ray-oh / ˈlaː-reːɔw): Teacher.

leahter, noun (LEH-ah-h'ter / ˈlɛax-tɛr): Sin, crime, vice.

leornung, noun (LEH-or-nung / ˈlɛɔr-nʌŋ): Learning, study, reading,
meditation.

leornung-cild, noun (LEH-or-nung-CHILLD / ˈlɛɔr-nʌŋ-ˌtʃɪld): Child
engaged in study, pupil.

leornung-cniht, noun (LEH-or-nung-K'NIH'T / ˈlɛɔr-nʌŋ-ˌknɪxt): Youth
engaged in study, scholar, disciple.

leornung-cræft, noun (LEH-or-nung-KRAFT / ˈlɛɔr-nʌŋ-ˌkræft):
Learning, erudition.

leornung-hūs, noun (LEH-or-nung-HOOS / 'lɛɔr-nʌŋ-ˌhuːs): School (learning-house).

leornung-mann, noun (LEH-or-nung-MAHN / 'lɛɔr-nʌŋ-ˌman): Scholar, student, disciple.

leðer-wyrhta, noun (LEH-ther-WUER-h'ta / 'lɛ-θɛr-ˌwyrx-ta): Tanner, currier, someone who works in leather.

mæstling-smiþ, noun (MAST-ling-SMITH / 'mæst-lɪŋ-ˌsmɪθ): Brazier, someone who works in brass.

mete-gafol, noun (MEH-tuh-GA-voll / 'mɛ-tə-ˌga-vɔl): Food paid as tax or tribute.

meter, noun (MEH-ter / 'mɛ-tɛr): Metre, versification.

meter-cræft, noun (MEH-ter-KRAFT / 'mɛ-tɛr-ˌkræft): Art of making poetry or verses.

munuc, noun (MUH-nuck / 'mʌ-nʌk): Monk.

nunne, noun (NUN-nuh / 'nʌn-nə): Nun.

scippan, verb (SHIP-pahn / 'ʃɪp-pan): To shape, form, create; to assign as a person's lot.

scippend, noun (SHIP-pend / 'ʃɪp-pɛnd): Creator, God.

scip-wyrhta, noun (SHIP-WUER-h'ta / 'ʃɪp-ˌwyrx-ta): Shipwright, someone who builds ships.

scop, noun (SHOP / 'ʃɔp): Poet.

sealm-wyrhta, noun (SEH-alm-WUER-h'ta / 'sɛalm-ˌwyrx-ta): Psalmist.

sēamestre, noun (SAY-ahm-es-truh / 'seːam-ɛs-trə): One who sews, tailor; (specifically) woman who sews, seamstress.

sib-sum, adjective (SIB-sum / 'sɪb-sʌm): Peaceable, friendly.

slītan, verb (SLEE-tahn / 'sliː-tan): To bite, tear, rend.

smiþ, noun (SMITH / 'smɪθ): Smith, usually someone who works in metals or wood.

smiþ-cræft, noun (SMITH-KRAFT / 'smɪθ-ˌkræft): 'Smith-craft', the craft of working in metals or wood.

stān-wyrhta, noun (STAHN-WUER-h'ta / ˈstaːn-ˌwyrx-ta):
Stonemason.

stæf, noun (STAFF / ˈstæf): Written character, letter.

stæf-cræft, noun (STAV-KRAFT / ˈstæv-ˌkræft): Grammar (letter-craft).

stig, noun (STIH / ˈstɪj): Wooden enclosure, part of a house, perhaps
a hall.

stig-weard, noun (STIH-WEH-ard / ˈstɪj-ˌwɛard): Steward,
superintendent of household affairs (especially in matters to do
with the table).

tungol-cræft, noun (TUNG-goll-KRAFT / ˈtʌŋ-gɔl-ˌkræft): Astronomy,
astrology (star-craft).

þēow, noun (THAY-oh / ˈθeːɔw): Enslaved person, servant.

þrǣl, noun (THRAL / ˈθræːl): Enslaved person, servant.

wægn-wyrhta, noun (WAYN-WUER-h'ta / ˈwæjn-ˌwyrx-ta):
Wainwright, someone who makes wagons or carts.

weard, noun (WEH-ard / ˈwɛard): Guard, watchman; guardian,
protector.

webbestre, noun (WEH-bes-truh / ˈwɛ-bɛs-trə): Weaver; (specifically)
female weaver.

wēod-hōc, noun (WAY-odd-HOAK / ˈweːɔd-ˌhoːk): Hoe (weed-hook).

weorold-cræft, noun (WEH-oh-rold-KRAFT / ˈwɛɔ-rɔld-ˌkræft): Secular
(non-religious) craft or art (world-craft).

wīs, adjective (WEES / ˈwiːs): Wise.

wōþ, noun (WOATH / ˈwoːθ): Voice, song, speech.

wōþ-cræft, noun (WOATH-KRAFT / ˈwoːθ-ˌkræft): 'Song-craft', the art
of poetry or song.

wrīting-feþer, noun (WREE-ting-FEH-ther / ˈwriː-tɪŋ-ˌfɛ-θɛr): Pen
(writing-feather).

wyrhta, noun (WUER-h'ta / ˈwyrx-ta): Worker, labourer; maker,
creator.

5

Playing (and More Drinking)

Well-comers and hall-joy

TODAY A PERSON CAN BE welcome, welcomed, or welcoming. A welcomer makes guests feel welcome. But there are no well-comers, people who 'come well'. Old English **wil-cuma** (well-comer) is a welcome visitor or a good guest, a person or thing whose arrival is pleasing.

The Geatish warrior Beowulf and his companions are 'well-comers' in two locations: the land of the Danes when they begin their mission and the land of the Geats when they return home. When Beowulf goes to King Hrothgar of the Danes to offer his services, his reputation precedes him. Beowulf is renowned in battle and his hand-grip has the strength of thirty men, so as long as he's on your side, what's not to welcome? Hrothgar is thrilled to have a foreign warrior offer to take on Grendel, the murderous creature who plagues his people. The king commands one of his men to greet the Geats and assure them that they are *wilcuman* (the plural of *wilcuma*). After slaying not one but *two* monsters, Beowulf is heading home, and the coastguard who sees him off declares that he and the other Geats will be *wilcuman* in their homeland. It's hard to have your strongest and bravest warrior abroad slaying other people's monsters, but the inconvenience is sweetened by the reward he brings back with him, a ship full of treasure.

Beowulf visits Hrothgar's mead-hall for only three nights, just enough time to slay Grendel and Grendel's mother and receive his reward. Perhaps it seems strange that he would depart so soon after his victories, but a *wil-cuma* must take care not to overstay their welcome. There's an old Danish saying that a fish and a guest begin to stink on the third day. The historian Alban Gautier explains how, in the context of early medieval hospitality, a guest is always 'ambiguous' and 'a potential danger'. A stay of longer than three nights starts to threaten the existing social hierarchy of the hall. A guest has the potential to create expectations of allegiance inadvertently in the host's mind. A limit of three nights for a host receiving a guest is actually specified in the law codes of two seventh-century Kentish kings. As with all law codes of this period, it's impossible to know to what extent the rules were actually followed or enforced, but a law's existence can still tell us something about contemporary attitudes and ideals. During the twelfth century (in the Middle English period) a similar rule appears in the law code attributed to Edward the Confessor but with more detail: a guest is only a guest for the first three days; after that, the host can be held responsible for the guest's actions. It's possible that a similar logic informed the seventh-century law codes.

Perhaps a guest simply should not be viewed as trustworthy. A guest is someone who takes advantage of a host's resources without making a formal alliance. Gautier notes that the Latin words *hospes* (guest) and *hostis* (enemy) share a common root, and in Old English wordplay on ***gyst*** (guest, stranger) and ***gāst*** (ghost, demon) was common. Both *gyst* and *gāst* can be spelled *gæst*.

But sometimes the demons are inside to begin with, not visitors from afar. In the Old English poem *Descent into Hell*, Christ goes down to the underworld to save its lost souls, an event known as the Harrowing (see page 44). The first person to witness Christ's arrival is his old friend John the Baptist, who is understandably overjoyed to see him. The poem says of John:

> Then the leader of the city-dwellers, brave before the multitude, boldly proclaimed, spoke to his kinsman, greeted the <u>welcome guest</u> (*wilcuman*) with words . . .

In this case, describing Christ as a 'welcome guest' seems like a bit of an understatement; after all, the guy who is going to save John from an eternity of hellish torments has just arrived.

But you don't have to be a Beowulf or a Christ to be a *wil-cuma*. A 'well-comer' might be your spouse, a seafarer returning home from a long journey, or maybe it's a friend, the person who brings you a snack while you work in the fields. A 'well-comer' could be your child coming home after fighting a battle. And all of us are 'well-comers' to God himself, if we make it into heaven on Judgement Day. In a poem on the subject of Judgement Day, God says to the fortunate souls on their way to heaven, *Ge sind wilcuman* (you are 'well-comers')!

Ideally, you will be a *wil-cuma* not to hell or to a monster fight but to **sele-drēam** (hall-joy). *Sele-drēam* refers to the mirth and festivities of a mead-hall. Although **drēam** looks like modern English 'dream', it is in fact a false friend. The etymology of modern English 'dream' is disputed, and it is unknown whether 'dream' and *drēam* are related in any way, but what is known is that the Old English word for 'dream' is actually **mǣting**. Not very dreamy.

In Old English literature some people long for *sele-drēam*, but others wish to leave it behind. Take, for instance, St Andrew: as soon as he finished converting the heathen cannibals of Mermedonia in the Old English poem *Andreas*, he was ready to move on to other projects. What's the point of hanging around in a place where everyone loves you for your teachings? The poem says:

> He was ready to set out. He wished to depart from that gold-city, the <u>hall-joy</u> (*seledream*) of men and treasure, the radiant ring-hall. He wished to seek a ship at the sea's edge.

The saint knows that the ultimate 'hall-joy' is in heaven, so you shouldn't waste time on mere earthly delights.

The poem *Beowulf* tells a different story. The last survivor of a soon-to-be defunct clan laments that his comrades who once knew *seledrēam* are all dead now:

> Death in battle, cruel mortality, snatched every soul of my people, those who lost their lives, who had once seen the <u>joy of the hall</u> (*seledream*). I have no one to bear a sword or to serve a gilded cup, a precious drinking-vessel. The old troops have gone elsewhere.

In another poem, *The Wanderer*, a wandering exile mournfully contemplates the companionship and 'hall-joy' he has left behind:

> Where has gone the horse? Where has gone the man?
> Where has gone the treasure-giver?
> Where has gone the house of feasts?
> Where are the <u>joys of the hall</u> (*seledreamas*)?

If you've read *The Lord of the Rings*, these lines might sound familiar. J. R. R. Tolkien, a philologist and a professor of English literature at the University of Oxford, used these lines as inspiration for his own 'Lament for the Rohirrim', which begins:

Where now the horse and the rider? Where is the horn that was blowing?
Where is the helm and the hauberk, and the bright hair flowing?

The Rohirrim seem to be longing for 'battle-joys' more than 'hall-joys', but the sense of loss is the same.

How tragic that *sele-drēam* is either elusive or oppressive, either something long gone or the very thing keeping us from true joy beyond the hall.

Aswim in ringing phrases

There were no castles in early medieval England: the first were constructed in the eleventh century after the Old English period. The closest you came to a royal residence prior to the Norman invasion was a great hall. But what was it like, this home of *sele-drēam*?

Great halls are in fact rare in the archaeological record. The handful of these large rectangular buildings that have been excavated date mostly from the seventh century. They are typically surrounded by various smaller buildings, so sometimes they are described as 'great hall complexes', a term which does not assume royal status (since this cannot necessarily be known). Halls like these were once common across Northern Europe. The largest known great hall in England is around 100 feet in length (three London double-decker buses), and around thirty feet in width; the largest on the Continent, a Viking hall at Lejre in Denmark, is twice that size. Halls were made mostly of wood, with wattle-and-daub walls and thatched roofs. There might be an entrance in the centre of a long side-wall, or that of a shorter end-wall. Curtains or drapes may have been used to further subdivide the hall's interior, as is illustrated in contemporary manuscripts, but the archaeological record leaves little to indicate how common these internal partitions might have been. A central *heorþ* (hearth) would have provided a hall with warmth and light (but also smoke). The *heorþ*'s importance is reflected in a word in King Cnut's law code for someone who owns their own property: **heorþ-fæst**, or 'secure at a hearth'.

The great hall was a place for sharing news, telling stories, playing games and making music, perhaps enjoying the sound of a **hearpe** (harp) or **gamen-wudu** (mirth-wood). Old English **gamen** (mirth, joy, amusement) would eventually become modern English 'game'. *Gamen-wudu* appears only twice in Old English, both times in *Beowulf*, describing the music and entertainment of King Hrothgar's mead-hall. In each instance the *gamen-wudu* is plucked while a poem is recited, and the second example calls the 'mirth-wood' a 'joyful harp' (*hearpan wynne*).

Joy, happiness . . . one might also call it glee. Modern English 'glee' comes from Old English **glīw**, which has a number of possible definitions – 'joy', 'merriment', 'mirth', 'entertainment', 'music'. The 'music' definition became obsolete after the sixteenth century, but the meaning of 'mirth' or 'joy' endured. The first recorded use of 'glee club' is from 1814; this London 'Glee-Club' met ten times a year for dining and singing 'when any glee is called for'. Although we still have glee clubs, we no longer have 'glee-wood'. Old English **glīw-bēam** (glee-wood) was some sort of musical instrument, possibly a harp, drum or tambourine.

'Music' in Old English is practically synonymous with 'joy' because the craft of *drēam* (joy) is in fact **drēam-cræft** (music). Yet the music, song and poetry of the hall is what ultimately drives the lake-dweller Grendel to attack and murder the Danes. In *Beowulf* Grendel 'suffered wretchedly' because, while waiting in darkness, he could hear joy (*dream*) loud in King Hrothgar's hall each day: 'There was the sound of the <u>harp</u> (*hearpan*), the sweet song of the <u>poet</u> (*scop*).' Grendel, unable to endure the 'joy-craft' of men, eventually begins his nightly murder spree.

John Gardner narrates this story from the antagonist's point of view in his novel *Grendel* (1971). While the Old English poem portrays Grendel's furious response to the music as senseless contempt for human happiness, Gardner provides a reason for it. In the novel, Grendel's mind is 'aswim in ringing phrases, magnificent, golden, and all of them, incredibly, lies'. He is angry because the poet's words have created a world in which there are heroes and villains, one race that is saved and another that is cursed. Grendel fumes, 'It was a cold-blooded lie that a god had lovingly made the world', a lie which the poet makes true 'by the sweetness of his harp, his cunning trickery'. Grendel despises the storyteller who can make people believe anything as long as his songs can make it beautiful.

Don't get drink-eager

If the music that reaches Grendel's ears is insufferably joyous, neither do the Danes' noisy parties endear them at all to their neighbour.

Heorot, King Hrothgar's hall, is a place for feasting, making speeches and even sleeping, but it's not called a food-hall, speech-hall or bed-hall. Heorot is first and foremost a **medu-heall**, a mead-hall. Although inebriation was not its raison d'être, the mead-hall in medieval England was a place of entertainment, and as the historian Martha Bayless observes, a habit of drinking 'substantial quantities' of alcohol 'may have sufficed to make everything that much more entertaining'. The focus on drinking in the hall was not due to pervasive alcoholism; it's just that one way to belong to a group is to drink with that group, the same reason we have wine receptions at conferences or after-work drinks at the pub.

Another word for a drinking hall is **bēor-sele** (*bēor*-hall). **Bēor** wasn't 'beer' exactly, nothing like the beer we drink today anyway. *Bēor* had different ingredients (honey, plus the juice of a fruit other than grapes) as well as a different process of manufacture. *Bēor* was both sweet and inebriating, with an alcohol content as high as 18 per cent. It was stronger than **wīn** (wine) and possibly the strongest alcohol available to drink in early medieval England, most likely imbibed from tiny drinking cups. **Medu** (mead) was less alcoholic than both *bēor* and *wīn*, around 10 per cent alcohol, about twice as strong as **ealu** (ale). While *bēor* is sometimes used interchangeably with *medu* in Old English poetry, it is never equated with *ealu*, which is a malt-based alcohol. It wasn't until the sixteenth century that 'beer' became a common word for hopped, malted liquor.

A feast or big social gathering could also be called a **bēor-þegu** (*bēor*-taking) or a **ge-bēor-scipe**. The Old English suffix *-scipe* (pronounced SHIP-uh) became '-ship' in modern English, appearing in words like 'friendship' and 'fellowship'. Unfortunately, we don't have a useful word like 'beer-ship' (although 'beer-ship' isn't right anyway, since *bēor* is different from beer). And one does not necessarily serve *bēor* at a *ge-bēor-scipe*. The Latin word *convivium* (a meal eaten in company) is used in the Old Testament to describe Pharaoh's birthday feast. The poet translating the narrative into Old English uses *ge-bēor-scipe* in place of *convivium*. *Ge-bēor-scipe* also appears as a translation for Latin *convivia* (company) in the Old English Gospel of Luke. When Christ has to feed 5,000 men with only five loaves of bread and two fish, he tells his apostles to have the people sit in companies (*gebeorscypas*) of fifty. Alcohol is not mentioned in either the Old English or Latin versions of this story, so the word *ge-bēor-scipe* here simply means a formal shared meal. And, as merry as it sounds, a *ge-bēor-scipe* is not necessarily a festive occasion: the Last Supper is called a *ge-bēor-scipe* in the Gospel of John. The word can also be a religious metaphor, referring either to God's eternal feast in heaven or to the spiritual feast of holy doctrine.

Another word for a feast is **symbel**, a word of unknown origin. Old Saxon *sumbal* and Old Icelandic *sumbl* (both of which mean 'feast') are *symbel*'s cognates, words that share a linguistic derivation (the same original word or root) with another word. Think of a cognate as a cousin: you and your cousin descend from common grandparents. Old English *symbel* became modern English 'symbol', which was used until the nineteenth century to mean 'a contribution to a feast or picnic'. And this obsolete 'symbol' that means 'feast' has nothing to do with the word 'symbol' that means 'a thing that stands for, represents, or denotes something else'.

A *symbel* itself is a pleasant thing, but from it derive some rather unsavoury Old English adjectives. **Symbel-gāl** (feast-lustful) is when you are so overwhelmed by the pleasures of food and drink that you are unable to focus on what's important. The word is a hapax in a Judgement Day poem, which tells about a man who spends too much time thinking about the pleasures of worldly life. The man forgets to pay attention to the fate of his soul: 'Little does he think about that, he who enjoys pleasures, cheerful with wine, sitting <u>feast-lustful</u> (*symbelgal*).' The *symbel-gāl* man doesn't care about how it will be for him in the afterlife, when his actions in life will be judged by God. Another *symbel* compound is **symbel-wlanc** (feast-proud), a word for the obnoxious, unwarranted arrogance of a person who has had too much to drink. A *symbel-wlanc* person is weighed down by wine and makes cutting remarks and foolish boasts, inciting quarrels with their treacherous words.

Symbel-wērig (feast-weary) sounds like it could simply mean 'tired from eating', but contextually it is aligned with drunkenness. When the Old English poem *Genesis A* (and yes, there's also a *Genesis B*) has God visit King Abimelech in a dream, it includes details that are absent from its Latin source text. In the Old English poem, the king is 'drunk with wine' (*wine druncen*) and 'feast-weary' (*symbelwerig*). Earlier in the same poem, Noah (of ark-building fame) is rudely introduced to the ill effects of alcohol: he too becomes 'drunk with wine' and sleeps 'feast-weary'. It seems pretty clear from these contexts that *symbel-wērig* has less to do with overeating and more to do with passing out in a drunken stupor.

Druncen-georn (drink-eager) sounds like it has to do with the beginning of the night, when you're eager for a drink, but it actually has more to do with the end, when you're already intoxicated. The word *druncen-georn* appears in an abbot's letter that explains proper behaviour for priests. Among other things, says the letter, a priest shouldn't be a merchant, be proud, make boasts, wear fancy clothes or adorn himself in gold. He must not be quarrelsome or argumentative, and he must not make a habit of frequenting wine-houses and becoming intoxicated (*druncengeorn*). Another word describing intoxication is the wonderfully evocative **hēafod-swīma** (drunkenness), which literally means 'head-swimming'. A drunk person is **druncen-lǣwe** (drink-weakened). **Lǣwe** means 'weakened' or 'mutilated' and can be found in other compounds like **hungor-lǣwe** (famished, hunger-weakened) and **lim-lǣweo** (injured, limb-weakened). *Druncen-lǣwe* appears in an Old English psalm in which the speaker discovers that they are 'drink-weakened' by the contents of God's chalice. God's cup overflows with goodness, an intoxicant far stronger than *bēor* or *medu* that inebriates the faithful soul.

For the wynn

Wynn, the name of the W-rune ᚹ, means 'joy', 'pleasure' or 'delight'. *The Rune Poem* says that ᚹ is enjoyed by a person who 'knows little of woe, suffering, and sorrow', and who has 'prosperity and bliss, as well as a sufficient stronghold'.

The thing about joy in Old English literature is that it's almost always followed by sorrow. With every feast, there is famine ahead. For every time of peace, there is a battle in the future. If an Old English poet ever describes present sorrow and *future* joy, it is the joy that is to be found in heaven . . . after you're dead.

Still, there is plenty of *wynn* to discover in Old English. **Symbel-wynn** is the joy you experience at a feast, whether because of food, companionship or entertainment – the term is not that specific. When King Hrothgar congratulates Beowulf on his victory, he orders him to partake in the 'feast-joy' at Heorot: 'Go now to your seat and experience <u>feast-joy</u> (*symbelwynne*)!' Of course, Hrothgar's amiable command is preceded by a speech of seventy-ish lines of doom and gloom. After admitting he never thought he would spend twelve years of his life at Grendel's mercy, like a prisoner in his own hall, Hrothgar proceeds to list all the ways in which he can imagine that Beowulf might die. These predicted deaths include sickness or sword, the grip of fire or surge of water, the blade's bite or the spear's flight, or wretched old age. The king warns ominously, 'The brightness of your eyes will diminish and darken. Suddenly, warrior, death will overcome you!' But please go, dear Beowulf, and enjoy the feast! Such is the way of Old English *wynn*.

Lēod-wynn (people-joy) is what you feel when you're with your people, a joy that comes from a sense of community. The hapax appears in a prayer for patience and humility in the poem *Resignation*. A solitary being, says the poem, cannot live long without 'people-joy' (*leodwynna*), without friends. Perhaps it's no surprise that the one appearance of this Old English 'joy' word is in a passage about its absence. Although we don't have a word for 'people-joy' in modern English, the concept is both universal and timeless.

Another joy, **līf-wynn** (life-joy), appears in one of Cynewulf's runic signatures, in a poem about Judgement Day. Cynewulf warns that life's pleasures are fleeting:

> The joy (ᛈ, W) of earth's ornaments will flee. Formerly (ᚢ, U) the share of life-joys (*lifwynna*) was long enclosed by the waters of the sea (ᛚ, L), wealth (ᚠ, F) on earth. Then the treasures shall burn in fire.

This is rather confusing – why is *līf-wynn* (life-joy) enclosed by the waters of the sea? Probably because Cynewulf needed to work the L-rune into his poem. **Lagu** (ᛚ) means sea or lake. Runic signatures are clever in theory but not easy to write. If it were me, for instance, I'd have to end everything I write with the words 'hail' (**hægel**), 'oak' (*āc*), 'need' (*nȳd*) . . . and then 'oak' again: ᚻᚪᚾᚪ (hana). There are only so many things to say using the words of a runic signature, so it ends up sounding rather awkward and contrived. In another runic signature, Cynewulf again writes of transient 'life-joys' in the sea: 'Life-joys (*lifwynne*) are gone as the sea (ᛚ) withdraws.' It's not entirely clear what *līf-wynn* is meant to be: perhaps the joy we experience while living, the happiness of being alive. This joy is notable in its absence – often the case in Old English.

Or if joy is still around in Old English, it won't be for long, as we see in the poem *Beowulf*. When Beowulf describes how he mortally wounded Grendel, he says: 'He got away, enjoyed life-joys (*lifwynna*) for a little while.' It was in fact a *very* little while, since he died upon his return home after the fight. Grendel probably had few 'life-joys' to enjoy anyway. Near the end of the poem, a dragon experiences **lyft-wynn** (air-joy), the pleasantness of the air or the joy experienced when flying: 'At times during the night it possessed air-joys (*lyftwynne*).' The joy of soaring unimpeded through the night sky sounds nice enough, but the description is quickly followed by the dragon's violent death.

If *lyft-wynn* is a particular joy reserved for dragons (and maybe birds), then there is also joy for us earth-bound creatures: **mann-drēam** (human-joy). But this promise of happiness is, of course, short-lived; by this point, it's barely worth saying that *mann-drēam* appears in negative contexts to describe instances where it *used* to exist. In a poetic retelling of the Book of Daniel, God punishes King Nebuchadnezzar for his pride, and Daniel tells him:

> He will cut you off from your kingdom and send you, friendless, into exile, where he will change your heart, so that you will not remember human-joy (*mandreame*), nor will you have the power of reason beyond that of wild beasts.

Mann-drēam seems here to be more than the pleasure of being *among* humans but also the joy of *being* human. Like a wild beast, the king must live without intellectual stimulation, conversation with friends, appreciation of art, a relationship with God.

Mann-drēam also appears in a poem known as *The Ruin*. (The manuscript is a bit of a 'ruin' itself, the result of time and physical damage.) The poem describes the ultimate downfall of human accomplishment, and might be referencing the crumbling ruins of the Romans who inhabited Britain centuries earlier.

> There were bright city buildings, many bathhouses, high gables, the great clamour of an army, many mead-halls full of human-joy (ᛗ *dreama*), until mighty Fate changed that.

Here *mann-drēam* is spelled with a rune, the M-rune **mann** (ᛗ). Although our word 'man' derives from *mann*, many scholars argue that the word is gender-non-specific: 'human'. The poet imagines *mann-drēam* in mead-halls of bygone years, perhaps overlooking the 'human-joys' of their own present. Can we never truly see or understand joy until it has passed?

But to counter that pessimism is the wonderful word ***wyn-drēam***, which literally means 'joy-joy' or 'pleasure-joy'. It's so abundantly joyful that one 'joy' is not enough! In Old English such happiness can only be found in religious texts like the Psalms: 'Sing to him a new song, and sing well to him in joy-joy (*wyndreame*) and in love' (Psalm 32), and 'Blessed are the people who know joy-joys (*wyndreamas*) and exultation' (Psalm 88).* These instances of *wyn-drēam* gloss the Latin word *iubilatio* (rejoicing, shouting, cry of joy), from which we get modern English 'jubilation'. Double-joy in Old English is a lot of happy noise.

The joyful sound of *wyn-drēam* contrasts with the sound of hail (ᚻ) pelting down on an oak (ᚩ) tree. Without a hall at which to be a *wil-cuma*, I must take shelter, out of necessity (ᚾ), under the branches of this oak (ᚩ). Such is my attempt to end this chapter with a runic signature. (I told you it would sound awkward and contrived.)

Fifth *wordhord*

bēor, noun (BAY-or / ˈbeːɔr): Alcoholic drink brewed from various fruits and honey.

bēor-sele, noun (BAY-or-SEH-luh / ˈbeːɔr-ˌsɛ-lə): Hall where (alcoholic) drink is served.

bēor-þegu, noun (BAY-or-THEH-guh / ˈbeːɔr-ˌθɛ-gʌ): Carousal, drinking of *bēor* (*bēor*-taking).

drēam, noun (DRAY-ahm / ˈdreːam): Joy, pleasure, gladness.

drēam-cræft, noun (DRAY-ahm-KRAFT / ˈdreːam-ˌkræft): Music (joy-craft).

druncen-georn, adjective (DRUNK-en-YEH-orn / ˈdrʌnk-ɛn-ˌjɛɔrn): Drunk (drink-eager).

* Biblical quotations are from the Latin Vulgate Bible (Douay-Rheims), with the Psalms numbered accordingly.

druncen-lǣwe, adjective (DRUNK-en-LAE-wuh / ˈdrʌnk-ɛn-ˌlæː-wə):
Drunk (drink-weakened).

ealu, noun (EH-ah-luh / ˈɛa-lʌ): Ale.

gamen, noun (GAH-men / ˈga-mɛn): Amusement, merriment,
entertainment.

gamen-wudu, noun (GAH-men-WUH-duh / ˈga-mɛn-ˌwʌ-dʌ): Harp
(merriment-wood).

gāst, noun (GAHST / ˈgaːst): Ghost, spirit, demon.

ge-bēor-scipe, noun (yeh-BAY-or-SHIP-uh / jɛ-ˈbeːɔr-ˌʃɪ-pə): Feast at
which (alcoholic) drink is served; group or gathering arranged for
drinking and eating.

glīw, noun (GLEE-ew / ˈgliːw): Glee, joy, mirth; amusement,
entertainment; music.

glīw-bēam, noun (GLEE-ew-BAY-ahm / ˈgliːw-ˌbeːam): Musical
instrument (glee-wood), possibly a harp, drum, timbrel or
tambourine.

gyst, noun (YUEST / ˈjyst): Guest, visitor, stranger.

hægel, noun (HAE-yell / ˈhæ-jɛl): Hail (ice pellets); name of the H-rune ᚻ.

hēafod-swīma, noun (HAY-ah-vod-SWEE-ma / ˈheːa-vɔd-ˌswiː-ma):
Dizziness, intoxication (head-swimming).

hearpe, noun (HEH-ar-puh / ˈhɛar-pə): Harp.

heorþ, noun (HEH-orth / ˈhɛɔrθ): Hearth, fireplace; home, household.

heorþ-fæst, adjective (HEH-orth-FAST / ˈhɛɔrθ-ˌfæst): Having a house
of one's own.

hungor-lǣwe, adjective (HUNG-gor-LAE-wuh / ˈhʌŋ-gɔr-ˌlæː-wə):
Hungry, famished (hunger-weakened).

lagu, noun (LAH-guh / ˈla-gʌ): Sea, water; name of the L-rune ᛚ.

lǣwe, adjective (LAE-wuh / ˈlæː-wə): Weakened, mutilated.

lēod-wynn, noun (LAY-odd-WUEN / ˈleːɔd-ˌwyn): Joy of being among
one's own people.

līf-wynn, noun (LEEV-WUEN / ˈliːv-ˌwyn): Pleasure or joy of life.

lim-lǣweo, adjective (LIM-LAE-weh-oh / 'lɪm-ˌlæː-wɛɔ): Injured, maimed (limb-weakened).

lyft-wynn, noun (LUEFT-WUEN / 'lyft-ˌwyn): Pleasantness of the air (air-joy).

mann, noun (MAHN / 'man): Man, human being; name of the M-rune ᛗ.

mann-drēam, noun (MAHN-DRAY-ahm / 'man-ˌdreːam): Human joy; joyous noise, jubilation.

mǣting, noun (MAE-ting / 'mæː-tɪŋ): Dream.

medu, noun (MEH-duh / 'mɛ-dʌ): Mead, alcoholic drink made from honey.

medu-heall, noun (MEH-duh-HEH-all / 'mɛ-dʌ-ˌhɛal): Mead-hall.

nȳd, noun (NUED / 'nyːd): Need, necessity, inevitableness, affliction; name of the N-rune ᚾ.

sele-drēam, noun (SEH-leh-DRAY-ahm / 'sɛ-lɛ-ˌdreːam): 'Hall-mirth', joy of the hall.

symbel, noun (SUEM-bell / 'sym-bɛl): Feast, banquet.

symbel-gāl, adjective (SUEM-bell-GALL / 'sym-bɛl-ˌgaːl): Lustful with feasting.

symbel-wērig, adjective (SUEM-bell-WAY-rih / 'sym-bɛl-ˌweː-rɪj): Weary with feasting.

symbel-wlanc, adjective (SUEM-bell-WLAHNK / 'sym-bɛl-ˌwlank): 'Feast-proud', high-spirited or arrogant with feasting.

symbel-wynn, noun (SUEM-bell-WUEN / 'sym-bɛl-ˌwyn): 'Feast-joy', pleasure or delight in feasting.

wil-cuma, noun (WILL-KUH-ma / 'wɪl-ˌkʌ-ma): One whose coming is pleasant; a welcome person or thing.

wīn, noun (WEEN / 'wiːn): Wine.

wyn-drēam, noun (WUEN-DRAY-ahm / 'wyn-ˌdreːam): Joyful sound, jubilation.

6

Making Friends and Enemies

Friendship and fiend-ship

THERE WERE NO ENEMIES in early medieval England. 'Enemy' didn't enter the English language until the fourteenth century, via Old French, ultimately deriving from Latin *inimīcus*: the negative prefix *in-* + *amīcus* (friend). Instead of a friend or enemy, in Old English you might have a ***frēond*** or ***fēond***. Given what happens to joy in Old English poetry – how often *wynn* is outweighed by sorrow – perhaps it won't surprise you to learn that the word *fēond* appears nearly three times as often as *frēond*. For whatever reason, fiends are easier to come by.

Another word for 'friend' in Old English is **wine** (pronounced WIN-uh). Both *wine* and *frēond* had a broader range of meanings than 'friend' does today, their definitions encompassing 'kinsman', 'close ally' and even 'lover'. *Wine* does not appear often in prose; according to the medieval literature scholar David Clark, this is presumably 'to avoid confusion with the beverage'. By the end of the Middle Ages, friendly *wine* became obsolete, with alcoholic 'wine' winning the linguistic battle. In Old English *wine* appears mainly in poetry, and it is also a popular ending for given names: the male names Ælfwine (elf-friend), Godwine (God-friend), and Eadwine (happiness-friend or wealth-friend), for instance, which would eventually become the names Alvin, Godwin and Edwin.

Old English also has **un-wine** (un-friend), a noun that means 'enemy' or 'adversary'. The earliest appearance of *un-wine* is in an eleventh-century will. A man named Ketel was planning a pilgrimage from England to Rome. As this was not a journey without dangers in the 1050s, he took the sensible step of creating a will before his departure. The will requests that in the event of Ketel's failure to return to England, would the reader please not allow his enemies (*unwinan*) to take hold of his estate and property. Such an unjust action, the will warns, would forever vex and injure him!

Despite its usefulness, *un-wine* did not last beyond the thirteenth century, and ended its short career as a surname: there are records from the thirteenth century for a Gilbert Unwine and a William Unwin. Early alternate spellings of the name are Hunwine or Hunwyn, which would support the theory that the name comes from *hūn*. *Hūn* appears in Old English names like Hūnbald and Ælfhūn, most likely related to Old Norse *húnn* (young bear). That would make Unwin a 'young bear-friend', a much nicer name than 'un-friend'.

Middle English dropped *un-wine* and used 'unfrēnd' instead. For a while modern English had the familiar-looking 'un-friend' (a noun, not a verb), but the noun went out of fashion in the nineteenth century. The verb 'un-friend' may strike you as modern, given its recent rise to prominence on social media platforms like Facebook, but its usage goes back at least as far as the 1650s. It's funny how a word that becomes obsolete can regain popularity, finding a niche in a new context. Perhaps the noun 'un-friend' will return one day as well.

Frēond-scipe (friendship) is one of the Old English *-scipes* that sailed happily into our modern language, while others foundered on the way. Along with the obsolete '*bēor*-ship' (*ge-bēor-scipe*, page 93), we no longer find ourselves in a state of 'fiend-ship'. Nowadays we're more likely to use the word 'enmity' to describe being enemies (or 'un-friends') with someone, but there is something about Old English *fēond-scipe* that captures the malice and viciousness that can characterise such a relationship. Unfortunately, *fēond-scipe* became obsolete after the thirteenth century, and although 'fiendship' did reappear briefly in the Victorian period, it was unrelated to the Old English word. Just as one might refer to the king as 'his Worship', Victorian novelists chose to call the Devil 'his Fiendship' – the perfect honorific for the person who is the thorn in your side.

Since the world of Old English has more *fēonds* than *frēonds*, you should take care to be **frēond-spēdig** (rich in friends). A word that literally means 'friend-speedy', *frēond-spēdig* might sound as if it describes a person who goes through their friends quickly, perhaps a serial un-friender, but that is far from the truth. Although 'speedy' acquires the meaning of 'swift' or 'quick' by the end of the Middle Ages, in Old English **spēdig** means 'prosperous', 'wealthy' or 'abundant'. The opposite of being *frēond-spēdig* is being **wine-lēas** (friendless), which aside from being lonely is a serious health and safety concern (remember trials like *cor-snæd* on pages 36–8). Old English wisdom poems impart such adages as:

> It is good for one to have a <u>friend</u> (*wine*) on each journey. It's often that someone will go far around a town where it is not certain that he will have a <u>friend</u> (*freond*). The <u>friendless</u> (*wineleas*), unhappy man has wolves for companions, very treacherous animals. Quite often such a companion will rip him apart.

Another maxim says:

> Wretched is he who must dwell alone, whom fate has decreed must

live <u>friendless</u> (*wineleas*). It would be better for him if he had a brother
… Such warriors will always be together, carrying equipment or
sleeping. May no one ever break their peace before death divides
them.

The simple truth is:

Hatred will be everywhere for the <u>friendless</u> (*wineleas*) man because
of his misfortune.

Just as being *frēond-spēdig* is a sure sign that you're doing something
right, being *wine-lēas* indicates a serious character flaw. What does it
say about you if no one will fight beside you and protect you from the
wolves?

As these adages show, the people who need a friend most of all are
those who bear arms – a friend, or better yet, a 'shoulder-companion'.
Eaxl-gestealla, a poetic compound of *eaxl* (shoulder) + *ge-stealla* (companion), is someone whose shoulder you can literally or metaphorically lean upon, a friend who is always at your side in a battle or adventure. The compound 'shoulder-companion' refers to the way in which
early medieval warriors would fight shoulder-to-shoulder to form an
impenetrable line against any *un-wine*. An *eaxl-gestealla* is trustworthy
and dependable in the most dire life-or-death situations.

An *eaxl-gestealla* might also be your **bēod-genēat** (table-companion)
or **heorþ-genēat** (hearth-companion), a friend with whom you share
food and drink while socialising at the dining table or near the warm
hearth. One of Beowulf's heroic qualities, according to the poem,
is that he would never 'drunkenly slay <u>hearth-companions</u> (*heorð-
geneatas*)'. Don't get drunk and kill your friends. (The bar for heroism
is lower than you think.)

One should give gold

A gift, no matter how artlessly or thoughtfully given, inspires a sense of obligation. What happens if you forget to give your friend a birthday present but they give one to you? You know they don't expect to be paid back, per se, but the friendship scales become unbalanced. And gift-giving among unequals can get even more complicated. Suppose your boss gives you and all your co-workers Christmas gifts. The gift isn't something you necessarily want, nor does it directly compensate you for the work you've done. Such a gift might make you feel obligated to be friendly with your boss or loyal to the company. If it's a particularly expensive gift, it may make it awkward for you to voice complaints at next week's meeting. A gift from a superior is not meant to be reciprocated in kind but in loyalty. It creates social alliances in a world that normally demands immediate remuneration.

The only thing that's changed about *gift* over a millennium is how you say it; in Old English it was pronounced YIFT. The importance of gifts is such that they have never gone out of style. In early medieval England, gifts were necessary to the success of a leader; in poetry the king's throne is even called a ***gif-stōl*** (gift-seat), possibly deriving from the tradition of the ruler distributing gifts from their seat of power. One should not accept a king's gift lightly; in so doing, you place yourself in a position of obligation to the king. Gifts were given publicly, before witnesses, representing the giver's hopes and expectations, the receiver's honour and the giver's power and generosity.

One Old English maxim states:

> The hand must work for the head. The hoard must await the treasure and the <u>gift-seat</u> (*gifstol*) stand ready for the treasure's distribution. He who receives gold is greedy – the man on the high seat has enough.

There must be a reward, if we do not want to deceive, for the one who has shown us favours.

Another says simply: 'One treasure turns into another. One should give gold.'

When Beowulf receives gifts from King Hrothgar, they don't stay in his possession for long. Upon returning home, Beowulf immediately presents the gifts to King Hrethel, who will distribute them as rewards to his men in exchange for their service and loyalty. Improper gift exchange has the potential to inflict great damage on friendships and alliances. When a gift is removed from circulation, hoarded rather than reciprocated or passed on, that is when the trouble begins. A gift hidden away in a dragon's hoard or locked in a greedy king's coffers will turn into poison. In fact, in some Germanic and Scandinavian languages *gift* means both 'gift' and 'poison'.

In Old English *gift* does not mean 'poison', but it does have a less common secondary definition of 'marriage'. Old English **gift-līc** (literally 'marriage-like') refers to all things nuptial or wedding-related. (Curiously, *gift* still means 'married' in modern Norwegian, Swedish and Danish – languages in which it also means 'poison'.)

Marriages in early medieval England required a **morgen-gifu** (morning-gift), a substantial sum of money and land paid to the wife on the morning after the marriage's consummation. It is worth noting that the *morgen-gifu* was paid to the wife, not to her father or any of her other family members. This gift was hers to sell, give away or bequeath as she saw fit. The *morgen-gifu* was by no means the only property of a married woman. Old English law codes, charters and wills make it clear that while both the man and the woman had control over money and property within a marriage, the *morgen-gifu* belonged solely to the wife.

Women in early medieval England were better off than their later medieval counterparts. A woman could not be forced to wed a man whom she disliked. In the case of a divorce, laws protected her custody of the children and her share of the property. If a woman took custody of her children, she was entitled to half the shared property outside of any that was already hers alone (like the *morgen-gifu*). In a law code from the late tenth century, the responsibilities of the bridegroom and the bride's own family are outlined and, as the historian Christine Fell says, 'Virtually every clause of the agreement is concerned with protecting and safe-guarding the woman's interests.'

Beyond their rights in marriage, early medieval women had other advantages over women of later historical periods. A woman could rule, either jointly with her husband or on her own after his death. Women could own, inherit and sell land, and they could decide who would inherit it. They could be litigants and oath-givers. They were responsible for their own crimes and not those of their husbands. A woman's life was equal to a man's in terms of compensation paid upon injury or death. According to the historian Doris Stenton, women in early medieval England were 'more nearly the equal companions of their husbands and brothers than at any other period before the modern age'. Equality would, in fact, be the greatest *gift* of all.

Truth-love was hot in their hearts

From Old English *lufu* to modern English 'love', this word (like *gift*) has not changed very much. *Lufu* is pronounced LUH-vuh, like our modern pronunciation only with an extra syllable. Old English, however, has a variety of compound words that have vanished over time, making it seem as though today's 'love' is somewhat diminished. *Lufu* can be named for the parts of the body that experience it (which is made all the more complicated by the ambiguity of certain Old English body parts): while **heort-lufe** is pretty clearly 'heart-love', **mōd-lufu** could be 'mind/heart-love', **gāst-lufu** 'soul/spirit-love', and *ferhþ-lufe* 'heart/soul/spirit/mind-love'. This terminology is not in more prosaic texts, and the variety is partly due to the need for alliteration, the building block of Old English poetry – yet arguably each of these loves means something slightly different. *Gāst-lufu*, for instance, is a spiritual love that better fits a context of worship than romance.

Some *lufu* words indicate the person for whom you feel love, or perhaps the person who feels love for you. A mother might feel **bearn-lufe** (son-love) for her child, and you might feel **sib-lufu** (kin-love) for your uncle. Although modern English 'sibling' comes directly from **sibling** (with the same root as *sib-lufu*), the Old English word means kin in general, not brothers and sisters specifically. *Sib-lufu* describes God's love for the angels, who are his children and therefore kin. But few siblings today are likely to describe each other as angels.

Frēond-lufu (friend-love) is something like platonic love, although there's never really an assumption that *lufu* is romantic. In any case, it appears in a context neither romantic nor friendly. In the Book of Genesis, Abraham and his wife Sarah travel to Egypt to start their new life there. Abraham worries that the Egyptian men will covet his beautiful wife and kill him, so he tells Sarah to pretend they are siblings (in the modern sense), not spouses. It's difficult to say what positive, long-term outcome he imagined could come from this cunning plan. In an Old English poetic version of the story, he says:

> Sarah, say that you are my sister, a blood-kinswoman, when strange men of the nation ask what the <u>friendship</u> (*freondlufu*) might be between us two foreigners who come from afar.

Here *frēond-lufu* is a non-sexual kind of intimacy, a love that won't make Abraham a target of deadly jealousy. Thus, a man tells lies for the sake of his own safety, putting his wife in danger ... not a story about *lufu* (*frēond-* or otherwise), if you ask me.

In contrast to the mendacious *frēond-lufu* of Abraham is **trēow-lufu** (truth-love). Today, when we talk about 'true love' we typically mean the kind of love found in romance novels and Disney movies, but Old English 'truth-love' is quite different. The passionate romance of later medieval texts does not often appear in Old English literature. Instead, we find 'truth-love' – passionate, faithful love – in relationships with God, Christ or one's hearth-companions. For example, when Christ ascends to heaven, leaving his disciples behind, 'There was a ring of weeping, surrounded by grief. <u>Truth-love</u> (*treowlufu*) was hot in their hearts, welled within their breasts, in the men's innermost thoughts.' The disciples' love of Christ is still full of passion, with the kind of desperation and turmoil we might expect from a Mills and Boon, but it is inspired by faith, spiritual rather than romantic.

One Old English poem actually does refer to a man's unrequited love of a woman, and here we find another kind of love: **sorh-lufu** (sorrow-love). The man's love is 'boundless, so that <u>sorrow-love</u> (*sorglufu*) deprived him of sleep'. His ardour only brings him frustration and sorrow because the woman doesn't return his affections. This word is so perfect for the kind of heartache connected to unrequited love, or the bittersweet feelings of lovers separated, that it's almost surprising it didn't last into our modern language.

If 'sorrow-love' sounds like what you feel when your beloved spurns your affection, then **ofer-lufu** (over-love) might be the way you feel about it a few years later – so over it. *Ofer-lufu* may sound like a word for a steamy romance novel, but it is better suited for a staid Rogationtide homily. In the medieval period, Rogationtide consisted of the three days (Monday, Tuesday, Wednesday) before Ascension Day. Ascension Day should not be confused with Easter, when Jesus ascends to heaven; it is actually the fortieth day after Easter, a Thursday. This is when Jesus leads his disciples to the Mount of Olives, blesses them and ascends to heaven to take his place at the right hand of God, the official end to his stint on earth. 'Rogation' comes from Latin *rogare* (to ask), since Rogationtide was a time to ask God to bless and nurture the newly sprouting crops. A time to celebrate spring's arrival and to pray for the earth's abundant gifts was also a time to remember the transience of such things. One Rogationtide homily says:

> What happened to the treasure of middle-earth? What happened to the wealth in the world? What happened to the beauty of the land? What happened to the people who strived most eagerly for possessions, and the others who were left in poverty? So transient is <u>excessive love</u> (*oferlufu*) of earth's treasures.

Lufu should be focused on things of permanence, like God and faith, not fleeting things like rain showers, bright sun or earthly riches. Like other humans. Whether you are finding it hard to let go of your ex, or simply can't resist splurging on a new pair of shoes, remember this: *ofer-lufu* is to be avoided!

The modern saying 'If you love something, set it free' feels delightfully close to the spirit of Old English, where love and freedom are closely linked. **Frēogan** (pronounced FRAY-o-gahn) primarily means 'to free, liberate', but its secondary definition is 'to love'. In the poem *Precepts* a father instructs his son, '<u>Love</u> (*freo*) with your heart your father and mother and each of your kindred, as long as they love God.'

Why is 'to free' and 'to love' the same word in Old English? It has cognates in other Germanic languages: Old Saxon *friohan* and Old Icelandic *frjá*, both of which mean 'to love'. The name of the Norse goddess of love is Frigg, whose name derives from the same root. It seems as though the 'love' meaning developed first, and the word acquired the definition 'free' later on. Although both definitions still applied to Old English *frēogan*, by the Middle English period the loving definition had ceded to freedom. But if freedom linguistically pushing out love makes you sad, take heart in knowing this is not the case everywhere: modern cognates of 'free' are German *freien* (to woo, court) and Dutch *vrijen* (to woo, caress, have sex with). The Indo-European base from which all these words derive may have meant something like 'one's own'. You love something because it is your own, and when you're free you are your own person.

Lone fliers and one-steppers

The phrase 'alone time' has appeared with steadily increasing frequency since the 1960s and 1970s. Its usage had a particularly sharp increase in the late 1990s, a time when the Internet and social media were making society increasingly connected. The concept of 'alone time' is appearing in more self-help books and lifestyle blogs. Alone time gives us a chance to 'know ourselves', to better understand who we are and even improve our relationships with other people.

A positive view of solitude is very modern. In his article 'The Virtues of Isolation' (2017), Brent Crane notes that although researchers have recently begun studying the productive, healthy nature of solitude in certain situations, solitude has long been stigmatised as 'an inconvenience, something to avoid, a punishment, a realm of loners'. In medieval literature, exiles face solitude as a punishment for their crimes. If you are alone, you have no friends or family to protect you from harm. Sometimes holy men and women willingly lived a life of solitude in order to test their spiritual strength against the Devil, but this was a trial, not a therapy. Mostly solitude is portrayed as involuntary, painful and wretched.

Like the ***ān-genga*** (solitary walker), a ***sundor-genga*** is someone who goes alone. ***Sundor*** (from which we get modern English 'asunder') means 'apart', 'by oneself', or 'in a manner different or separate from others', while ***ān*** is simply 'one'. The poem *Beowulf* comments on the antagonist Grendel's solitary ways on several occasions, and his solitude seems linked to his evil nature. For instance, the poem says, 'The enemy of mankind, the terrible, <u>solitary walker</u> (*angengea*), often performed many wicked deeds.' Is Grendel an *ān-genga* because he's the enemy of mankind, or is he the enemy of mankind because he walks alone?

A more positive example of an *ān-genga*, albeit one that still lacks the power to speak, appears in a homily for Epiphany. The homilist tells how the Three Wise Men learned about Christ's birth in Bethlehem:

> The eastern astrologers saw a bright new star, not in heaven between the other stars but a <u>solitary walker</u> (*angenga*) between heaven and earth. Then they understood that the strange star indicated the birth of the true king in the land over which it glided.

The solitude of this star does not mark it as evil or exiled but rather singled out for the important task of bringing heaven's message to earth.

Ān-genga is used to describe another non-human entity in an Old English homily. This time the entity is not a star but a proud, anti-social bull. The story concerns the Church of St Michael, a grotto chapel founded on Mount Garganus in southern Italy. The legend of the chapel most likely reached England via Ireland in the ninth century, and the chapel itself would have been a destination for English pilgrims travelling to Rome. We know this because of graffiti on the walls – medieval English names written in futhark. The homily tells the chapel's story:

There lived a very wealthy man called Garganus, and the mountain was named for him on account of his accident. It happened when his great herd of cattle was grazing on the mountain. There came a high-spirited bull, a <u>solitary walker</u> (*angencga*), and it scorned the herd. So Lord Garganus gathered a great many of his household servants and sought the bull everywhere in the wilderness. At last he found it standing upon a knoll of the high mountain at the entrance to a cave. He was moved with fury because the bull, the <u>solitary walker</u> (*angencga*), had scorned his herd, so he bent his bow, wishing to shoot him with a poisoned arrow. But the poisoned arrow turned back as if thrown by a blast of wind and straightaway killed the one who had shot it.

What does it mean that the bull scorns Lord Garganus's herd? Another version of this story claims that the bull was too proud to keep company with the rest of the herd. The arrogant bull became an *ān-genga*, a lone wanderer. Apparently the bull was doing the bidding of St Michael, who used him to show the world where he wanted his church to be built. Unfortunately, Garganus was unaware of this, and when he tried to kill the bull it backfired fatally. Personally, I think St Michael could have been a bit clearer with his hint, and I would pity Garganus but for the fact that he wanted to kill a bull whose only crime was a dislike of the man's herd. Let an *ān-genga* be an *ān-genga*, if that's what they desire.

A saintly bull, a holy star and a man-eating lake-dweller – all of them are quite exceptional, unnatural beings, and not just because they walk alone. Each *sundor-genga* inevitably has a **sundor-gecynd**, a one-of-a-kind nature. The word *sundor-gecynd* itself is one of a kind, a hapax. It appears in a poem about the Panther, who represents Christ in bestiary lore. The Old English poem known as *The Panther* is derived from the *Physiologus*, a book that was originally composed in Greek and later translated into Latin. Bestiaries are books of animal lore that were popular throughout the Middle Ages, and the *Physiologus* is thought to be the first. These books describe an animal's appearance and behaviour, often linking these qualities to a moralising tale or allegory.

The Old English poem details the remarkable Panther's *sundor-gecynd*. He is called an **ān-stapa** (one-stepper), a hapax for someone who walks on their own. The poem begins:

> We have heard tell of the wondrous nature of a certain wild beast who rules a region famous to people in faraway lands. He enjoys his home amidst mountain caves. This animal is known by the name of Panther, which the wise ones, children of men, make known in writings about the <u>lone wanderer</u> (*anstapan*) ... He has a <u>one-of-a-kind nature</u> (*sundorgecynd*), mild and modest. He is gentle, amiable, and loving, and will do no harm to anything aside from the serpent, that venomous killer, his old nemesis.

The Panther, shining and iridescent, is affectionate towards all but the Devil in his reptilian form. After his meal he retreats into his secret hideaway in a mountain cave for a three-day snooze. On the third day he arises, stronger than ever, at which point he draws animals to him with his lovely voice and pleasant-smelling breath. In the older, classical tradition the Panther used his breath and voice to lure unsuspecting animals to their doom, but in the Middle Ages the Panther was reinterpreted as one of the good guys. The Panther arises from a deep sleep the way Christ arises from the dead. Only the serpent fears him, as only the Devil fears Christ. And both the Panther's breath and Christ's word are good and sweet, more wholesome than honey and *bēo-brēad* (royal jelly or honeycomb, see pages 22–3).

The Panther and Christ are both alone in a sense, even though they are friends with nearly everyone; so it is for anyone with a *sundor-gecynd*. But the Panther is an exception, not the rule, for loners in medieval literature in that his solitude is a positive circumstance, a mark of greatness rather than one of exile. This is not the case for the poor ***ān-floga*** (one-flier), a lonely creature who flies alone through a poem known as *The Seafarer*. This poem describes the loneliness of a spiritual journey, a self-imposed exile from the world:

> My spirit, my mind, now journeys beyond my breast's locker with the sea tide, journeys far across the whale's home, the regions of the earth, and returns to me voracious and greedy. The <u>lone flier</u> (*anfloga*) cries, inciting the heart irresistibly on the whale's path across the expanse of oceans.

Is the *ān-floga* a solitary sea-bird, screeching as it soars above the whale's path? ('Whale's path' is a kenning or metaphor for the ocean: more on kennings in Chapter 7.) Or is the *ān-floga* the soul of the seafarer taking flight, attempting to leave behind worldly concerns and seek the heavenly kingdom?

The *ān-floga*'s solitude may be self-imposed, but that is not the case for the unfortunate ***ān-haga*** (solitary being). The *ān-haga* appears in the same passage of *Resignation* as *lēod-wynn* (Chapter 5), in which the very real troubles of a political or social exile describe metaphorical exile from God.

> A <u>solitary being</u> (*anhoga*), a friendless exile, cannot live long, without the <u>joy of being with his own people</u> (*leodwynna*). God is angry with him. He mourns his youth, and whenever men aid him, it adds to his misery. He endures it all, the bitter words of men, and his mind is always sad, his heart <u>sick in the morning</u> (*morgenseoc*).

The *ān-haga*'s existence is lonely and wretched. In Old English poetry, one becomes **morgen-sēoc** (morning-sick) from abandonment, not pregnancy.

Perhaps the loneliest exile of all is Death itself. Ever since Adam and Eve disobeyed God in the Garden of Eden, says the poem known as *Guthlac B*, humanity has had to pay a tax for their disobedience, partaking of 'that wretched drink, the deep cup of death'. No mortal can escape the greedy clutches of Death, 'the cruel, solitary one (*anhoga*), the warrior greedy for slaughter'. Death takes many yet is always alone.

Sixth *wordhord*

ān, adjective/noun/numeral (AHN / 'aːn): One.

ān-floga, noun (AHN-FLO-ga / 'aːn-ˌflɔ-ga): Lone flier.

ān-genga, noun (AHN-YENG-ga / 'aːn-ˌjɛŋ-ga): Solitary walker, lone wanderer.

ān-haga, noun (AHN-HA-ga / 'aːn-ˌha-ga): Solitary being.

ān-stapa, noun (AHN-STAH-pa / 'aːn-ˌsta-pa): Lone wanderer.

bearn-lufe, noun (BEH-arn-LUH-vuh / 'bɛarn-ˌlʌ-və): Love due to a son.

bēod-genēat, noun (BAY-odd-yeh-NAY-aht / 'beːɔd-jɛ-ˌneːat): Table-companion.

eaxl-gestealla, noun (EH-ahk-sul-yeh-STEH-ah-lah / 'ɛak-səl-jɛ-ˌstɛal-la): 'Shoulder-companion', fellow warrior.

fēond, noun (FAY-ond / 'feːɔnd): Enemy, foe; fiend, the Devil.

fēond-scipe, noun (FAY-ond-SHIP-uh / 'feːɔnd-ˌʃɪ-pə): Enmity, hostility.

ferhþ-lufe, noun (FER-h'th-LUH-vuh / 'fɛrxθ-ˌlʌ-və): Love of the heart/soul/spirit/mind.

frēogan, verb (FRAY-o-gahn / 'freːɔ-gan): To free, make free; to honour, like, love.

frēond, noun (FRAY-ond / 'freːɔnd): Friend.

frēond-lufu, noun (FRAY-ond-LUH-vuh / 'freːɔnd-ˌlʌ-vʌ): Friendship, love.

frēond-scipe, noun (FRAY-ond-SHIP-uh / 'freːɔnd-ˌʃi-pə): Friendship.

frēond-spēdig, adjective (FRAY-ond-SPAY-dih / 'freːɔnd-ˌspeː-dɪj): Rich in friends.

gāst-lufu, noun (GAHST-LUH-vuh / 'gaːst-ˌlʌ-vʌ): Spiritual love.

gif-stōl, noun (YIF-STOAL / 'jɪf-ˌstoːl): 'Gift-seat', the seat from which gifts are distributed, the throne.

gift, noun (YIFT / 'jɪft): Gift; (less common) marriage.

gift-līc, adjective (YIFT-leech / 'jɪft-liːtʃ): Of or pertaining to a marriage or wedding, nuptial.

heort-lufe, noun (HEH-ort-LUH-vuh / 'hɛɔrt-ˌlʌ-və): Love which comes from the heart, heartfelt love.

heorþ-genēat, noun (HEH-orth-yeh-NAY-aht / 'hɛɔrθ-jɛ-ˌneːat): Hearth-companion.

lufu, noun (LUH-vuh / 'lʌ-vʌ): Love.

mōd-lufu, noun (MOAD-LUH-vuh / 'moːd-ˌlʌ-vʌ): Heart's love, affection.

morgen-gifu, noun (MOR-gen-YIV-uh / 'mɔr-gɛn-ˌji-vʌ): Husband's gift to his wife on the morning after the consummation of their marriage.

morgen-sēoc, adjective (MOR-gen-SAY-ock / 'mɔr-gɛn-ˌseːɔk): Morning-sick.

ofer-lufu, noun (OV-er-LUH-vuh / 'ɔ-vɛr-ˌlʌ-vʌ): Excessive love.

sibling, noun (SIB-ling / 'sɪb-lɪŋ): Relative, kin.

sib-lufu, noun (SIB-LUH-vuh / 'sɪb-ˌlʌ-vʌ): Love or affection between kin.

sorh-lufu, noun (SOR-h'LUH-vuh / 'sɔrx-ˌlʌ-vʌ): Love accompanied by anxiety or sorrow, hapless love.

spēdig, adjective (SPAY-dih / 'speː-dɪj): Prosperous, rich, wealthy; abundant; powerful.

sundor, adverb (SUN-dor / 'sʌn-dɔr): Apart, aloof, by one's self; in a manner different from others.

sundor-gecynd, noun (SUN-dor-yeh-KUEND / 'sʌn-dɔr-jɛ-ˌkynd): Peculiar or unique nature.

sundor-genga, noun (SUN-dor-YENG-ga / 'sʌn-dɔr-ˌjɛŋ-ga): One who goes alone.

trēow-lufu, noun (TRAY-oh-LUH-vuh / 'treːɔw-ˌlʌ-vʌ): Faithful love (truth-love).

un-wine, noun (UN-WIN-uh / 'ʌn-ˌwɪ-nə): Enemy (un-friend).

wine, noun (WIN-uh / 'wɪ-nə): Friend.

wine-lēas, adjective (WIN-uh-LAY-ahs / 'wɪ-nə-ˌleːas): Friendless.

7

Caring for Body and Mind

Health and un-health

To avoid the greedy clutches of Death, you must take good care of your body and mind. *Wes hāl!* You may recall from Chapter 1 that this standard *grēting-word* means 'be well' or 'be healthy'. But what counted as 'healthy' in early medieval England?

Old English *hǣlþ* (pronounced HALTH) is another of those words so central to our everyday lives that it has barely changed over the centuries; from it we get 'health', and like our current word it can refer to either the condition of (good) health or the act of healing. Health, security, well-being and salvation . . . all of these are different kinds of *hǣlu* – physical, mental or spiritual health. From Old English *hǣlu* we also get modern English 'heal', 'hale' and 'whole'. Today 'whole' more often means 'undivided' or 'complete', but its original definition had to do with being in good health and free from injury.

Although English speakers today can be 'unhealthy', they rarely discuss their 'un-health' (even though that is, of course, what is *actually* concerning). In Old English, however, this highly practical term exists: **un-hǣlu** (un-health). *Un-hǣlu* appears in poetry, religion, law and medicine, referring to what we might call 'bad health' or simply 'illness'.

Like *hǣlþ*, **sēocness** (sickness) has changed little over the past millennium. Less familiar are terms like **wæter-sēocness** (water-sickness), **fylle-sēocnes** (falling-sickness) and **mōnaþ-sēocness** (month-sickness). While the simplicity of their names might suggest an easy interpretation, these illnesses' definitions are far from straightforward. *Wæter-sēocness* is the accumulation of excessive fluid in tissues or body cavities, what's known as oedema today. *Fylle-sēocnes* describes the symptom of the sufferer – falling – and may refer to epilepsy. *Mōnaþ-sēocness* is defined simply as 'lunacy'. Today 'lunacy' is synonymous with 'insanity', and although it's used in popular and sometimes even legal language, it's never a medical term. The original meaning of 'lunacy' was intermittent insanity, believed to be caused by changes of the moon. Latin *lūna* means 'moon', hence *luna*-cy for moon-sickness. You might remember from Chapter 3 that the *mōnaþ* (month) of *mōnaþ-sēocness* is related to the word *mōna* (moon). This 'lunacy', incidentally, had nothing to do with the condition that today we call premenstrual syndrome (and menstruating women in early medieval England weren't any more 'insane' than they are now). Both men and women could suffer from *mōnaþ-sēocness*.

The Old English *Herbarium*, an eleventh-century book of herbal medicine, suggests three remedies for *mōnaþ-sēocness*:

1. Using a red thread, tie clove wort (a kind of buttercup) to the patient's neck. This must be done during a waning moon, in either April or early October.

2. Apply peony to the patient's neck, either a topical ointment of its juice mixed with vinegar or its leaves and roots bound with a clean cloth.

3   The easiest remedy. Have the patient lie down. Place a peony on
     top of them. As soon as they get up, they'll be cured.

It seems as though best practice is to keep a peony on you at all times,
so you'll always have a remedy for lunacy to hand.

The *Herbarium* gets its name from being a book of herbal remedies,
but in general the medical texts of medieval England are called 'leechbooks'. Old English **lǣce-bōc** (leechbook) comes from **lǣce** (doctor).
'Leech' continued to be a word for 'doctor' through the nineteenth
century. But in Old English *lǣce* also means 'leech', the aquatic,
blood-sucking worm. This kind of leech was used to remove (for better
or worse) a supposed excess of blood. Leeches were a common remedy
for many ailments well into the nineteenth century, which raises the
question: which leech came first, the physician or the worm?

Despite their reputation for being a bizarre medieval remedy,
leeches are still used in medicine today, and medical leeches go back
much further in time than the Middle Ages. The earliest written reference to medical leeches is from the second century BCE, so the association of physicians with blood-sucking worms predates Old English
lǣce by at least a millennium. The concept of balancing the humours, the
four elements believed to make up the body (blood, phlegm, yellow bile
and black bile), goes back to ancient Greece, when bloodletting was the
most common method. An imbalance in the humours was believed to be
toxic, even deadly, so a physician might let blood to relieve an unhealthy
excess. Other methods for balancing the humours included pricking the
skin with a sharp object, vomiting, taking laxatives and even spitting.

In the eighth to eleventh centuries, bloodletting actually appears less
frequently in England than in the rest of Europe. While medical leeches
(the worms, not the physicians) are usually associated with the medieval period, they actually reached peak use in the nineteenth century.
In his book on medicine in early medieval England, the biologist and

ƿoht lice · ᵹeoƿine ſpaharcſ ſpa þin blodſie-
ſcunc ꝥulne · ᵹoſpa þonne þeþearſ ſie ·

. XX .

Ƿ iþ ſculdor pehꝼce · ealo ᵹſ ſpunᵹ- toƿid
þæſ þe ſeld ᵹanᵹtmoe- ſie- mdnᵹ ꝥið ealonc
ny ſele- ᵹe þynme- lᵹeon ꝥ amhƿiþ ſcul
dor pehꝼce- ᵹeꝥid ꝥ oꝥeheƿce- ƿiþ þwoſt
pehꝼce- ꝼ þiþ lſmoiuþ pehꝼce- ᵹᵹ Eᵹᵹ ꝥyl
betonican ꝼ nſpan onealod ſeledunean
ᵹelome- ꝼ ſimle- ættype ᵹeſmiꝥe- mid þn
þyꝼte- Eᵹᵹ ᵹenim ſpunᵹ ꝥ a þn þæſ þ
on dun lande- ꝼ þ yꝥtum libbe- mdnᵹ þi þ
ealone-þy ſele- lᵹeon ꝼ þinc betonican
on ᵹoſpæ dm þine- ᵹiſ ſeꝼſ habbe dun
æ onꝥæꝼhe- .   XXI .

Ƿi þ ſidan ſuꝥe- þeƿe ſpi þ þan boᵹfu
ꝥ ædie ꝼ hꝥ ꝥæ clæꝥ þan þy þo to clame-
ꝼ toþ þhuce- Pi þ þꝥe þme ſꝥan ſi dan

A remedy from *Bald's Leechbook*. Many of the remedies start with *wiþ* (against): against headache, against mistiness of the eyes, against *smēga-wyrm* (Chapter 2), etc. Each *wiþ* here begins with a decorated W-rune Ƿ (*wynn*, Chapter 5).

historian M. L. Cameron says that 'lip service' was paid to humoural theory, but bloodletting was by no means practised 'as a cure-all'. Old English leechbooks never actually mention leeches (the worms) in the sections on bloodletting. Presumably a physician already knew how to practise bloodletting, whether by leech or knife or some other means.

It seems obvious that Old English speakers would call doctors after leeches or vice versa, but, surprisingly, *lǣce* (doctor) and *lǣce* (leech) are two different words with distinct etymologies. Old English *lǣce* (leech, the worm), cognate of Middle Dutch *lieke*, appeared sometime before 900 CE; its earlier origins are unknown. *Lǣce* (doctor) was first used around the year 900, a cognate of Germanic words for 'healer': Old Frisian *letza*, Old Saxon *laki*, Old High German *lakki*. In their article for the *World Journal of Surgery*, the researchers Robert N. Mory, David Mindell and David A. Bloom argue that because 'leech' had two forms with distinct meanings early on, 'the joining or relating of the two meanings was a later development and an artificial one'. It's even possible that the words used to be distinct in Old English but assimilated to *lǣce* by popular etymology.

In Old English *lǣce* applied to all types of medical practitioners, but in Middle English there came more specialised terminology: 'doctour of phisik', 'phisicien', 'cirurgien' (surgeon), 'apothecarie', 'barbour' (barber-surgeon) and 'mid-wif'. By the end of the Middle Ages, people weren't using 'leech' very often because its meaning had become too vague. In his vast corpus of writing, Shakespeare uses the word 'leech' for a medical practitioner only once (in *Timon of Athens*). A 'leech' used to be someone respected for their skills in healing and desire to help people, but nowadays a 'leech' is someone who parasitically 'attaches' to another person to get some gain or benefit from them.

Completely unrelated to both *lǣce* (doctor) and *lǣce* (leech), the Old English word for 'body' is, coincidentally, pronounced LEECH. It must have got rather confusing in the sickroom.

Bone-lockers, earth-hoards and their many parts

Like 'body' in modern English, Old English **līc** can refer to a live body or a corpse, though it is more often the latter. By the end of the Middle Ages 'lich' referred exclusively to a dead body. 'Lich-gate' is an archaic word for the roofed gateway to a churchyard, where a corpse would await the clergyman's arrival. A funeral would process down a lich-path, preceded by someone ringing a lich-bell. The lich-owl (more commonly known as a screech-owl) would supposedly cry out to portend a death. Today 'liches' appear in fantasy games, books and movies as undead corpses and zombie-like creatures. So over the centuries *līc* has changed from a body that's dead *or* alive, to one that's *only* dead, to one that's *un*dead!

The early medieval body can also be described using a variety of kennings. A kenning is a metaphorical compound noun used frequently in Old English poetry. To create a kenning, combine two ordinary nouns to create a compound that is itself a sort of riddle. A 'day-candle' is the sun, 'whale-road' the ocean. Although kennings are common in Old English poetry, with some appearing in a number of different contexts, the exact meaning of a kenning is not always clear, particularly if it's a pesky hapax.

Bān-loca (bone-locker) appears five times in Old English, but while it is clearly anatomical it could refer to a muscle, the skin or the body as a whole. When Grendel comes to Hrothgar's mead-hall to kill a sleeping warrior, he bites the poor man's *banlocan*. In this instance *banlocan* could be either singular or plural. If it's plural, then perhaps Grendel is biting through muscles; if it's singular, he could be munching on the whole body. Later, during his battle with Beowulf, Grendel receives a mortal wound on his shoulder – his sinews spring apart, his *banlocan* (plural) burst! Here *banlocan* is the subject and, as such, must be plural (the singular form would be *banloca*). Grendel is one person, with only one body to burst, so *banlocan* can't be 'bodies' here. It makes more sense if *banlocan* is plural in both contexts and means 'muscles'.

Simple, right? But what about a different Old English poem that describes the death of St Guthlac:

> Guthlac's strength was spent at that dire time, but his thinking was very resolute. He was single-minded in courage. The illness was severe, feverish, and deadly fierce. His heart welled within, his <u>bone-locker</u> (*banloca*) burned.

In the context of St Guthlac's death, *banloca* must be singular, and the definition of 'muscle' does not make sense (the heart may be a muscle, but it has no bones inside it). Here *banloca* must mean 'body.' Perhaps kennings, like metaphors, can mean different things to different people. A 'bone-locker' might be a muscle for one poet, a body for another.

Other kennings for 'body' include **bān-hūs** (bone-house), **flǣsc-hama** (flesh-covering), **bān-fæt** (bone-vessel), **flǣsc-hord** (flesh-hoard), and **feorh-hūs** (life-house). **Grēot-hord** is a particularly evocative kenning that literally means 'earth-hoard', a repository for earth. St Guthlac describes his own body on his deathbed, saying: 'This <u>bone-vessel</u> (*banfæt*) weakens, this <u>earth-hoard</u> (*greothord*) grieves. The soul hastens to its eternal home, eager to depart for better dwellings.' The weakened body grieves for the soul who leaves it behind. The soul's place is in heaven with God, while the 'earth-hoard' must return to the earth.

All in all, the body doesn't have a great image in Old English poetry. A receptacle for dirt, it is constantly rebuked by the soul, who knows it deserves a better partner. I particularly feel for the body when the self-centred soul berates it in the poem *Soul and Body II*:

> Hey, you withered wretch, why have you troubled me? Foul earth,
> likeness of clay, you'll decay completely! How little you considered
> your soul's fate after it would be taken from the body!

The soul goes on to complain about all the time it was forced to spend
imprisoned by the body's flesh:

> I couldn't escape from you, surrounded by flesh, and your wicked
> desires oppressed me. It frequently seemed to me like 30,000 winters
> till your death-day. Oh, how I awaited our separation with difficulty!

The worst part is that, throughout the soul's diatribe, the body is
unable to respond. It must listen mutely because its tongue has been
torn into ten pieces. The poet describes the fate of the body in greater
detail, in case its situation is still in doubt:

> The head is split open, hands disjointed, jaws gaping, throat torn
> apart, sinews consumed, neck chewed through. Fierce worms plunder
> the ribs, partake of the corpse in swarms, thirsty for gore.

A poem like this one is meant to encourage its audience to consider
the great hereafter, when the luxuries and foolish desires of earthly
life will cease to have value or meaning. If the body doesn't do right by
the soul during life, the soul must go to hell – and apparently the soul's
only consolation is being able to mock the body as worms tear it apart.

But before the body is relegated to the earth, all its parts are pretty
valuable. The penalty for gouging out someone's eye in seventh-
century Kent, for instance, was fifty shillings – the same as the penalty
for killing a free man. So sight, it seems, was as precious as life itself.
It's no surprise, then, that another word for **ēage** (eye) is **hēafod-gim**
(head-gem, jewel of the head). Eyes in Old English have apples. An

æppel (pronounced the same in Old English as in modern English) was an apple or fruit, but it could also just be something round. Here the *æppel* appears in the *ēage*:

> He may see with the <u>apple of his eye</u> (*æpl ðæs eagan*), if the albugo does not reach it. But if the albugo spreads over it entirely, then he cannot see anything.

Albugo is an eye disease in which a white opacity forms on the cornea. The quotation sounds like it comes from a leechbook, but it is actually from an Old English translation of Pope Gregory's *Pastoral Care* (originally written in Latin). This albugo is a metaphor for blindness to God's truth. The *æpl ðæs eagan* (apple of the eye) refers to the pupil. Perhaps people once thought the round pupil was a solid sphere within the eye; the pupil does look round like an apple.

Today the expression 'apple of your eye' refers to someone you love and cherish over all others. The phrase appears in Psalm 16: 'Preserve me, Lord, and protect me, as one protects the <u>apples of his eyes</u> (*æplum on his eagum*) with his eyelids.' *Æplum on his eagum* is the Old English translation of Latin *pupillam oculi* (pupils of the eyes). The Hebrew version, of which the Latin is a translation, says *'iyshown 'ayin*, meaning 'dark part of the eye', although one theory suggests that *'iyshown* is a diminutive of *'iysh* (man), making the phrase 'little man of the eye'. Is this because you can see your reflection, a little person, in a friend's pupil? Apple or little man, it's an old idiom indeed.

Another part of the face, the *mūþ* (mouth), hasn't changed much over the millennium. Today you can mouth words (speak without vocalising), mouth off (express your opinion in an offensive manner), mouth against or at someone (argue), and bad-mouth (slander or verbally abuse). In the time of Shakespeare 'mouthing' was kissing, and an insult from *Measure for Measure* is 'he would mouth with a beggar, though she smelt brown bread and garlic'. (Brown bread apparently smelled musty.)

Old English has its own unique set of mouth-related words. *Mūþettan* means 'to chatter' or 'to let out a secret' (the *-ettan* part doesn't mean anything, it's just one of several suffixes that turn nouns into verbs). Someone who is *mūþ-frēo* (mouth-free) is at liberty to speak. *Mūþ-frēo* appears in Psalm 11, following a warning against boasting for the sake of your social status. The would-be braggarts counter with the Latin *Labia nostra a nobis sunt* (Our lips are our own), which is glossed in Old English *Hwi ne synt we muðfreo* (Why aren't we 'mouth-free'?). Grendel's epithet *mūþ-bana* (mouth-killer or mouth-bane) serves to further dehumanise him. Men kill with their hands, after all, not with their mouths. In a description of Grendel murdering one of King Hrothgar's men, Beowulf says: 'Grendel came to be his <u>mouth-killer</u> (*muðbonan*). He swallowed the body of that dear man whole.'

If you are the hapless victim of a *mūþ-bana*, your life both begins and ends in a **wamb**. 'Womb' today of course means uterus, but it was once a far less specific word, meaning some sort of body cavity, be it the stomach, uterus, chest, abdomen or bowel. The primary definition of Old English *wamb* was 'stomach', making it both a starting and (very unfortunate) end point. Modern English 'belly' comes from Old English, but perhaps not in the way you think. An Old English **belg** was a bag, sack, pouch or even a pair of bellows. Middle English 'beli' had all those meanings, but its primary definition had become 'stomach', what we call a 'belly' today.

In addition to *mūþ* and *wamb*, a number of other Old English body parts may look familiar: **fōt** (foot), **hand** (hand) and *finger* (finger). You can probably guess that *þūma* is the thumb, **middel-finger** is the middle finger, **hring-finger** is the ring finger and the **scyte-finger** is the . . .

The first time I saw that last word I have to admit that I thought of something rather unpleasant, but *scyte-finger* (index finger) literally means 'shooting-finger' or 'arrow-finger' (it is pronounced SHUE-tuh-FING-ger). Perhaps it's because of the position of that finger when you shoot, or maybe it's because that finger can point like an arrow. According to King Alfred's law code, you must pay fifteen *sceattas* for injuring someone's *scyte-finger*. A **sceatt** was a small, thick silver coin minted in Northern Europe during the early medieval period. But to what extent must the *scyte-finger* be injured in such a scenario? Are we talking jammed-in-a-door injured or chopped-off injured? The law code doesn't specify. The little finger is called the **ēar-finger** (ear-finger) because it's (apparently) the finger you use to clean out your ear; sometimes it's even called the **ēar-clǣnsiend** (ear-cleaner). A word for what we would call a ring finger is **lǣce-finger** (leech-finger or doctor-finger), both because a *lǣce* often used this finger to mix and apply medicines, and because of a belief that its veins flowed directly to the heart (which could be useful to a *lǣce*). Perhaps the association of this finger with the heart is why it's the finger for a wedding ring.

Old English words for this finger – *hring-finger* (ring finger) and **gold-finger** (gold finger) – point (no pun intended) to this wedding ring tradition. But how did the ring finger become associated with wedding rings? One theory says that, long before the circulatory system was fully understood, the ancient Romans and Egyptians believed (as above) that a vein ran directly from the ring finger on the left hand to the heart. The nineteenth-century lawyer Charles Edwards calls this theory a 'vulgar error' (i.e. too pagan), arguing that instead it has to do with the Holy Trinity:

> [I]n the ancient ritual of English marriages, the ring was placed by the husband on the top of the thumb of the left hand, with the words, 'In the name of the Father;' he then removed it to the forefinger saying: 'In the name of the Son;' then to the middle finger, adding: 'And of the

Holy Ghost;' finally he left it, as now, on the fourth finger, with the closing word 'Amen.'

An early Saxon burial site was uncovered at Harnham Hill near Salisbury in the 1850s, and one of the finds was a gold ring on the finger bone of a left hand. John Yonge Akerman, the lead archaeologist, frustratingly doesn't specify *which* finger of the hand it was on. Maybe the skeleton's hand had suffered too much damage for Akerman to tell, but in any case his report only says that there was a ring 'exactly resembling our modern wedding-ring'. It's impossible to tell whether this particular ring was actually symbolic of marriage, but ring exchanges were a part of medieval wedding ceremonies. And Old English *hring-finger* indicates that a specific finger was associated with ring-wearing in early medieval England.

If Old English words tell us something about life in the medieval period, nineteenth-century dictionaries tell us something about the Victorians. The *Bosworth-Toller Anglo-Saxon Dictionary*, published between 1882 and 1898, self-censors when it comes to certain words. For instance, *Bosworth-Toller* defines the words **teors** or **pintel**, synonyms for 'penis', with the Latin words *membrum virile*. A *membrum virile*, or 'virile member', was a safer choice than 'penis' because only people educated in Latin (in 1898 mostly men) would know what it was. We wouldn't want women to learn Old English words for 'penis' now, would we?

This prudishness also comes across in nineteenth-century translations of leechbooks. The only complete translated edition of the Old English medical texts was written by the Reverend Thomas Oswald Cockayne in the 1860s (with the enviable title *Leechdoms, Wortcunning, and Starcraft of Early England*). The edition has the helpful feature of a facing-page translation: the Old English text on the left side, a modern English translation on the right. But you'll occasionally encounter

Latin on the modern English side. The Latin was not in the original text, but the reverend uses it to obscure his translations of certain passages, particularly those discussing gynaecological concerns.

Victorian philologists were bothered by references to genitalia far more than medieval scribes. The tenth-century Exeter Book contains an assortment of riddles, some of which are indubitably suggestive. In one riddle a wondrous creature, erect and tall, brings joyful expectation to women, standing up in a bed; sometimes a girl assaults it and a tear comes to her eye. Another riddle tells of a curious thing that hangs at a man's **þēoh** (thigh): it is stiff, and the man lifts his cloak to put the head of the hanging thing into a familiar **hol** (hole). Although the Exeter Book provides no solutions to these riddles, the answer to the first is clearly 'onion' and the second 'key in a lock'!

The words *teors* and *pintel* don't actually appear much in Old English, and there's no word that shows up for a woman's privates. It seems at first that we have a candidate when looking up **scēaþ** (sheath), given as a translation of Latin *vagina*. But Latin *vagina* simply means 'sheath, scabbard'. The word 'vagina' is not used in English to describe the female reproductive tract until the seventeenth century. Middle English 'cunte' has cognates in Germanic languages like Old Frisian and Old Icelandic, so chances are a form of the word existed in Old English. Still, the *Oxford English Dictionary* says that in Old English such a word is 'not securely attested'.

The lack of evidence for women's reproductive organs does not necessarily denote a complete lack of interest in their sexual needs. At least one medical text gives instructions for *wifes willan* (woman's pleasure): take the bile of a male goat, mix it with incense and nettle seeds, and smear it on the *teors* before intercourse. (Don't try this at home: the remedy that follows – for epilepsy – advises consuming a goat's brain after pulling it through a golden ring, a cure definitely not recommended by today's health professionals.)

Heart, mind and soul-blood

What part of the body is most important for the circulation of blood? The heart, perhaps. The arteries and veins. *Bald's Leechbook*, a tenth-century Old English medical text, describes the **lifer** (liver) as the primary organ of the circulatory system; it collects the 'clean blood', which it sends through 'the four greatest veins' to the **heorte** (heart) and all throughout the body, all the way to the extremities. The *heorte*'s role in the circulatory system is thus secondary to the *lifer*. Our modern-day association of the heart and the blood is absent from early medieval England.

It's hard to come up with enough modern English equivalents to translate all the Old English 'blood' words. **Blōd** (blood) is the closest to the word we use today, and it is the most prosaic of the Old English options, the only one that appears in medical texts. **Swāt** means 'blood' in poetic contexts, but in leechbooks it refers to 'sweat', 'perspiration' or sometimes 'juice' (as in plant-juice for a herbal remedy). **Drēor** also means 'blood' and only appears in poetry. Sometimes an Old English poem uses multiple words for blood within a few lines, and when you attempt a modern English translation you find yourself lacking in synonyms. Take, for instance, this apocalyptic vision of Judgement Day:

> . . . *usses dryhtnes rod   ondweard stondeð,*
> *beacna beorhtast,   <u>blode</u> bistemed,*
> *heofoncyninges   hlutran <u>dreore</u>,*
> *biseon mid <u>swate</u>   þæt ofer side gesceaft*
> *scire scineð.*

. . . there the rood of our Lord will stand, the brightest of beacons, soaked with blood (*blōd*), the pure blood (*drēor*) of heaven's King, sprinkled with blood (*swāt*), which will shine clearly across the vast creation.

When you examine the Old English, you can see how a variety of blood words allows the poet more freedom to create the right sounds. *Blode* alliterates with the other three words in its line, and *swate* alliterates with the strong syllable 'se' in *biseon* and with *side*. *Dreore* doesn't add to the alliteration but echoes the 'eo' in *heofoncyninges*, bookending the line with assonance. And with three different words you can make the passage truly soaked in blood without repeating yourself.

The medievalist Caroline Walker Bynum describes the literature and art of the later Middle Ages as 'awash in blood'. Christ's blood became a hugely important symbol during the thirteenth century, when the Feast of Corpus Christi was established. This feast celebrated the Eucharist, bread and wine transformed by the power of God into Christ's own body and blood. But there is no evidence that the feast of Corpus Christi was celebrated in England prior to the fourteenth century. While Old English literature has its fair share of blood, it's not there for the same reason.

Blood's significance in Old English lies in its ability to interact with and affect the surrounding world, transferring qualities of sanctity and sin, health and illness, human-ness and divinity. Blood communicates vocally: when the earth swallows Abel's spilled blood in an Old English poem, the blood actually cries and calls out. In poetry and homilies, blood flows from strange sources like the trees and the clouds to remind sinners to think about Judgement Day. In medical remedies, blood transfers a person's illness from their body to a stick of wood or a stream of flowing water. In one story, a saint's blood mixed with earth cures a king's blindness when it's applied to his eyes. In the poem *Andreas* St Andrew's blood falls to the ground, germinating beautiful, blossoming trees, for the blood transfers his sanctity to the earth. Old English literature is not always awash in blood, but when it is the blood transforms the world, affecting everyone who touches, sees, hears or consumes it.

Despite our modern association of blood with violence, this does not necessarily hold true for Old English *blōd*. There is, however, another Old English word that does: **heolfor** (blood, gore). *Heolfor* is not a common word, appearing only twelve times in extant Old English literature. It is used in descriptions of torture, decapitation and death in battle. While *blōd*, *swāt* and *drēor* are not always present in scenes of battle and physical combat, the word *heolfor* is *only* associated with violence. Thus, the usual translation for *heolfor* is 'gore', which is itself defined as 'blood in the thickened state that follows effusion'. Modern English 'gore' appears often in poetry, referring specifically to blood shed in violence. But if *heolfor* is 'gore', then what is Old English **gor**? In early medieval England *gor* had a different meaning than it does now: 'dung', 'faeces', 'filth', 'dirt', 'slime'. So, etymologically speaking, it seems that, over time, blood spilled in violence became conceptually dirty or unclean.

The most intriguing of the Old English blood words is **sāwel-drēor**, which is often translated 'life blood' but literally means 'soul blood'. But what exactly is the relationship between the soul and the blood? In a dialogue between the wise King Solomon and the Chaldean Prince Saturn, Saturn asks Solomon to tell him 'where a man's soul rests when the body sleeps'. Solomon replies, 'It is in three places: in the brain, in the heart, and in the blood.' Whether corporeal or not, the soul is very much enmeshed in the flesh of the body.

Like the soul, which is linked to a unique body, blood corresponds with a specific individual, at least according to the leechbooks. Because blood not only came from but represented a particular body, remedies involving blood taken from a person's body could, by extension, treat that body. Some Old English medical remedies call for blood, saliva, an article of clothing or even a footprint to represent the individual receiving treatment. For example, a remedy for swelling instructs the leech to do the following:

1   Write the patient's name on a stick of hazel or elder. Make three cuts in it.

2   Put some of the patient's blood in the carved-out parts of the stick.

3   Throw the stick over your shoulder or between your thighs into flowing water.

Performing this ritual on the patient's blood is meant to affect the well-being of the patient, even though the blood is no longer in the body. In Old English literature blood – intrinsic to one's identity – is not unlike the soul.

Even more challenging than translating the numerous Old English blood words is making sense of the many words for 'heart', 'mind' and 'soul'. **Mōd** (from which we get 'mood'), **hyge** and **sefa** can all be translated as 'mind' or 'heart'. Additionally, *mōd* can refer to the spirit, *hyge* to the soul and *sefa* to one's understanding. Old English poetry also refers to the 'thoughts of the heart' (*heortan geþohtas*) on a couple of occasions. To further complicate things, *mōd* and *sefa* combine to make **mōd-sefa**, a compound that can mean 'mind', 'spirit', 'soul' or 'heart'. On top of that there are also **ferhþ** (soul, spirit, mind, life) and **hreþer** (breast, heart, mind). And then there are the mind's many kennings. The mind is a **hord-loca** (hoard-locker), a chest in which thoughts are locked away, and a **feorh-hord** (life-hoard), a treasure trove of life itself. Another kenning for the mind, **brēost-loca** (breast-locker), seems to indicate that intellect resides in the heart – the organ located in your breast – not the brain.

In addition to all these poetic and metaphorical words for the mind, there's **brægen** (from which we get 'brain'), a word that only appears in medical texts. Despite considerable overlap of 'heart' and 'mind' in Old English, a description of how a baby forms in the mother's womb clearly distinguishes between the two: the *brægen* forms in the first month of pregnancy, but the *heorte* doesn't show up until the eighth.

Today mental illness is associated with the brain, but the word for 'insanity' in Old English is **wōdheortness**, literally 'mad-heart-ness'. The physiological cause of *wōdheortness* is never explained, at least not in any of the early medieval English texts that survive. And the concept of 'heart-madness' does not only appear in medical contexts; the poem *Andreas* tells of a potion that drives people mad, specifically targeting the *hyge* and *heorte*.

Hearts and minds are often vulnerable to outside influences, so perhaps there's good reason to keep them locked away. A hoard is good for safekeeping, as is a locker, so as a *hord-loca* the mind is doubly secure.

From devil-sickness to ancientbiotics

Wherever the mind is located, in the heart or in the brain, it is vulnerable to insanity or **dēofol-sēocnes** (devil-sickness), an illness that shows up in leechbooks as well as in homilies and scripture. In the Old English Gospel of Matthew, Christ comes upon two men who suffer from *dēofol-sēocnes*. He convinces the devils to leave the men's bodies and move into the bodies of a nearby herd of pigs. (The herd then runs off into the sea and drowns, getting rid of the devils more permanently.) One leechbook uses the word *dēofol-sēocnes* interchangeably with **ge-wit-lēast** (witlessness), while another associates it with **scīn-lāc** (necromancy causing apparitions and delusions).

Wolf meat and mandrake root are effective remedies for *dēofol-sēocnes*, as well as a number of different herbs. Mugwort not only drives away *dēofol-sēocnes*, it protects against 'evil medicine' (poison? sorcery?) when kept in the house by turning away 'the eyes of evil men'. Mugwort, a medicinal herb used by many cultures over the centuries, is recommended in Ayurvedic medicine to treat feelings of unease, unwellness and general malaise, mental and emotional complaints that might equate to whatever *dēofol-sēocnes* was in early medieval England. Smear wort (*Aristolochia*) is another *dēofol-sēocnes* remedy, also useful against fevers, poisonings and sore nostrils. (Today *Aristolochia* has been identified as a potent carcinogen and kidney toxin, so don't always take 1,000-year-old medical advice to heart.)

The Devil is often called *fēond* (Chapter 6), so **feond-sēocnes** (fiend-sickness) is presumably quite similar to *dēofol-sēocnes*. One way to cure *fēond-sēocnes* is with magic soil. Where do you find magic soil, you might ask? Well, according to Bede (the pagan-obsessed historian of Chapter 3), you can find it at Bardney Monastery, where the bones of St Oswald were translated around the year 679 CE. In a religious context, 'translation' is the moving of saints' bodies from one location to another. A saint's body might need to be translated due to war or Vikings, or even because the saint appeared in someone's vision demanding a change in their final resting place. St Oswald, King of Northumbria, died in 642. Where his bones resided for the thirty-odd years following his death is unknown, but around the year 679 St Oswald's bones were translated to Bardney Monastery. The bones were washed before their burial, and the water used for washing them fell upon a particular patch of soil at one end of the church. Later it was discovered that this soil from Bardney had the power to cure *fēond-sēocnes*.

Abbess Æthelhild used some of Bardney's miracle soil on a guest who suffered from *fēond-sēocnes*, afflicted at night by an 'unclean spirit'. According to Bede, the guest's symptoms were as follows:

> All of a sudden he was seized by the Devil and began to call out and chatter and gnash his teeth, and then foam came out of his mouth, and he began to twist his limbs with various motions.

It sounds very much like a scene from *The Exorcist*, except the priest's incantations accomplish nothing. It is only when the man receives Bardney's miracle soil that his attack of *fēond-sēocnes* ceases.

Dēofol-sēocnes and *fēond-sēocnes* appear to be terms used for illnesses that affect the patient's mind in a way that makes them lose control of their own body. It's possible these illnesses would be diagnosed today as epilepsy and the 'demonic attacks' called seizures. During a seizure a person may cry out repeatedly, stiffen their body, and then make rhythmic motions with their arms and legs. Excess saliva and foam may come from the mouth, and blood may appear if the person inadvertently bites their tongue or cheek. After a seizure the person may remain confused for minutes or hours.

Peter Dendle, who has written peer-reviewed articles on cryptozoology and demonic possession as well as a two-volume encyclopaedia on zombie movies, published an article on 'devil-sickness' in the Johns Hopkins *Bulletin of the History of Medicine* in 2001. Dendle observes that in the primary Old English medical texts, every condition that refers to a demonic or supernatural element (*dēofol-sēocnes* or *fēond-sēocnes*, for instance) has at least one remedy containing **elehtre** (lupine, a flowering plant). Dendle notes that *Lupinus albus*, a species of lupine likely cultivated in early medieval England, is particularly rich in manganese. The brain requires manganese to function properly, and medical studies have shown that a lack of manganese may be both a cause and result of repeated seizures.

In modern medicine the ingestion of manganese is not recommended for treating seizures – it's considered 'clumsy' and potentially dangerous. But in early medieval England the options for an epileptic would have been limited, and although increasing manganese in an epileptic's diet wouldn't have cured the seizures, it may have helped a little. Dendle says that the 'general seizure threshold' might have been raised, resulting in fewer and less intense seizures. Lupine extracts have been found to have a slight sedative effect on the central nervous system. Manganese's absorption through digestion isn't great, but it does increase when combined with alcohol, and some leechbook remedies say to mix the *elehtre* in *ealu* (ale, Chapter 5) for drinking.

It's strange how medical science and medieval literature cross paths. M. L. Cameron, well known among Old English scholars for his work on medicine in early medieval England, was in fact a professor of biology for most of his career. In his book *Anglo-Saxon Medicine* (1993) Cameron argues for the logic behind many leechbook remedies, explaining that things that seem superstitious to us may have had practical, therapeutic effects. For instance, boiling a potion in an **ār-fæt** (brass or copper vessel) might actually allow salts to form that may kill some bacteria. A recipe that calls for a **galdor** (incantation) to be sung while stirring may serve as a timer in a world before stopwatches. (In fact, in early medieval England there wasn't a smaller unit of measurement than an hour.) **Dryhtenlic gebed** (the Lord's Prayer), something that anyone reading a leechbook would know, was not a bad way to measure time. An instruction to 'stir while reciting the Lord's Prayer three times' could be like a recipe saying 'stir for *x* minutes'.

As the challenge of antibiotic resistance continues to increase, some scientists are turning to the humble *lǣce-bōc* for new (old) ideas on medical treatments. Researchers are looking for what they call 'ancientbiotics'. In 2015 a team of medievalists from the University of Nottingham and scientists from the Texas Tech University Health Sciences Center published a paper on an Old English remedy for an eye infection or sty from *Bald's Leechbook*. The 1,000-year-old recipe was for an **ēag-sealf** (eye salve) that combined garlic and other herbs from the genus *Allium* (like leek or onion) with wine and ox bile in an *ār-fæt*. The individual ingredients were already known to have beneficial effects, although none of them particularly robust. Garlic, leeks and onions produce 'a range of antimicrobial compounds', and bile may also be antibacterial. Wine may be another source of antimicrobials, or simply a solvent for the other ingredients. The copper of the *ār-fæt* can prevent the growth of bacteria. But the researchers learned through experimentation that the *ēag-sealf* was highly effective when the ingredients were combined according to the leechbook's precise instructions, which allowed the various ingredients to interact within a brass vessel for a period of nine days. The ancientbiotics researcher Erin Connelly says: 'Methicillin-resistant *Staphylococcus aureus* (or MRSA) is resistant to many current antibiotics. Staph and MRSA infections are responsible for a variety of severe and chronic infections, including wound infections, sepsis and pneumonia.' The *ēag-sealf* from *Bald's Leechbook* not only prevented further growth of MRSA bacteria, it killed those already present in artificial wounds. Who would have thought that knowing Old English would assist us in medical research?

Well, Bald probably did.

Seventh *wordhord*

ār-fæt, noun (AR-VAT / 'aːr-ˌvæt): Brass or copper vessel.

æppel, noun (AP-pell / 'æp-pɛl): Apple, fruit; something round, ball.

bān-fæt, noun (BAHN-VAT / 'baːn-ˌvæt): 'Bone-vessel', the body.

bān-hūs, noun (BAHN-HOOS / 'baːn-ˌhuːs): 'Bone-house', the body.

bān-loca, noun (BAHN-LOCK-ah / 'baːn-ˌlɔ-ka): 'Bone-enclosure', 'bone-locker', muscle or the body.

belg, noun (BELG / 'bɛlg): Bag, pouch, sack; bellows.

blōd, noun (BLOAD / 'bloːd): Blood.

brægen, noun (BRAE-yen / 'bræ-jɛn): Brain.

brēost-loca, noun (BRAY-ost-LOCK-ah / 'breːɔst-ˌlɔ-ka): 'Breast-enclosure', the mind.

dēofol-sēocnes, noun (DAY-ov-ol-SAY-ock-ness / ˈdeːɔ-vɔl-ˌseːɔk-nɛs):
'Devil-sickness', possession by devils, insanity.

drēor, noun (DRAY-or / ˈdreːɔr): Blood.

dryhtenlic gebed, noun (DRUE-h'ten-litch yeh-BED / ˈdryx-tɛn-litʃ
jɛ-ˈbɛd): Lord's Prayer.

ēage, noun (AY-ah-yuh / ˈeːa-jə): Eye.

ēag-sealf, noun (AY-ah-SEH-alf / ˈeːaj-ˌsɛalf): Eye salve, ointment for
the eye.

ēar-clǣnsiend, noun (AY-ar-KLAN-zi-yend / ˈeːar-ˌklæːn-zɪ-ɛnd): Little
finger (ear-cleaner).

ēar-finger, noun (AY-ar-FING-ger / ˈeːar-ˌfiŋ-gɛr): Little finger
(ear-finger).

elehtre, noun (EL-eh-h'truh / ˈɛ-lɛx-trə): Lupine.

fæt, noun (FAT / ˈfæt): Vessel or container, mainly for fluids.

fēond-sēocnes, noun (FAY-ond-SAY-ock-ness / ˈfeːɔnd-ˌseːɔk-nɛs):
'Fiend-sickness', possession by devils, insanity.

feorh-hord, noun (FEH-or'h-HORD / ˈfɛɔrx-ˌhɔrd): 'Life-treasure', 'life-
hoard', the soul or spirit.

feorh-hūs, noun (FEH-or'h-HOOS / ˈfɛɔrx-ˌhuːs): 'Life-house', the
body.

ferhþ, noun (FER-h'th / ˈfɛrxθ): Soul, spirit, mind, life.

finger, noun (FING-ger / ˈfiŋ-gər): Finger.

flǣsc-hama, noun (FLASH-HA-ma / ˈflæːʃ-ˌha-ma): 'Flesh-covering',
the body.

flǣsc-hord, noun (FLASH-HORD / ˈflæːʃ-ˌhɔrd): 'Flesh-hoard', the body.

fōt, noun (FOAT / ˈfoːt): Foot.

fylle-sēocnes, noun (FUE-luh-SAY-ock-ness / ˈfy-lə-ˌseːɔk-nɛs): 'Falling-
sickness', possibly epilepsy.

galdor, noun (GAL-dor / ˈgal-dɔr): Poem, song; incantation, charm.

ge-wit-lēast, noun (yeh-WIT-LAY-ahst / jɛ-ˈwɪt-ˌleːast): Witlessness,
madness.

gold-finger, noun (GOLD-FING-ger / ˈgɔld-ˌfɪŋ-gər): Ring finger.

gor, noun (GOR / ˈgɔr): Dung, faeces, filth, dirt, slime.

grēot-hord, noun (GRAY-ot-HORD / ˈgreːɔt-ˌhɔrd): 'Earth-hoard', the human body.

hand, noun (HAHND / ˈhand): Hand.

hǣlþ, noun (HALTH / ˈhæːlθ): (Good) health, freedom from sickness; (act of) healing.

hǣlu, noun (HAL-uh / ˈhæː-lʌ): Health, security, sound physical condition, well-being.

hēafod-gim, noun (HAY-ah-vod-YIM / ˈheːa-vɔd-ˌjim): Eye (head-gem).

heolfor, noun (HEH-ol-vor / ˈhɛɔl-vɔr): Blood, gore.

heorte, noun (HEH-or-tuh / ˈhɛɔr-tə): Heart.

hord-loca, noun (HORD-LOCK-ah / ˈhɔrd-ˌlɔ-ka): 'Hoard-locker', 'treasure-locker', the mind.

hreþer, noun (HREH-ther / ˈhrɛ-θɛr): Breast, heart, mind.

hring-finger, noun (H'RING-FING-ger / ˈhrɪŋ-ˌfɪŋ-gər): Ring finger.

hyge, noun (HUE-yuh / ˈhy-jə): Heart, mind, soul.

lǣce, noun (LATCH-uh / ˈlæː-t͡ʃə): Doctor, physician; a leech (species of worm).

lǣce-bōc, noun (LATCH-uh-BOAK / ˈlæː-t͡ʃə-ˌboːk): Leechbook, book of medical remedies.

lǣce-finger, noun (LATCH-uh-FING-ger / ˈlæː-t͡ʃə-ˌfɪŋ-gər): Ring finger (leech-finger).

līc, noun (LEECH / ˈliːt͡ʃ): Body.

lifer, noun (LIV-er / ˈlɪ-vɛr): Liver.

middel-finger, noun (MID-dell-FING-ger / ˈmɪd-dɛl-ˌfɪŋ-gər): Middle finger.

mōd, noun (MOAD / ˈmoːd): Mind, heart, spirit.

mōd-sefa, noun (MOAD-SEH-va / ˈmoːd-ˌsɛ-va): Mind, spirit, soul, heart.

mōnaþ-sēocness, noun (MO-nath-SAY-ock-ness / ˈmoː-naθ-ˌseːɔk-nɛs): Lunacy (month-sickness).

mūþ, noun (MOOTH / ˈmuːθ): Mouth.

mūþ-bana, noun (MOOTH-BAH-na / ˈmuːθ-ˌba-na): 'Mouth-killer', one who destroys with the mouth.

mūþettan, verb (MOO-thet-tahn / ˈmuː-θɛt-tan): To chatter, let out a secret.

mūþ-frēo, adjective (MOOTH-FRAY-oh / ˈmuːθ-ˌfreːɔ): At liberty to speak (mouth-free).

pintel, noun (PIN-tell / ˈpɪn-tɛl): Penis.

sāwel-drēor, noun (SAH-well-DRAY-or / ˈsaː-wɛl-ˌdreːɔr): 'Soul-blood'.

sceatt, noun (SHEH-aht / ˈʃɛat): Piece of money, coin.

scīn-lāc, noun (SHEEN-LAHK / ˈʃiːn-ˌlaːk): Magic or necromancy that causes apparitions and delusions.

scyte-finger, noun (SHUE-tuh-FING-ger / ˈʃy-tə-ˌfiŋ-gər): Index finger (shooting-finger or arrow-finger).

sefa, noun (SEH-va / ˈsɛ-va): Understanding, mind, heart.

sēocness, noun (SAY-ock-ness / ˈseːɔk-nɛs): Sickness, illness.

swāt, noun (SWAHT / ˈswaːt): (In medicine) sweat, perspiration, plant juice; (in poetry) blood.

teors, noun (TEH-ors / ˈtɛɔrs): Penis.

þūma, noun (THOO-ma / ˈθuː-ma): Thumb.

un-hǣlu, noun (UN-HAE-luh / ˈʌn-ˌhæː-lʌ): Bad health, disease, sickness, unsoundness.

wamb, noun (WAHMB / ˈwamb): Belly, stomach; womb.

wæter-sēocness, noun (WAT-er-SAY-ock-ness / ˈwæ-tɛr-ˌseːɔk-nɛs): 'Water-sickness', oedema.

wōdheortness, noun (WOAD-HEH-ort-ness / ˈwoːd-ˌhɛɔrt-nɛs): Insanity, madness.

8

The World Outside

Weather and un-weather

IF HEALTH AND UN-HEALTH are popular topics of conversation, the weather is even more so. In 2018 Bristol Airport commissioned a study polling 2,000 adults on their conversations about weather. According to the study, a British person spends around four and a half months of their life discussing the weather, an average of three weather-related exchanges a day! The weather is probably the first thing you notice when you go outside. It affects the quality of your day and what you're able to accomplish, even more so if you're a farmer. This has not changed over the past millennium; if anything, the weather was more significant in a time when most people did work on farms.

Another thing that has barely changed is the word itself: *weder*. Old English **weder** became modern English 'weather', which, aside from a change from d to th, is pronounced the same. The negation of weather, **un-weder**, is less common in Old English, but it was a word that referred specifically to bad weather. This raises the question: if there is a word for bad weather that essentially means 'not-weather', is 'weather' itself inherently good?

You might think **weder-tācen** (weather-token) would be a sign of rain or a storm, perhaps a dark cloud or rough winds, but it means just the opposite. *Weder-tācen*, a hapax that appears in a poem about St Guthlac, refers unambiguously to a sign of *good* weather. The poet describes the heavenly light of dawn on the morning of the saint's death:

> Glory's brightness, noble around the noble one, shone clearly throughout the night. The shadows withdrew, dissipating under the heavens. The bright light, a heavenly candle, was around the holy house from twilight until daybreak, coming from the east across the deep ocean, the warm <u>weather-token</u> (*wedertacen*).

The sunrise is a *weder-tācen*, a sign of beautiful weather but also a sign of Guthlac's saintliness. The *weder-tācen* lights his way to heaven. For saints, death is seen as a joyous time, when they leave behind their fleshly prisons for eternal life in heaven.

The definition of 'weather' that was inherently favourable became obsolete after the Middle Ages. Nowadays, if someone warns you to keep an eye on the weather, that weather is assumed to be bad. If you're looking out for weather, you aren't thinking of sunshine and clear skies (certainly not in Britain). Although the good-weather 'weather' stuck around for a while longer, the bad-weather 'weather' appears as early as the twelfth century. A chronicle entry for the year 1097 reports that King William had planned to hold his court at Winchester but was delayed in Normandy due to *weder*. This late Old English *weder* has an unfavourable implication – it is dangerous and destructive, referring to storms and not heavenly weather-tokens.

Although contemporary historians like this chronicler rarely describe good weather (what would the interest in that be?), the English may have enjoyed what's now called the Medieval Warm

Period. It's misleading to call this period an 'improvement', as some historians do, because it came with both positive and negative consequences. While warmer weather meant that most regions of early medieval England could grow grapes and make wine, it also meant that diseases were introduced that were normally limited to warmer parts of the world. The marshland in eastern England became 'an ideal breeding ground for the mosquito', says the historian Christina Lee, who theorises that Old English **lencten-ādl** (spring-disease) may have referred to malaria.

The term 'Medieval Warm Period' is itself misleading. The climate of Europe during the Middle Ages is thought to have been warmer and drier than what preceded or followed, but temperatures during this period did not indicate a steady trend in one direction or the other. Sometimes they reversed for several years, and there were good and bad seasons alike. And unlike climate change today – an indisputable global phenomenon caused by human industry, not merely a change in wind patterns – the Medieval Warm Period affected a limited geographical area, not the whole world. The glacial geologist Nicolás Young says: 'The Medieval Warm Period was certainly not a global event and probably didn't even span the entire North Atlantic region', while the climate historian Astrid Ogilvie notes that the concept of such a period is itself 'greatly exaggerated'.

Whatever the weather was like in the Middle Ages – warm or otherwise – you can be sure English people enjoyed talking about it.

Welkin-faring and slaughter-mist

In 1596 William Barlow, Bishop of Lincoln, wrote about writers of almanacs who made astrological predictions. He called these individuals 'Welkin Wisards' – a truly magical name compared to today's boring old 'meteorologist' or even 'weatherman'! 'Welkin' comes from Old English **wolcen** (cloud or clouds).

Today we have seafaring, but in Old English there was also welkin-faring. **Wolcen-faru** is the movement or journey of clouds across the sky. An Old English prayer calls upon all the elements to praise God, with an alliteration that is difficult to capture in modern English:

> Mighty Lord, the frosts and snows, <u>winter-bitter weather and moving</u> <u>clouds</u> (*winterbiter* **w***eder and* **w***olcenfaru*), may they praise you in the air! And the lightning, shining and flashing – may it bless you!

The prayer goes on to call upon the praise of the ground, the hills, the plains, the mountains, the sea waves and even the whales. *Hwalas ðec herigað* (the whales praise you) – now *that* is a useful phrase.

Clouds move, and sometimes they collide. Both *wolcen-faru* (cloud-movement) and **wolcen-gehnāst** (cloud-collision) appear in an Old English riddle:

> I cause the beginning of that strife, then go pressing through the <u>collision of clouds</u> (*wolcengehnaste*), the tumult, with great force, over the stream's embrace. The press of troops on high bursts loudly, then sinks beneath the air's helm near land, and on my back I must carry a burden, strengthened by my lord's might. A powerful servant, I thus strive at times. Sometimes I must descend low under the earth or beneath the waves. Sometimes I stir the currents over the ocean. Sometimes I ascend, rousing the <u>passing clouds</u> (*wolcnfare*), travelling widely, swift and violent.

The riddle describes an epic battle, with clouds colliding like opposing forces. The tenth-century manuscript in which this riddle is preserved offers no answers. One popular, potential solution is the wind.

The language of battle is used for the weather, so is it any surprise that weather words appear in descriptions of actual warfare? Take, for instance, the hapax **hilde-gicel** (battle-icicle), which appears in *Beowulf*:

> Then that sword, the war-blade, began to diminish from the war-sweat in battle-icicles (*hildegicelum*). It was wondrous when it completely melted, just like ice.

The 'war-sweat' here is Grendel's blood. Beowulf has just decapitated his corpse. *Hilde-gicel* could be a metaphor for a number of things – the sword, the blood on the sword, the molten metal corroded by Grendel's supernaturally hot corpse-blood.

Another martial, meteorological phenomenon is **wæl-mist** (slaughter-mist). The word, which appears only twice in extant Old English literature, is thought to be a mist that enshrouds those killed in battle. In an Old English poetic version of the Book of Exodus, the Egyptians chase the Israelites through the divinely parted waters of the Red Sea. Once the Israelites are safely across, God releases the waters. The Egyptians are all drowned and, according to the poem, a *wæl-mist* rises over bloody waves. Really, it's quite a lot of blood and gore for a drowning scene, as if the poet couldn't resist adding in some more conventional Old English battle imagery.

The other occurrence of *wæl-mist* is in the poem *The Fortunes of Men*. One possible fortune is, of course, being hanged as a convict:

> One must ride on the gallows extended. He hangs there at death until his soul-hoard breaks, his bloody bone-chamber. The dark-cloaked raven takes his eyes, tearing into the man without a soul. He cannot ward off the loathsome, treacherous sky-robber with his hands. His life is gone. Pale on the beam, enveloped in slaughter-mist (*wælmiste*), he awaits his fate without feeling, with no hope for life.

Neither the convict nor the Egyptians receive an honourable or peaceful death. Whatever it might be, *wæl-mist* appears in only the most dire and dreadful of scenarios.

If bloody slaughter-mists seem like miserable weather, don't worry: sunny skies are ahead.

Heaven's candle

England has a reputation for clouds and rain, but Old English has plenty of words for sunny weather. If the sunshine is particularly radiant, the weather is **sunn-beorht** (sun-bright). When the sun comes out after days of gloom, you may be pleased at how **sunn-wlitig** (sun-beautiful) it is outside. If you get overly **sunn-hāt** (sun-hot), you might seek the cool shadows of a **lēaf-scead** (place shaded by trees and foliage).

Modern English 'sun' hasn't changed much from **sunne**, but Old English has another, less familiar word: **sigel**. Not only does *sigel* mean 'sun', it's the name of the lightning-bolt-shaped S-rune ᛋ. Here it appears in *The Rune Poem*:

> ᛋ *semannum   symble biþ on hihte,*
> *ðonn hi hine feriaþ   ofer fisces beþ,*
> *oþ hi brimhengest   bringeþ to lande.*

The <u>sun</u> (*sigel*) is always a joy to seafarers, when they journey across the fish's bath, until their sea-steed brings them to land.

'Fish's bath' (*fisces beþ*) is a kenning for the ocean and 'sea-steed' (*brimhengest*) for a ship. Most kennings for the sun are candles of some sort: **dæg-candel** (day-candle), **heofon-candel** (heaven-candle), **weder-candel** (weather-candle), **swegel-candel** (sky-candle), and the rather odd *mere-candel* (sea-candle). The sun might be called a *mere-candel* because it rises from and sets into the sea. Or maybe the poet just needed a sun word to alliterate with *midne dæg* (midday) in their Old English translation of Boethius:

> . . . *ofer **midne** dæg,   **me**recondel scyfð* . . .
> . . . past **midd**ay, the sea-candle advances . . .

Another less obvious kenning is **friþ-candel** (peace-candle). The sun might be a *friþ-candel* because its light protects one from harm; there was a belief that evil spirits ceased to operate at sunrise. The compound *friþ-candel* is a hapax, with its single occurrence in the poem *Genesis A*. The Latin Vulgate Bible simply has *Sol egressus est super terram* (The sun was risen upon the earth), but the Old English says:

> *Þa sunne up,*
> *folca friðcandel,   furðum eode.*

The sun was up, the peace-candle of peoples went forth.

This so-called 'peace-candle' rather inappropriately precedes God sending heavenly brimstone, welling fire and dark flame down to earth for the punishment of men. The scene upon which the peace-candle shines is hardly peaceful.

Winter-weeds

Today weeds are plants that are considered neither useful nor pretty, nuisances of the wild that hinder the growth of the cultivated. These weeds should not be confused with the ones worn by widows. The words are homonyms, sharing the same spelling and pronunciation but having nothing to do with each other in terms of meaning and origin.

In Old English the words were easily distinguishable. The item of clothing you wore was a **wǣd** (pronounced WADD), and the undesirable plant was a **wēod** (WAY-odd). For example:

> *Martinus me bewǣfde efne mid ðyssere <u>wǣde</u>.* (WADD-uh)
> Martin even clothed me with this <u>garment</u>.

vs.

> *Cuom feond his ond oferseow <u>weod</u> in midle þæs hwætes.* (WAY-odd)
> His enemy came and over-sowed <u>weeds</u> amidst the wheat.

Wǣd could describe any sort of garment. **Here-wǣd**, or 'war-weed', was armour. A person's *wǣd* could indicate their occupation, status or gender, depending on the context. It wasn't until Middle English that 'widwe wedes' was used to describe the clothing worn by a widow during her period of mourning (usually a black or dark-coloured dress and veil).

The earliest cited use of widow's weeds is in what's known as the *Middle English Metrical Paraphrase of the Old Testament* from the early fifteenth century. In the Book of Genesis, a woman named Thamar is married to the sons of Judah: firstly to Er (but God kills him), secondly to Onan (but God kills him), and thirdly . . . well, it is supposed to be to Judah's third son Shelah, but by then Judah is a bit concerned about the emerging pattern. Judah tells Thamar to go and live with her father in widow's clothing until Shelah is older. But after 'many days' have passed, Thamar decides to do a peculiar thing. According to the Latin, Thamar takes off her *viduitatis vestibus* (garments of widowhood): the Middle English says, 'Hyr wedow wedes scho layd away'. Thamar removes her widow's weeds, puts on a veil to disguise herself, and waits for Judah to walk by – who of course mistakes her for a harlot and ends up sleeping with her. Later she gives birth to twins, the sons of her own father-in-law, and Judah, ashamed, realises he should have given her Shelah as he'd promised. Widow's weeds are so essential to the way her father-in-law sees her that Thamar might as well be a complete stranger to him without them!

There may not have been 'widow's weeds' in Old English, but there were 'winter-weeds'. The hapax **winter-gewǣde** (winter-weeds) appears in a tenth-century poem describing the arrival of winter, 'when frost and snow with great force cover the earth with <u>winter-weeds</u> (*wintergewǣdum*)'. 'Winter weed' appears in the *Oxford English Dictionary* as a rare, archaic, primarily literary term, defined as 'clothes worn, or suitable to be worn, in winter'. The earliest cited use is from a fifteenth-century poem: a tree without leaves or fruit on its branches is dressed in 'wynters weede'. But *winter-gewǣde* is in fact nearly 500 years older.

In these early- and late-medieval texts, *wintergewǣdum* and 'wynters weede' are metaphorical, referring to the frost and snow or a lack of leaves as the clothing of winter. An April 1918 ad from the *Charleston Daily Mail* uses the term more literally: 'Back go the hands of the clock – Away go our Winter weeds . . . One more hour a day to wear our new Spring clothes.' These twentieth-century 'Winter weeds' are the clothing worn by people during the winter, not the metaphorical clothing worn by winter itself. Winter weeds, *winter-gewǣde* (WIN-ter-yeh-WADD-uh) . . . we continue to be captivated by alliteration, whether in advertising or in poetry.

In leek-towns and wort-yards

The word **tūn** grew from its humble beginnings as one house and its surrounding land to a collection of homes, what we'd call a town today. The word can simply mean 'enclosure' – a house, land or buildings encompassed by walls, fences or hedges. In early medieval England, *tūn* was often used to refer to the old towns of Roman Britain, which is why 'ton' appears in many British place names: Luton, Tonbridge, Southampton, etc.

A **wyrt** is a plant. *Wyrt* becomes 'wort', found in modern plant names like St John's wort and mugwort. Put *wyrt* and *tūn* together and you have a 'plant-town', or **wyrt-tūn**, an Old English word for 'garden'.

And what might grow in a plant-town? Modern English 'leek' comes from Old English **lēac**, a garden herb or plant. But *lēac* could be any herb, not only the specific vegetable we call a leek today. This is an example of semantic narrowing, when a general word becomes more specific over time (like *brēad* or *mete* in Chapter 2). Perhaps in another millennium the word 'vegetable' will refer specifically to a carrot.

Just as a *wyrt* grows in a *wyrt-tūn*, a *lēac* grows in a **lēac-tūn**, a herb or kitchen garden. The warden of the *lēac* is a **lēac-weard**, the gardener, who keeps watch over their veggie wards. A *lēac-tūn* might contain such 'leeks' as **enne-lēac** (onion) and **gār-lēac** (garlic). The word **gār** means spear or arrow, so a *gār-lēac* is really a 'spear-herb', a name that makes sense when you see the plant's pointy leaves.

Another word for a garden is **wyrt-geard**. Like a *tūn*, a **geard** is an enclosure, anything from a small garden to an entire household to a land or region. In modern English the British call a house's grassy area a garden, while Americans call it a yard. Both 'garden' and 'yard' come from *geard* (pronounced YEH-ard). An **ort-geard** is an orchard, although I personally prefer **æppel-tūn**, a word that could be translated 'apple-town'.

A garden can have many a **wyn-wyrt**, not just fruits and vegetables. *Wyn-wyrt* means 'pleasant plant' – one might call it a winsome wort. A *wyn-wyrt* is most lovely when it's 'blowing', which it does even when the air is perfectly still. The Old English verb **blōwan** means 'to bloom' as well as 'to blow'. A common *wyn-wyrt* is the **dæges ēage**, 'day's eye' or 'eye of the day', the petals of which supposedly close at night and open in the morning. Today the *dæges ēage* is known as a daisy.

The most winsome worts of the *wyrt-geard* have a lovely 'wort-stink'. **Wyrt-stenc** is used in positive contexts, so a better translation might be 'plant-scent'. Although it eventually becomes modern English 'stink', Old English **stenc** is not necessarily bad and can even be pleasing, a sweet perfume of flower blossoms. Even Paradise has a *stenc*:

> The plain is all beautiful, blessed with joys, with the sweetest <u>scents</u> (*stencum*) of the earth.

Paradise is called **neorxnawang** in Old English. The -*wang* element means 'plain' or 'field', but no one knows what *neorxna* means, although there is no shortage of theories. Gudbrand Vigfússon, one of the foremost Scandinavian scholars of the nineteenth century, thought *neorxnawang* meant 'Garden of the Norns', the three goddesses of fate or destiny in Norse mythology. Other scholars, like Jacob Grimm of fairy-tale fame, dismissed this theory, which, although appealing, made no sense linguistically or contextually. In 1913 the American philologist James Bright suggested that *neorxna* came from *ne wyrcan* (Old English for 'no work'), an explanation that sounds more pleasing than probable. Other translations for *neorxnawang* include pagan 'Asgard' (home of the gods in Norse mythology) and 'garden of perpetual change', particularly strange for the Christian Paradise, which in every description is characterised by a *lack* of change. In 1973 the Old English professor Alan K. Brown theorised that the word was coined deliberately to be mysterious and obscure, combining a rune with a word spelled backwards. Brown explains that the x could actually be the rune ᚷ (*gyfu*), which makes a g-sound. If you change the x for a g and reverse the letters, you get 'groen'. *Groene* is a potential eighth-century spelling of 'green', so it would be a way of saying 'green plain' or 'green field'. But then shouldn't it be 'eneorᚷwang'? Well, says Brown, 'eneorxwang' is hard to pronounce, so . . . how about *neorxnawang*? More recently, in 2015 the English professor Sandra M. Hordis has taken *neorxnawang* as a compound word: *neor* (near) + *na* (not) + *wang* (garden, field). That would make *neorxnawang* either 'garden-not-near' or 'near-not-garden'. And the x, a letter found relatively infrequently in Old English? Well, says Hordis, 'a certain mystery lies in the intrusive x'. It sure does. Although scholars will never stop trying to solve the puzzle, it may be that Old English Paradise will always remain a mystery.

Neorxnawang, as well as gardens in general, produces many a lovely *wyrt-stenc*, but if you suffer from allergies, a *wyn-wyrt* might be less winsome. If this is the case, you can at least take comfort in the wonderfully onomatopoeic word for 'sneeze' in Old English: **fnēosung** (F'NAY-oh-zung). Or perhaps you can treat those allergies with a **wyrt-drenc**, a potion made of plants or herbs.

Acquiring a *wyrt-drenc*, however, means trusting your health to a **wyrt-gælstre**, a woman who uses herbs for magic charms. *Wyrt-gælstre* appears only once in extant Old English in a prognostics text. Whether folklore or pseudo-science, medieval prognostics make predictions about the future based on astronomy, numerology, the days of the week, dreams and the human body. They address many uncertainties: birth, health, weather, harvest and the course of one's life. They also specify which dates are best for activities such as bloodletting and giving birth.

The Old English prognostics that survive are from the eleventh century. By that time England was fully Christian and had been so for quite some time. Some people of the Church, like Abbot Ælfric of Eynsham, condemned the use of divination (far too pagan!), although some Christians clearly believed in it, since the prognostics were recorded in manuscripts created in monasteries.

One Old English prognostic text, known as the *Birth Lunarium*, makes predictions based on the age of the moon at one's birth. For instance, if you were born when the moon was one night old, you will be long-lived and prosperous. A lunar month is thirty days, the time between two new moons. According to the *Birth Lunarium*, a birthday on the fifth of a lunar month was unlucky: a boy would be unlikely to survive beyond age five, and a girl would die the *wyrst swelt* (worst death). The girl's age of death is not specified, but she must have lived significantly longer than the boy, long enough to have the occupation of *wyrt-gælstre*, because it is through the making of herbal charms that the girl's unlucky, early demise would supposedly come about.

If you were born a boy on the fifth of a lunar month and are reading this book, you have presumably proven that first prediction wrong (unless you are an extraordinarily precocious five-year-old). Even if you were born a girl on this unlucky date and are herbologically inclined, I wouldn't be too concerned, since bad luck is predicted for many different birthdays and predictions often contradict each other. For instance, I was born on a three-night-old moon: according to one lunarium, I will neither live to be an old woman nor will I die a good death, but according to a second lunarium I will live a long time indeed.

Whether you are a knowledgeable *wyrt-gælstre* or simply admire a *wyn-wyrt* as much as the next person, the most beautiful *wyrt-tūn* of all is the garden of Paradise, *neorxnawang* – yet this pleasant place is where humankind discovered death.

Every evil began to sprout

In the Book of Genesis, Adam and Eve eat fruit from a forbidden tree in the Garden of Eden. That tree is known as the 'Tree of Knowledge of Good and Evil', or simply the 'Tree of Knowledge'. In Old English it has a more sinister name: ***dēaþ-bēam*** (death-tree). The word *dēaþ-bēam* appears in the poem *Genesis B*. The Latin Vulgate Bible describes the tree as a 'Tree of Life' in the same verse in which God brings forth from the ground 'all manner of trees, fair to behold, and pleasant to eat of'. When Eve observes it later, the tree is 'fair to the eyes, and delightful to behold'. But the Old English description of this tree is quite different:

> It was completely black, dim and dark. That was the <u>Tree of Death</u> (*deaðes beam*), which bore much that was bitter. Every person who tasted what grew on that tree must know the turn of evil and good in this world, and live ever after in pain, with sweat and sorrow.

Adam eats from the tree and lives to be 930 years old, so the *dēaþ-bēam*'s 'death' is far from instantaneous. Nine hundred and thirty years sounds like a long time to us with our fleeting lifespans, but it was short for a man who, if he hadn't failed to obey God's command, could have been immortal. The *dēaþ-bēam* brought death into the world.

The *Genesis* poems are truly a botanist's experiment gone horribly wrong. In *Genesis A* there is yet another unholy plant, one that grows from the blood of the world's first murder. Cain kills his brother Abel out of jealousy and malice, an act that brings God's curse upon himself and his descendants. The Latin Vulgate Bible says only that Abel's blood soaks into the earth and then cries out to God, but the Old English poem adds a unique detail – a tree that grows from Abel's spilled blood:

Then Cain carried out an unwise deed with his hands, slew his kinsman, his brother, and spilled Abel's blood. This earth swallowed up the slaughter-blood, the man's blood, after the deadly blow. Woe reared up, the progeny of sorrow. For a very long time since then, cruel fruit has grown from this branch with hostility. The branches of strife have reached widely among the nations of men. The <u>harm-branches</u> (*hearmtanas*) have touched the sons of multitudes severely and sorely – as they still do. From those broad leaves every evil began to sprout.

These **hearmtanas**, 'harm-branches' or 'sorrow-twigs', extend across all humanity, spreading murder, jealousy and every evil across the world. This is often read as metaphorical, but the eleventh-century Old English Hexateuch actually depicts a tree-like growth watered by Abel's gushing red blood.

But the most mysterious of Old English trees is the **wulfhēafod-trēow** (wolf-head tree). A 'wolf head' is associated with outlawry in early medieval England. The eleventh-century law code of King Edward the Confessor states that an outlaw 'wears the head of a wolf from the day of his outlawry', which is called *wlvesheved* in Old English. Like a wolf, an outlaw could be killed without fear of penalty. (Wolves got a pretty bad rap in the Middle Ages.) Thus, a 'wolf-head tree' might be a way to describe a gallows, a 'tree' from which an outlaw is hanged. As a hapax, *wulfhēafod-trēow* is already difficult to interpret, and the challenge is made even greater since the one text in which it appears is a tenth-century riddle with no solution:

I saw in the hall, where warriors drank, four of a kind carried across the floor: an adorned tree, twisted gold, treasure artfully bound, some silver, and the sign of the cross of he who raised a ladder to the heavens for us before destroying the city of hell-dwellers.

Cain killing Abel in the Old English Hexateuch

I can easily tell men of the tree's noble nature. There were maple, oak, hard yew and <u>yellow</u> (*fealwa*) holly. All together, they are useful to the lord and have one name: <u>wolf-head tree</u> (*wulfheafedtreo*).

It often <u>received/repelled/proffered/prayed for</u> (*abæd*) a weapon for its lord, a treasure in the hall, a gold-hilted sword.

Now reveal to me the answer of this riddle, he who presumes to say with words what the wood is called.

Proposed solutions for this riddle include a scabbard, sword rack, sword carrying box (though there is no evidence for such an item's existence), harp, cross, gallows, reliquary, or mead barrel with drinking bowl. Of these solutions I find the latter two, though far from perfect, the most compelling.

The medievalist Claire Fanger proposed the reliquary solution in 1986. A reliquary is a container for sacred relics, which could be anything from a saint's finger bone to a shred of cloth from a saint's garment to a sliver of the cross on which Christ was crucified. A reliquary could be made of wood, elaborately decorated and marked with the sign of the cross. The four kinds of wood are ones that would have been available in early medieval England, but more significantly they could symbolically point to the four more exotic types of wood that were supposedly used to make Christ's cross. The 'hall' across which the reliquary is carried could be the hall of a church during a liturgical ritual, and 'where warriors drank' could refer to Christians receiving the wine of the Eucharist. Fanger translates the troublesome word *abæd* as 'asked' or 'prayed for', reasoning that the cross might have prayed for a weapon its lord (Christ) could use to smite his enemies.

In 1995 the medievalist Keith P. Taylor proposed the mead barrel and drinking bowl (or mazer) solution. (Although Taylor uses the term 'mazer', which historians use now to refer to the wooden drinking bowls common during this period, a drinking bowl was not called a mazer until around 1200, the Middle English period.) Mead barrels in early medieval England were often made of yew and oak, and the word 'mazer' itself has cognates in Old Norse (*mǫsur-r*) and Middle High German (*maser*) that mean 'maple'. In Old English literature mazers are often decorated with silver, and it's possible this cup was especially fancy, decorated with gold and a cross-shaped design. A warrior who has overindulged from the barrel and mazer might try to fight but fumble, as though their own weapons were repelling them (Taylor taking *abæd* as 'repelled').

Taylor points out that Old English poetry has plenty of drunk warriors doing stupid things. An especially drunk and unlucky warrior might even commit crimes severe enough to merit outlawry. If a wolf-head represents an outlaw, the *wulfhēafod-trēow* (booze barrel and bowl) could be a tree that produces outlaws (drunk warriors), in the way that the metaphorical *dēaþ-bēam* produces evil and sorrow. Perhaps the riddle serves as a warning not to overindulge.

The biggest stretch in Taylor's solution is his explanation for the yellow holly. Yellow holly doesn't make sense (a holly tree's wood is white), so Taylor suggests that the tree is yellow from a swarm of bees, which would pollinate the hollies when they're in bloom. Bees make you think of honey, which makes you think of mead. Hence, a barrel and mazer. This logic is far from straightforward, and then there's the fact that bees in medieval England weren't yellow. Until 1850, the Dark European honeybee was exclusively used in beekeeping in all of Europe north of the Alps. A swarm of these bees would appear dark brown or black, not yellow.

Although the yellow holly explanation is faulty, Taylor does address *all* aspects of this puzzling riddle. Fanger does not include the holly's colour in her explanation, although she translates the colour word *fealwa* as 'fallow'. Today the word 'fallow' can mean a pale-brown or reddish-yellow colour, which doesn't accurately describe holly wood either. For its definition of **fealu**, the Toronto *Dictionary of Old English* says:

> A colour-term of varied meaning; the corpus yields the most evidence
> for a colour basically yellow but variously tinted with shades of red,
> brown or grey, often pale but always unsaturated, i.e. not vivid.

The white-coloured wood of holly is not vivid, so the definition could work in this context. It would not work, however, for Taylor's swarm of bees, which would have been dark-coloured.

The scribe who copied down the puzzling riddle left no solutions, so we will probably never know exactly what a *wulfhēafod-trēow* is. The truth behind the 'wolf-head tree' remains obscured.

Truth, however, is intrinsically linked to trees, because in Old English the words are homonyms: **trēow** (truth) and **trēow** (tree). The truth-*trēow* makes sense if you're familiar with 'trow', an obsolete word for 'belief', 'faith', 'trust', 'pledge' or 'covenant'; and it's from the word *trēow* that we get 'true'. The *Oxford English Dictionary* suggests that a distant Indo-European base may have connected the words 'tree' and 'truth' semantically, pointing to classical Latin *robustus*, which means 'made of oak' as well as 'strong, firm'. Whether or not the words are semantically related, the fact that 'tree' and 'truth' are both *trēow* is perfect for Old English wordplay and religious symbolism. Not only is the cross on which Christ was crucified often referred to as a tree (*trēow*), it is a symbol of faith and truth (*trēow*) among Christians.

Eighth *wordhord*

æppel-tūn, noun (AP-pell-TOON / ˈæp-pɛl-ˌtuːn): Orchard.

blōwan, verb (BLO-wan / ˈbloː-wan): To bloom, flourish, blossom.

dæg-candel, noun (DAIE-KAHN-dell / ˈdæj-ˌkan-dɛl): 'Day-candle', the sun.

dæges ēage, noun (DAIE-yes-AY-ah-yuh / ˈdæ-jɛs-ˌeːa-jə): Daisy (day's eye).

dēaþ-bēam, noun (DAY-ath-BAY-ahm / ˈdeːaθ-ˌbeːam): 'Death-tree', the Tree of Knowledge.

enne-lēac, noun (EN-nuh-LAY-ock / ˈɛn-nə-ˌleːak): Onion.

fealu, adjective (FEH-ah-luh / ˈfɛa-lʌ): Colour-term of varied meaning, often yellowish and pale, never vivid or saturated.

fnēosung, noun (F'NAY-oh-zung / ˈfneːɔ-zʌŋ): Sneeze.

friþ-candel, noun (FRITH-KAHN-dell / ˈfrɪθ-ˌkan-dɛl): 'Peace-candle', the sun.

gār, noun (GAR / ˈgaːr): Dart, spear, arrow; a weapon with a pointed head.

gār-lēac, noun (GAR-LAY-ock / ˈgaːr-ˌleːak): Garlic.

geard, noun (YEH-ard / ˈjɛard): Enclosure, yard, garden, court, dwelling, region; fence, hedge.

hearmtanas, plural noun (HEH-arm-TAH-nas / ˈhɛarm-ˌta-nas): 'Sorrow-twigs', branches of evil or strife.

heofon-candel, noun (HEH-ov-on-KAHN-dell / ˈhɛɔ-vɔn-ˌkan-dɛl): 'Heaven-candle', the sun.

here-wǣd, noun (HEH-ruh-WADD / ˈhɛ-rə-ˌwæːd): Armour.

hilde-gicel, noun (HILL-duh-YI-chell / ˈhɪl-də-ˌjɪ-t͡ʃɛl): 'Battle-icicle', drop of blood or blood dripping from a sword.

lēac, noun (LAY-ock / ˈleːak): Herb, plant.

lēac-tūn, noun (LAY-ock-TOON / ˈleːak-ˌtuːn): Herb garden, kitchen garden.

lēac-weard, noun (LAY-ock-WEH-ard / ˈleːak-ˌwɛard): Gardener.

lēaf-scead, noun (LAY-ov-SHEH-odd / ˈleːav-ˌʃɛad): 'Leaf-shade', place shaded by leaves or foliage.

lencten-ādl, noun (LENK-ten-AH-dull / ˈlɛnk-tɛn-ˌaː-dəl): 'Spring-disease', fever.

mere-candel, noun (MEH-ruh-KAHN-dell / ˈmɛ-rə-ˌkan-dɛl): 'Sea-candle', the sun.

neorxnawang, noun (NEH-ork-snah-WAHNG / ˈnɛɔrk-sna-ˌwaŋ): Paradise.

ort-geard, noun (ORT-YEH-ard / ˈɔrt-ˌjɛard): Orchard.

sigel, noun (SI-yell / ˈsɪ-jɛl): Sun; name of the S-rune ᚻ.

stenc, noun (STENCH / ˈstɛnt͡ʃ): Smell, scent, odour.

sunn-beorht, adjective (SUN-BEH-orh't / ˈsʌn-ˌbɛɔrxt): 'Sun-bright', bright with sunshine.

sunne, noun (SUH-nuh / ˈsʌ-nə): Sun.

sunn-hāt, adjective (SUN-HAWT / ˈsʌn-ˌhaːt): 'Sun-hot', heated by the sun.

sunn-wlitig, adjective (SUN-W'LI-tih / ˈsʌn-ˌwlɪ-tɪj): 'Sun-beautiful', beautiful with the sun.

swegel-candel, noun (SWEH-yell-KAHN-dell / ˈswɛ-jɛl-ˌkan-dɛl): 'Sky-candle', the sun.

trēow, noun (TRAY-oh / ˈtreːɔw): Tree; wood.

trēow, noun (TRAY-oh / ˈtreːɔw): Truth.

tūn, noun (TOON / ˈtuːn): Enclosure, yard, court; estate, farm; village, town.

un-weder, noun (UN-WEH-der / ˈʌn-ˌwɛ-dɛr): Bad weather.

wǣd, noun (WADD / ˈwæːd): Article of dress, garment; (in plural) clothing.

wæl-mist, noun (WAEL-MIST / ˈwæl-ˌmɪst): 'Slaughter-mist', mist that covers the bodies of the slain.

weder, noun (WEH-der / ˈwɛ-dɛr): Weather.

weder-candel, noun (WEH-der-KAHN-dell / ˈwɛ-dɛr-ˌkan-dɛl): 'Weather-candle', the sun.

weder-tācen, noun (WEH-der-TAH-ken / ˈwɛ-dɛr-ˌtaː-kɛn): 'Weather-token', sign of good weather.

wēod, noun (WAY-odd / ˈweːɔd): Useless or injurious plant, weed.

winter-gewǣde, noun (WIN-ter-yeh-WADD-uh / ˈwɪn-tɛr-jɛ-ˌwæː-də): Wintry garment.

wolcen, noun (WOL-kun / ˈwɔl-kən): Cloud.

wolcen-faru, noun (WOL-kun-FAH-ruh / ˈwɔl-kən-ˌfa-rʌ): Passing of clouds, moving clouds.

wolcen-gehnāst, noun (WOL-kun-yeh-H'NAST / ˈwɔl-kən-jɛ-ˌhnaːst):
   Collision of clouds.

wulfhēafod-trēow, noun (WULF-hay-ah-vod-TRAY-oh / ˈwʌlf-heːa-vɔd-
   ˌtreːɔw): 'Wolf-head tree' (definition uncertain).

wyn-wyrt, noun (WUEN-WUERT / ˈwyn-ˌwyrt): Pleasant plant.

wyrt, noun (WUERT / ˈwyrt): Plant, herb.

wyrt-drenc, noun (WUERT-DRENCH / ˈwyrt-ˌdrɛntʃ͡): Herbal drink,
   potion made from herbs.

wyrt-gælstre, noun (WUERT-GAL-struh / ˈwyrt-ˌgæl-strə): Woman
   who uses herbs for charms.

wyrt-geard, noun (WUERT-YEH-ard / ˈwyrt-ˌjɛard): Kitchen garden.

wyrt-stenc, noun (WUERT-STENCH / ˈwyrt-ˌstɛntʃ͡): Scent from a
   plant.

wyrt-tūn, noun (WUERT-TOON / ˈwyrt-ˌtuːn): Garden.

9
Wildlife

What is nature?

THERE IS NO WORD FOR nature in Old English. **Ge-cynd** can be translated as 'nature', but really it refers to one's condition or kind – human nature, for example. 'Nature' didn't appear in English until the thirteenth century (with Middle English 'nātūr'), and it wasn't until the end of the fourteenth that 'nature' referred to plants and animals as opposed to humans and human-made objects.

Instead of nature, Old English had **sceaft** (creation). *Sceaft* could refer to the entire created world or a single creature. Not only did *sceaft* encompass the things we think of as nature today (animals, plants, the rain, the soil, the sea, etc.), it included human beings and even supernatural entities. All these things were the creation of God. It didn't matter if the created thing or creature was evil or good, threatening or salutary – a dragon was still a part of God's creation no matter how many mead-halls it burned down.

In the nineteenth century, Romantic poets and artists saw nature as an escape from the over-development of the industrial age, a haven to be found among hills, meadows and forests. In early medieval England, however, beauty and splendour were found in humans and human-made things, if not in God. The Old English poem *The Dream of the Rood* tells of a tree's journey from the forest to its transformation into the cross on which Christ was crucified. Its beauty comes from its proximity and intimacy with Christ, not from its leaves and branches. The narrator of the poem, who is having a dream-vision of the cross, says that he saw it 'changing garments and colours; sometimes it was drenched, soaked by the flowing of blood, and sometimes it was adorned with treasure'. There is nothing natural about this tree or its beauty. The medieval literature scholar Jennifer Neville explains that in Old English the value of a horse or a piece of land *comes* from its human adornment and cultivation, not *in spite of* human intervention. A poet might admire the beauty of plants and animals *after* their transformation to fit into the civilised world. Humans made the wilderness beautiful by cultivating it with fruitful gardens and farmland. A **hors** (horse) was made beautiful with human adornments: gold, gems, an intricately wrought saddle. When left untouched by humans, *sceaft* was wild, often incomprehensible, inspiring fear and awe rather than joy and admiration.

Animals were beautiful as expressions of God's wisdom. Bestiaries, books of animal lore, were medieval bestsellers for wealthy patrons, filled with impressively time-consuming and expensive illustrations. Although bestiaries point to a fascination with the creatures of different lands, the animals' significance lay in the lessons they offered from God. There are animals that still carry the bestiary symbolism today. The **lēo** (lion) is still called 'king of beasts', and the fantastical **fēnix** (phoenix) still represents resurrection and rebirth.

Other animals' symbolism has not survived into modernity. Take the **befer** (beaver), for instance, who was 'a gentle animal, hunted not for its pelt but for its testicles, which contained, it was thought, a medicine of great value'. According to medieval bestiaries, the beaver would bite off its own testicles when fleeing hunters. It would then stand on its hind legs, exposing itself so the hunters would know that capture would be fruitless – no balls here! The manuscript curator Ann Payne says that the beaver represented 'a right-minded man [who] must sever himself from sins of all kinds and throw them in the face of the Devil'. As one bestiary says, 'the Devil will see that that man has nothing belonging to him and will leave him, ashamed'. For some reason, the ball-biting beaver doesn't live on in modern fiction like Aslan the lion or Fawkes the phoenix.

Bestiary animals that are similar in appearance can be quite different symbolically. In medieval England the **wudu-bucca** (wild goat) lived up in the highlands, while the **gāt-bucca** (domestic goat) was raised on farms. Even though the *wudu-bucca* and the *gāt-bucca* look pretty much the same in medieval illustrations, they represent opposing concepts.

The domesticated *gāt-bucca* was considered overly lustful, symbolic of lechery and licentiousness. A common guise used by the Devil was a male goat – with horn, tail and cloven hooves – and this did nothing for the *gāt-bucca*'s reputation. Domestic goats were associated not only with the Devil but with paganism, due to their resemblance to the satyrs and the Greek fertility god Pan, who had a man's head and torso but a goat's hindquarters, legs and horns.

It was a different story for the wild *wudu-bucca*. Wild goats dwelt in the high hills in the manner of Christ: 'Behold he cometh leaping upon the mountains, skipping over the hills' (Song of Songs 2:8). The wild goat had very keen eyesight, allowing it to see great distances, the way God was all-seeing and all-knowing. Wild goats could tell from a long way off if a man was a hunter or a harmless traveller, the way Christ could see through the wiles of his betrayers: 'Behold he is at hand that will betray me' (Matthew 26:46). Their ability to identify which plants were edible was compared to a wise preacher's ability to identify which ideas were worthy. It was believed that a wild goat would seek dittany if wounded, a plant that would supposedly expel the metal of a weapon from a wound. Bestiaries likened dittany's ability to cast out harmful metals to Christ's ability to cast devils out of sinners, if only those sinners confessed and sought forgiveness for their sins.

From the keen-sighted *wudu-bucca* to the ball-biting *befer*, such marvellous creatures as all these must be the creation of God, part of his great *sceaft*.

Worms big and small

Many Old English animal names have endured for over 1,000 years. **Cat** is still 'cat'. **Bera** became 'bear' and **scēap** (pronounced SHAY-op) 'sheep'. In Old English **hund** (hound) was far more common than the antecedent of 'dog': **docga** (DODGE-ah), a hapax. The word 'fowl' isn't used quite as often as 'bird' these days, but **fugel** was the word used in Old English. **Bridd**, from which we get 'bird', referred specifically to a young bird or chick. We don't get the word 'pigge' until Middle English; in Old English the word **swīn** (SWEEN) was used, which became modern English 'swine'.

After all these examples, you might guess that the word **dēor** means 'deer', but it is a false friend. In modern English only a particular kind of animal is called a 'deer'. Although Old English *dēor* became modern English 'deer', *dēor* was a far more inclusive term. A *dēor* could be what we call a deer, but it could in fact be *any* animal.

Several words that mean 'animal' ultimately derive from Old Germanic *deuzom*: Old English *dēor*, Old Saxon *dier*, Old High German *tior* and Gothic *dius*, as well as modern Icelandic *dýr*, Swedish *djur* and Danish *dyr*. The root of *deuzom* is *dhus*, which means 'to breathe'. 'Animal', a word that has only been around since Middle English, is also related to breathing, derived as it is from Latin *animalis* (having the breath of life), from *anima* (air, breath, life). *Anima* also gives us modern English 'animate'. An animal is a creature that is animated with *anima*, a creature that lives and breathes.

Like modern English 'deer', the word 'worm' used to have a far broader definition. A **wyrm** could be a snake, earthworm, insect, parasite or essentially anything reptilian. Old English *wyrm* has a number of cognates in other Germanic languages: Old Frisian *wirm*, Old Saxon *wurm*, Old Icelandic *orm-r*, all of which can refer to a worm, snake, dragon or any creepy-crawly. The Latin cognate, however, is *vermis* and specifically means 'worm', not 'dragon'. Vermicelli pasta looks like little worms, after all, not little dragons.

So if you read about a hero fighting a *wyrm* in an epic poem, it's probably not a giant killer earthworm. Beowulf's final battle is against a fifty-foot-long *wyrm*, grim and dreadful, that has been wreaking havoc, killing people, destroying villages and burning down mead-halls with his fiery breath. The poet calls this fearsome opponent both a *wyrm* and a **līg-draca** (flame-dragon). **Draca**, a less ambiguous word for a dragon, comes from Latin *dracō*, a word you might recognise from the *Harry Potter* series. Hogwarts student Draco Malfoy shares his name with the dragon constellation Draco, and (appropriately) he belongs to Slytherin, the house with a serpent mascot. Technically, Latin *dracō* can mean 'devil' as well as 'dragon', but either way it is a threatening and dangerous creature. In Old English, the Latin-derived *draca* is joined with the Germanic **līg** (flame, lightning) to create a *līg-draca*, a 'flame-dragon' or fire-breathing dragon. Another name for Beowulf's dragon is **lyft-floga**, which literally means 'air-flier'. Technically, a *lyft-floga* could be anything that flies in the air, be it bird or bumblebee, but the word is a hapax and its only context describes a fearsome, fire-breathing dragon. Definitely not one to confuse with a bee.

A smaller, garden-variety *wyrm* is the **lēaf-wyrm**, but this *wyrm* is equally destructive. In Psalm 77, Asaph, a great singer and musician from around 1000 BCE, reminds the Israelites of God's power and warns them not to repeat the errors of past generations. Asaph lists many of God's miracles, including the plagues on Egypt that allowed the Israelites to escape Pharaoh. The plagues were meant to oppose each of the principal Egyptian deities, demonstrating how God's powers surpassed those of the idols. For instance, with the plague of the locusts God shows that his power exceeds that of the Egyptian god Set, protector of crops. In the Latin Vulgate Bible the psalm reads:

> And he gave up their fruits to the <u>blast</u> (Latin *aerugini*), and their labours to the <u>locust</u> (Latin *locustae*).

A blast, also called a *Bruchus*, is a lentil-loving member of the leaf beetle family that wreaks havoc on crops. The Old English translations of this psalm use *lēaf-wyrm* (leaf-worm) to gloss Latin *aerugini*. Bosworth-Toller defines *lēaf-wyrm* as 'caterpillar', but really if it's a *Bruchus* or blast from the Egyptian plagues, it's more accurately a beetle. Latin *locustae* is translated with Old English **gærs-stapa** (grass-stepper) or **gærs-hoppa** (grass-hopper). Modern English still has the 'grasshopper', but it's very different from a locust, and its pleasingly descriptive name is highlighted when paired with the lovely but obsolete 'grass-stepper'.

The classification of *lēaf-wyrm* within the broader category of *wyrm* came not from England but from seventh-century Spain. The scholar Isidore of Seville designed a classification system that influenced bestiaries throughout the Middle Ages. Isidore's 'worm' list included 'earth-worms' (scorpions, beetles, millipedes, snails), 'air-worms' (spiders), 'water-worms' (leeches), 'clothing-worms' (moths), 'wood-worms' (termites), 'leaf-worms' (silkworms, caterpillars) and 'flesh-worms' (see *smēga-wyrm* in Chapter 2 – or don't, if you have a weak stomach). In addition to being a scholar, Isidore was a saint, and because of his obsession with recording and sharing all information in the known world, today some people call him the patron saint of the Internet.

Walking-weavers and bee-gangs

When I taught Old English in undergraduate seminars, I always introduced the language with kennings, for no better reason than they are one of my favourite things in the world. Kennings (introduced in Chapter 7) are a language of riddles and metaphors. What kind of creature do you suppose a ***gongel-wæfre*** (walking-weaver) is? A common guess among my students was a snake. A snake moves with a weaving motion, but it doesn't really walk. A *gongel-wæfre*, or a ***wæfer-gange*** (weaver-walker), is in fact a spider.

Gongel and *gange* are forms of the noun ***gang***, which means 'going' or 'moving', particularly by foot – it lives on in modern English 'gangplank'. 'Gang' is still used in Scots today: if someone has a 'ganging fit', they've got wanderlust, and if two people 'gang together', they're getting married. And in the wise but cynical words of the Scottish poet Robert Burns, 'The best laid schemes o' Mice an' Men / Gang aft agley', or often go ('gang') wrong ('To a Mouse', 1785).

Gang could also refer to a journey, a stream bed or a step of a flight of stairs. It wasn't until Middle English that 'gang' began to refer to a set of objects that were produced, sold or used together, such as 'ganges de spyndellez et cogges' (sets of spindles and cogs). By Shakespeare's time, the definitions of 'gang' had expanded to sets of *people* who 'go around together', 'associate with one another regularly', or are 'joined together by a shared interest or common cause'. This 'gang' was often associated with violence and disrepute, and later especially applied to groups of youths. Its earliest usage to denote an organised group of criminals was in 1652. In the latter half of the nineteenth century, 'gang' began to refer to organised groups of young urban people who went by a particular name and claimed control over a specific territory. In 1920s America, 'gang' recovered a bit of respectability as an informal way to address a group of people. Hey, gang!

One bee in Old English is a *bēo*; a swarm is a *bēo-gang*, a word that evokes a group of winged outlaws, drones trading in black-market pollen. But if *gang* means 'going' or moving', then a *bēo-gang* is not a gang or even a group of bees but a movement of bees. In modern English we call a group of bees a 'swarm', a word which (like Old English *gang*) refers to a type of motion. Swarms don't sit around in their hives. Swarms *swarm*, flying about in a mass, constantly moving in a purposeful cloud of kinetic energy.

A gang these days might have a godfather (particularly in Hollywood), but in Old English a *bēo-gang* had a *bēo-mōder* (bee-mother). This *bēo-mōder*, the female bee who rules the hive, has only been called a 'queen bee' since the seventeenth century. *Bēo-mōder* evokes a caring, benevolent leader, and perhaps people came to prefer less sentimental terminology. It's true, after all, that a newly hatched *bēo-mōder* will immediately slaughter all the unhatched queens (and the less murderous hatched ones) in the hive. A behaviour more queenly than motherly?

While bees went from being mothers to queens, hens did just the opposite. Granted, we usually call a hen a hen, and one hen doesn't direct the actions of all the other chickens (except in *Animal Farm*). 'Mother hen' began to be used in the nineteenth century for someone who takes care of others, especially in an overprotective, 'motherly' manner. But in early medieval England, any female bird was a *cwēn-fugol* (queen-bird). Although it eventually became modern English 'queen', Old English *cwēn* more often meant 'woman' or 'wife'. In contrast, Old English *cyning*, which became modern English 'king', is never used to refer to simply a 'man' or 'husband'. Once upon a time, every woman was a *cwēn*.

The unexpected scorpion

The word **þrowend** (scorpion) appears in an Old English version of a parable in which Jesus asks his disciples:

> What father will give his child a stone, if he asks for bread? Or a serpent, if he asks for fish? Or a <u>creepy-crawly</u> (*wyrm*), a <u>scorpion</u> (*þrowend*), if he asks for an egg?

The ubiquitous *wyrm*! This time *wyrm* refers to a predatory arachnid, which I have translated very scientifically as 'creepy-crawly'. (Snakes, dragons, predatory arachnids – they're all different kinds of creepy-crawlies, aren't they?) In this parable, Jesus tells his disciples that they should never expect bad things from God, their heavenly father, when they've prayed for good. Each good thing represents a more abstract benefit. Bread, the foremost of foods, signifies true love, the foremost of virtues. A fish symbolises faith, since a fish grows stronger fighting the current, the way faith grows stronger fighting persecution. The egg represents hope because it holds the promise of a baby bird in the future. What, then, about the stone, serpent and scorpion? In opposition to true love, the stone represents hard-heartedness (because it's hard). The serpent tricked Adam and Eve in the Garden of Eden, so it symbolises deceit. Finally, the scorpion signifies despair because it looks back at hope and attacks, killing it with its venomous stinger. Thus, what first appears to be a series of questions about irresponsible parenting is actually a parable on how to pray.

If *þrowend* is 'scorpion', is **þrowend-hād** 'scorpion-hood'? In an Old English translation of his *Dialogues*, Pope Gregory the Great says:

> Truly even when there is a lack of external persecution, *þrowendhad* is earned in secret when a man's might burns eager and quick in the mind for suffering.

Why would internal angst, secret suffering, make you more like a scorpion, and why would anyone aim to achieve this?

Old English *þrowend* didn't only mean 'scorpion'; it also meant 'martyr'. If you're **þrowend-lic**, you're 'like a martyr', or 'passive'. Pope Gregory is explaining how it is possible to become a martyr even if no one is actively persecuting you. *Þrowend-hād* (martyrdom) can be earned in secret, if you are eager for suffering in your mind.

But is scorpion-*þrowend* actually related to martyr-*þrowend*? The verb **þrowian** means 'to suffer', and a martyr-*þrowend* does suffer. A scorpion-*þrowend* can *cause* suffering with its venomous stinger. In the heavenly parenting parable, the scorpion represents despair, and despair is itself suffering.

At first glance the words appear to be related, but they in fact have different roots. Martyr-*þrowend* comes from Old English *þrowian* (to suffer), a verb with Germanic origins. The word 'throw' was used throughout the Middle Ages to mean 'suffer', and we still refer to 'throes' of pain or despair when describing extreme suffering.

The scorpion-*þrowend* is not Germanic in origin. Scorpions are not native to England, although some make their home there today. These arachnids may have hitched a ride to England on Italian merchant ships back in the eighteenth century, but there weren't any around in the Middle Ages. Unless an English person travelled south to the Mediterranean, the only place they would encounter a scorpion was in the Bible. So the fact that scorpion-*þrowend* derives not from a Northern European language but a biblical one (Greek) makes sense. The version of the Bible familiar to Christians in medieval England was Jerome's Latin Vulgate (or an Old English translation of it). The Latin Vulgate was translated from Greek in the fourth century. Scorpion-*þrowend* actually derives from Greek *troo*, which means 'injury' or 'harm'.

Þrowend has yet another meaning in the Old English poem *Widsith*. In this text a poet unlocks his *wordhord*, listing off the names of famous rulers with whom he has allegedly spent time, as well as the nations in which he has lived. He says:

> I've been with the Saxons and the Sycgs and the Sweordweras. I've been with the Hronas and the Danes and the Heathoremas. I've been with the Thuringians and the *þrowendum* and the Burgundians.

Has the poet been with scorpions? With martyrs? No. Old English *þrowend* may also refer to a person from northern Norway, one of the Thrönder or Thronds. The Thronds gave their name to *Þrónd-heimr*, a county in northern Norway, now called Trondheim. The Thronds were not martyrs, and medieval scorpions never made it to the Arctic North.

Adorned mice and grey-cloaks

In early medieval England animals wore clothes – sort of. In Old English animals were clothed linguistically, if not literally.

For instance, there's the **hrēaðe-mūs**, the 'adorned mouse'. Something that is **hroden** is 'decorated', 'adorned' or 'ornamented', like ale cups, war banners, the Virgin Mary, or even a **mūs** (mouse). If I asked you to envision an adorned mouse, would you picture the dressmaking rodents in Disney's *Cinderella*? Or perhaps the housewifely

Hunca Munca of Beatrix Potter? The 'ornaments' in which the *hrēaðe-mūs* is adorned are actually its wings. A *hrēaðe-mūs* is a bat.

Another word for 'bat' in Old English is **hrēre-mūs**. The archaic name 'rearmouse' can still be heard in some regions of England. The name comes from Old English **hrēran** (to shake, move, stir, agitate). So technically a rearmouse is an agitated or shaking mouse. The first time the bat was classified in English was in 1667, in a description written by the physician Christopher Merret, who compiled the first lists of British birds and butterflies. He was a bit off the mark when he put bats on his 'bird' list, but we can forgive him this error because of the marvellous word he recorded for posterity. Merret called the bat a 'rearmouse' or a 'flittermouse'. While 'flittermouse' tragically slipped out of English use, it does live on in German. The Austrian composer Johann Strauss II wrote the well-known operetta *Die Fledermaus* (*The Flittermouse*, i.e. *The Bat*). This operatic flittermouse premiered in 1874 and continues to be performed to this day.

Whether flittering, agitated or adorned, bats lose some of their whimsical charm in a story from Alexander the Great's travels in Central Asia. Alexander, King of Macedon and conqueror of the Persian Empire, made observations about the local wildlife while travelling to Bactria, a flat region straddling modern-day Afghanistan, Tajikistan and Uzbekistan. In a purported letter written in Greek, Alexander described his adventures to Aristotle, his old tutor. The Greek letter did not survive, but a medieval Latin translation of it did. The Latin version (written no later than the seventh century) was translated into Old English, the text of which appears in the same tenth-century manuscript as *Beowulf*. The Old English letter describes many awe-inspiring and threatening creatures that Alexander encountered while sleeping rough. As Alexander says, 'Such hardships and animal-related challenges befell us in the black night and darkness!' First, Alexander and his men were rushed by white lions, as big as bulls, roaring loudly. Next came boars of immense size, tigers and other wild animals. Then came the adorned mice:

> <u>Bats</u> (*hreaþe-mys*) as big as doves also came, striking our faces and plucking out our hair. The bats had human-like teeth, which they used to wound and tear apart my men.

Of all these creatures, bats with human teeth are by far the most disturbing.

A *hrēaðe-mūs* can come in handy when you are unwell. According to *Bald's Leechbook*, there is a remedy that uses bat blood for 'a dangerous disease that makes a man vomit faeces from his mouth'. Apparently you should smear the blood of a bat on your stomach. (Consuming dill soaked in oil or water with some hot bread may also do the trick.) Bat's blood has been used in medicine in various cultures throughout history, but the only other topical bat-blood treatments I've found are for combatting baldness or (paradoxically) for making your skin smooth and hairless.

The adorned mouse is not the only clothed critter in Old English. There is the **grǣg-hama**, which translates literally as 'grey-covering' or 'grey-cloak'. Scholars disagree on what creature precisely wears this grey cloak, and there are even divided opinions on whether *grǣg-hama* is an adjective or noun ('grey-cloaked' versus 'grey-cloaked one'). Either way, *grǣg-hama* is an evocative word that Tolkien borrowed for the name of a wizard in *The Lord of the Rings*: Gandalf Greyhame.

Because *grǣg-hama* is a hapax, there is only one context on which to base a definition. The word appears in the poem *The Battle of Finnsburh*, in the rousing speech of young King Hnæf. Before the battle Hnæf says to his men:

This is not the day dawning in the east. No <u>dragon</u> (*draca*) flies here, nor do the gables of this hall burn here. But here [our foes] carry forth weapons. <u>Birds sing</u> (*fugelas singað*), <u>the grey-cloaked one cries out</u> (*gylleð græghama*), the wood spear resounds, the shield echoes back to the shaft. Now the moon shines, wandering under the clouds. Now deeds of woe arise, which will advance the hatred of that people. Rouse yourselves now, my warriors! Take your shields, turn your minds to courage! Toil on the line of battle, and be bold!

Epic fights in Old English poetry are often accompanied by the 'beasts of battle' triad. These three animals are a literary trope for battle scenes, traditionally a **hræfn** (raven), **earn** (eagle) and **wulf** (wolf), who follow warriors to the fight. These creatures wait patiently beside the battlefield, prepared to feed upon the inevitable corpses.

The *earn* and *hræfn* are already represented in the passage by the word *fugelas* (birds), who *singað* (sing) before their supper. Technically, a word like *græg-hama* could refer to either a bird of some sort or a wolf. *Græg-hama* is paired with the verb **gyllan** (pronounced YUEL-lahn), from which we get modern English 'yell'. *Gyllan* can refer to a drunk man's shout, a wolf's howl or a bird's screech, so the verb itself doesn't do much to narrow down *græg-hama*'s possible definitions. *Gyllan* can even refer to the strident, grating or crashing noise of an inanimate object, such as the clang of spear against shield. Some scholars have suggested that *græg-hama* is actually a spear or even chain mail, which would take **hama** (covering) more literally. But it would be strange to omit the *wulf* from the famous battle scene triad, so it seems most likely that the wolf is represented by the poetic word *græg-hama*.

Some Old English animal names are beautifully evocative, riddling words like *græg-hama*, *hrēaðe-mūs*, *gongel-wæfre*: 'grey-cloak', 'adorned mouse', 'walker-weaver'. Others' names aren't far from the words we use today: *cat, befer, wulf, hors*. From the small garden *wyrm* to the larger fire-breathing variety, the creatures of God's *sceaft* surprise and delight.

Ninth *wordhord*

befer, noun (BEH-ver / 'bɛ-vɛr): Beaver.

bēo, noun (BAY-oh / 'be:ɔ): Bee.

bēo-gang, noun (BAY-oh-GAHNG / 'be:ɔ-ˌgaŋ): Swarm of bees.

bēo-mōder, noun (BAY-oh-MO-der / 'be:ɔ-ˌmo:-dɛr): Queen bee (bee-mother).

bera, noun (BEH-ra / 'bɛ-ra): Bear.

bridd, noun (BRID / 'brɪd): Young bird, chick.

cat, noun (KAHT / 'kat): Cat.

cwēn, noun (KWAIN / 'kwe:n): Woman; wife; queen, empress.

cwēn-fugol, noun (KWAIN-FUH-gol / 'kwe:n-ˌfʌ-gɔl): Female bird, hen.

cyning, noun (KUE-ning / 'ky-niŋ): King, emperor.

dēor, noun (DAY-or / 'de:ɔr): Animal.

docga, noun (DODGE-ah / 'dɔd͡ʒ-a): Dog.

draca, noun (DRAH-ka / 'dra-ka): Dragon.

earn, noun (EH-arn / 'ɛarn): Eagle.

fēnix, noun (FAY-niks / 'fe:-nɪks): Phoenix.

fugel, noun (FUH-yel / 'fʌ-jɛl): Bird.

gang, noun (GAHNG / 'gaŋ): Going, movement; power or manner of walking; coming or going from one place to another.

gāt-bucca, noun (GAHT-BUCK-ka / 'ga:t-ˌbʌk-ka): Domestic goat (male).

gærs-hoppa, noun (GARZ-HOP-pa / 'gærz-ˌhɔp-pa): Grasshopper.

gærs-stapa, noun (GARZ-STAH-pa / 'gærz-ˌsta-pa): Locust (grass-stepper).

ge-cynd, noun (yeh-KUEND / jɛ-'kynd): Nature, kind, condition.

gongel-wæfre, noun (GONG-gell-WAV-ruh / 'gɔŋ-gɛl-,wæv-rə): Spider (walker-weaver).

grǣg-hama, noun?/adjective? (GRAIE-HA-ma / 'græ:j-,ha-ma): 'Grey-covering' or 'grey-cloaked', possibly a wolf, bird, spear or chain mail.

gyllan, verb (YUEL-lahn / 'jyl-lan): (Of birds) to make a loud cry, to screech; (of wolves or dogs) to bay, howl; (of inanimate objects) to make a strident, grating or crashing noise; to yell, utter a loud cry.

hama, noun (HA-ma / 'ha-ma): Covering.

hors, noun (HORS / 'hɔrs): Horse.

hræfn, noun (H'RAV-un / 'hræ-vən): Raven.

hrēaðe-mūs, noun (HRAY-ah-thuh-MOOS / 'hre:a-θə-,mu:s): Bat (adorned mouse).

hrēran, verb (HRAY-rahn / 'hre:-ran): To move, stir, shake; to stir up, agitate.

hrēre-mūs, noun (HRAY-ruh-MOOS / 'hre:-rə-,mu:s): Bat.

hroden, adjective (HROD-en / 'hrɔ-dɛn): Decorated, ornamented, adorned.

hund, noun (HUND / 'hʌnd): Hound, dog.

lēaf-wyrm, noun (LAY-ahv-WUERM / 'le:av-,wyrm): 'Leaf-worm', blast or *Bruchus* (a kind of leaf beetle known for destroying crops).

lēo, noun (LAY-oh / 'le:ɔ): Lion.

līg, noun (LEE / 'li:j): Flame, lightning.

līg-draca, noun (LEE-DRAH-ka / 'li:j-,dra-ka): 'Flame-dragon', fire-breathing dragon.

lyft-floga, noun (LUEFT-FLO-ga / 'lyft-,flɔ-ga): 'Air-flier' (dragon).

mūs, noun (MOOS / 'mu:s): Mouse.

sceaft, noun (SHEH-oft / 'ʃɛaft): Creation, what is created, creature.

scēap, noun (SHAY-op / 'ʃe:ap): Sheep.

swīn, noun (SWEEN / 'swi:n): Pig, swine.

þrowend, noun (THRO-wend / 'θrɔ-wɛnd): Scorpion; martyr; Thrond
(member of a people in northern Norway).

þrowend-hād, noun (THRO-wend-HAWD / 'θrɔ-wɛnd-ˌhaːd):
Martyrdom.

þrowend-lic, adjective (THRO-wend-litch / 'θrɔ-wɛnd-lɪtʃ): Passive,
martyr-like.

þrowian, verb (THRO-wi-yahn / 'θrɔ-wɪ-an): To suffer; to suffer
martyrdom; to pay for, atone for.

wæfer-gange, noun (WAV-er-GAHNG-guh / 'wæ-vɛr-ˌgaŋ-gə): Spider
(weaver-walker).

wudu-bucca, noun (WUH-duh-BUH-ka / 'wʌ-dʌ-ˌbʌ-ka): Wild goat
(male).

wulf, noun (WULF / 'wʌlf): Wolf.

wyrm, noun (WUERM / 'wyrm): Worm, insect, snake, dragon, reptile.

10

Travel

Through the wide-ways

To SEE THE FULL EXTENT of *sceaft*, God's creation, one needs to travel.

In a tenth-century poem Christ bids his apostles, 'Travel now throughout all the great earth, through the <u>wide-ways</u> (*widwegas*).' This is not for their own education but rather to help the people in distant lands who need the 'bright faith' of Christ's teachings, as well as the opportunity to be baptised. **Wīd-wegas**, literally 'wide-ways', are distant regions, places 'far and wide', we might say today. Like the standard beginning of a fairy tale – 'Once upon a time in a faraway land' – *wīd-wegas*, which appears only in poetry, evokes an impressively distant, non-specific locale. Instead of going *everywhere*, Christ's apostles are asked to visit the 'wide-ways'.

Where might one have travelled in early medieval England? As early as the seventh century, Christians were travelling from Britain to spread their faith to and trade with Frisia and Saxony (modern-day Netherlands and north-west Germany). One of the earliest and most influential of these was the **weg-fērend** (traveller, 'way-farer') Willibrord of Northumbria. Shortly after his death in 739, Willibrord was deemed a saint. Supposedly, holy wells sprang up wherever he went, and his miraculous generation of wine must have made this traveller especially popular. One time, when visiting the (now German) archipelago of Heligoland, he shocked and offended the local pagans by baptising three people in their holy well. To push the point further, Willibrord had a few of the pagans' cattle slaughtered to eat, cattle reserved for their god Fosite. Much to the astonishment of the locals, Fosite didn't strike Willibrord down for his offences, and, luckily for Willibrord, the pagan king was so impressed by the man's sheer audacity that he released him with full honours. (Still, the king refused to convert.)

Even if you weren't going around slaughtering cattle without permission, as a **nīw-fara** (stranger, 'new-farer' or 'new-traveller') you couldn't count on a warm-hearted welcome. The seventh-century law code of King Wihtred of Kent says:

> If a stranger or a man who has come from afar strays off the track and neither calls out nor blows a horn, he should be taken for a thief, either to be killed or to be redeemed.

The Old English scholar Lisi Oliver observes: 'Any foreigner straying from the public way without giving notification of his presence thus may be assumed to be up to no good!' King Wihtred is certainly not alone in history as a leader who shoots first and asks questions later.

If one was not travelling to trade or evangelise, a *weg-fērend* might have been travelling to work. An artist, for example, who wasn't tied to a monastery might move between England and Francia, wherever fine manuscripts were in need of illumination. Nor was it uncommon for English people to be seen journeying to Rome on pilgrimage. During the ninth century, they were travelling all throughout the Baltic, with evidence for contacts as distant as Greece. Even English travellers to *wīd-wegas* like the Baltic would have been supplied with precise and detailed information: which routes were safest or quickest, what goods you could buy in different places, which ports were the most convenient, and so on.

As for travel within England, the system of roads hadn't been improved upon, or even properly maintained, since the Romans left in the fifth century. There wasn't a lot of heavy traffic, so roads weren't relied upon as much and fell into disrepair. Settlements that were too far away from a Roman road made do with lesser paths that would eventually connect to the main roads. The wealthy would travel on horseback, while the poor would have simply walked. Moving heavy loads would have required a wooden **wægn** (wagon) or **cræt** (cart), perhaps with open sides, which could be pulled by a pair of oxen.

Old English **hwēol** (wheel) reveals why the modern English word is spelled as it is, with a silent h. Modern English words that begin with wh- (whale, which, whine, etc.) were spelled with hw- in Old English. During the early Middle English period, the spellings hw-, wh- and w- were all used, without any single spelling taking precedence. By the end of the thirteenth century, most of the words we now spell with wh- were spelled with w-, and the use of hw- had begun to decline. Eventually the h and w of Old English *hwēol* swapped positions, producing the Middle English spelling 'whēl'. This phonological change is called the 'wine-whine merger' because it's when the pronunciations of 'wine' and 'whine' become identical. People in most of England, Wales, the West Indies, South Africa and Australia pronounce w- and wh- the same. In other places, like in Scotland and most of Ireland, the wine-whine merger is absent: words spelled wh- are still pronounced hw-. In New Zealand, the older population still distinguishes between w- and wh-, but younger people do not. And while most English speakers in North America have the merger, some regions of the United States retain the hw- pronunciation. Americans living in the Southeast are most likely to differentiate their wines from their whines.

A two-wheeled open *cræt*

The word **stræt** (street) has hardly changed over the past 1,000 years. What, then, is a **ranc-stræt** . . . a street that smells rank? 'Rank' is a curious word, with numerous Germanic cognates (in Dutch, German, Swedish, Icelandic, etc.) that mean everything from 'thin' or 'slender', to 'straight' or 'upright', to 'proud' or 'bold'. But the English 'rank' went on a different etymological journey from all these cognates.

The Old English adjective **ranc** meant 'proud', 'arrogant', 'showy in dress', 'bold', or 'valiant'. The Middle English noun 'rank' could mean 'pride' but also 'a festering sore or wound'. (Both pride and a festering sore will poison one from the inside, after all.) In the 1300s 'rank' referred to vegetation that grew too rampantly, its fruits becoming distended or overripe. From festering wounds or overripe fruit, we move to another iteration in the 1400s, when the Middle English adjective 'rank' meant 'having a strong or unpleasant smell' (from which we get modern English 'rancid'). The word 'rank' has not been used to mean 'pride' or 'arrogance' since the 1600s, although in some regions of England it still means 'brave' or 'strong'.

Ranc-strǣt is a hapax and thus tricky to define. One dictionary goes with 'splendid street', while another has the very specific definition of 'road in which bravery is displayed'. The latter definition is followed by a bracketed question mark (?), so it's certainly not a definition in which confidence is displayed.

The one occurrence of *ranc-strǣt* is in the poem *Genesis A*. In the Book of Genesis, King Melchizedek of Sodom and his allies are at war, and Lot, one of the king's men, is captured. (This is the same Lot whose daughters seduced him and whose wife turned into salt.) Lot's uncle Abraham comes to his rescue and wins victory in battle. After an exciting sequence with his enemies perishing in slime pits, King Melchizedek is obviously very pleased with Abraham. Abraham receives God's blessing for saving the day.

The story told in the Old English poem is far more concerned with depicting acts of epic heroism as well as the king's praise for his victorious warrior. You can really see the influence of Germanic heroic poetry, in which the king praises his men's glorious performance in battle. Melchizedek says:

> Be honoured to be of the count of men in sight of the one who granted you spear-glory in battle! That is God himself, who broke the armies of enemy warriors in his power, allowing you to clear a <u>bold-road</u> (*rancstræte*) forward with weapons, recovering plunder and slaying men. The dead were left behind.

> The army on expedition could not succeed in battle but were put to flight by God – who with his hands, alongside princes, shielded you from the terror of a force superior in battle – and by the holy covenant, which you kept correctly with the Guardian of the heavens.

Sometimes we can determine the meaning of an Old English word because it is a direct translation from a Bible verse, but in Genesis 14 all King Melchizedek says is:

> Blessed be Abraham by the most high God, who created heaven and earth. And blessed be the most high God, by whose protection the enemies are in thy hands.

No battle spears. No plundering or slaying. No *ranc-strǣt* (which I've translated as 'bold-road'). The Old English poet adds their own details to the fight. God doesn't just protect Abraham from his enemies; he breaks through armies of warriors, giving Abraham 'spear-glory in battle'. Those who 'sat in the track' are the corpses of warriors slain on the warpath. *Ranc-strǣt* isn't a translation of anything in the Book of Genesis, but it adds to the scene of heroism and bravery, with Abraham and his warriors clearing a 'bold-road' before them.

So a *ranc-strǣt* is a road for the bold. But if there is as much slaying going on as the *Genesis A* poet indicates, then it can't smell all that great either. I'd rather make my journey on a ***gamen-wāþ*** (joyful path). *Gamen-wāþ*, another hapax, appears in *Beowulf*. Like *ranc-strǣt*, it's a road for victorious warriors, but at least this one is clear of corpses. Beowulf and his warriors ride back to King Hrothgar's mead-hall after Beowulf successfully kills Grendel's mother in her own underwater abode. They 'went back on a <u>joyful path</u> (*gomenwaþe*), high-spirited, riding horses from the mere, warriors on shining steeds'. The word *gamen* (Chapter 5) means 'amusement' or 'joy', while **wāþ** means 'roving' or 'wandering'. Yes, the men are on their way back to Heorot, but they are enjoying the ride, a journey on high-spirited horses. When travelling itself is joyful, your concern is not the destination but the *gamen-wāþ*.

House of wisdom, house of woe

Old English **hūs**, from which we get modern English 'house', is a home, building or temporary shelter. Modern English 'husband' comes from Old English **hūs-bōnda**, which means 'householder' or 'master of a house'. From the thirteenth century 'husband' took on the meaning of a male partner in a marriage, and by the end of the Middle Ages the 'householder' meaning was obsolete, although 'husbandry' is still used today to describe the work of a farmer.

Some of the houses in Old English will look familiar. You can probably guess the meaning of the following houses: **æppel-hūs**, **bæþ-hūs**, **bell-hūs**, **bōc-hūs**, **fisc-hūs**, **drenc-hūs**. (If you are stumped, check the answers below.)*

These words may look familiar, but it's important not to get carried away with guessing. Old English is full of false friends. A **bēd-hūs** may look like a dormitory or mattress store, but it's actually a place of worship. Old English **bēd** means prayer, so a **bēd-hūs** is an oratory, a house for prayer. Modern English 'beadhouse' (or 'bedehouse') is an old-fashioned word for an almshouse, a private charity for the poor and elderly. The inmates of a **bēd-hūs** would pray for the soul of the charity's founder or patron, helping them get to heaven.

Hlāf-hūs, literally 'loaf-house' or 'bread-house', sounds like the name of a bakery, and it is indeed a place name. It is the Old English name for the town of Bethlehem. An explanation of the name appears in Ælfric of Eynsham's homily for Christmas:

Bethlehem (*Betleem*) should be interpreted as bread-house (*hlafhus*). It was there that Christ, the true bread (*hlaf*), was born, he who said of

---

* Apple-house (storehouse for fruit); bathhouse; bell-house (belfry); book-house (library); fish-house (building for storing and possibly selling fish); drink-house (tavern).

himself: 'I am the living bread, descended from heaven, and he who eats this bread will never die.'

This reasoning from the tenth-century English abbot is lovely, metaphorical and appropriately Christian, but the name of the town existed long before Christ's birth. Over 1,000 years earlier, the polytheistic Canaanites settled in the region and dedicated their town to Lachama, a fertility god of the Chaldeans (who called him Lachmo). The town's name, *Beit Lachama*, meant 'house of Lachama'. When the Hebrews – faithful monotheists – arrived a millennium or so later, they decided a town named for a Chaldean fertility god would never do. They altered the name ever so slightly to *Beth-Lechem*, which was Hebrew for 'house of bread'. There was plenty of grain in this fertile region, so even before Christ, 'the living bread', came along, the name made sense. Really, it isn't surprising that Hebrew and Chaldean, both Semitic languages, share a common root for 'bread' and 'fertility'.

A far less appealing *hūs* is a **morþor-hūs**, a 'murder-house' or 'torment-house'. The word *morþor*, from which we get modern English 'murder', inspired Tolkien when he came up with the name Mordor for the black, volcanic plain of doom in *The Lord of the Rings*. In modern English we just say 'hell', but Old English has far more evocative terms. Here an Old English poem describes a scene on Judgement Day, when the Holy Spirit imprisons the wicked souls in hell:

> Wretched is he who does wicked deeds, for he, marked, will be severed from his Creator on Judgement Day. Down to death he must go, among hell's creatures, into hot fire in a locker of flame. There they will stretch out his limbs – binding, burning, flogging – as punishment for his sins. Then the Holy Spirit will lock up hell, full of fire and the Devil's army, the <u>greatest of murder-houses</u> (*morþerhusa mæst*), by the might of God and the word of the King.

Not only is hell a *morþor-hūs*, it is *morþerhusa mæst*, the greatest of murder-houses, which should give you pause. (After all, the poet clearly has other murder-houses in mind.)

A similar name for hell is **morþor-hof** (murder-house), but Old English also has **sūsl-hof** (torment-house), **heolstor-hof** (darkness-house), and **grorn-hof** (woe-house). **Hof** is another word for 'house', 'hall' or 'dwelling'. In modern German, the word *Hof* can mean 'court', 'courtyard', 'yard', 'farm' or 'farmyard'. If you've ever been to Munich's Oktoberfest, chances are high that you visited Hofbräu-Festzelt, one of the largest beer tents. The Munich brewery Hofbräu, also known as Staatliches Hofbräuhaus, was founded in 1589 by the Duke of Bavaria. It was the royal brewery of the court (*Hof*) of the Bavarian kingdom.

If you've ever been out for a drink in Seoul, you'll find that the word *hof* is ubiquitous. Signs on windows advertise 'Hof and Beer'. In Korea 'hof' is draft beer, so a bar advertising 'Hof and Beer' sells draft in addition to bottled. Beer was only introduced to Korea in the early nineteenth century, and up until 2011 strict laws greatly limited the success of microbreweries. Over the past decade the market for craft beer in Korea has exploded, and German-style brewpubs have opened their doors for business in Seoul. Even the bars that didn't go the route of schnitzel and goulash use the word 'hof' in their trade names or advertising, possibly to add an exotic German flavour. So the Korean 'hof' actually goes back to German and, by extension, to medieval Germanic languages like Old High German and Old English. 'Hof' became obsolete as a house in English centuries ago, but it took on a boozy new life in the bars of Gangnam and Hongdae.

These merry drinking houses are – hopefully – quite far from the hell compounds where we first encountered the *hof* (*grorn-hof*, etc.). *Hof* appears in some other rather unpleasant dwelling places. Take a *sand-hof*, for instance. This hapax, literally 'sand-house' or 'sand-dwelling', may sound like a beach hut, but that is not the case. In early medieval England, sand was associated not with beaches but with graves. On his deathbed, St Guthlac asks his disciple to pass on a message to his sister. The holy man says:

> Tell her to entrust this <u>bone-vessel</u> (*banfæt*: a kenning for 'body') to the
> hill, enclose it in clay, a soulless body in a dark chamber, where it must
> dwell awhile in a <u>sand-house</u> (*sondhofe*).

Less poetically, Guthlac is saying, 'When I'm dead, please bury me in this hill.' His body will dwell in a house made of clay, soil, gravel and grit.

A *mearc-hof* (mark-dwelling) is not particularly nice either. 'Mark' is a word for the countryside, the borderlands, the edges of civilisation. The hapax *mearc-hof* appears in the Old English poem *Exodus*. In the Latin Vulgate Bible, the Book of Exodus tells how Moses leads the Israelites out of Egypt by way of the desert; they make camp in Etham, in 'the utmost coasts of the wilderness' (*in extremis finibus solitudinis*). An Old English direct translation of this from the eleventh or twelfth century is *on þam ytemestan ende þæs westenes* (at the utmost end of the wilderness).

But the *Exodus* poem, copied down in the latter part of the tenth century, evokes a more haunting setting. The poet says that Moses and his people passed through a great number of strongholds, travelling 'narrow lonely paths, an unknown way' (*enge anpaðas, uncuð gelad*) to 'mark-dwellings of the mountain fastness' (*mearchofu morheald*). The Israelites must battle the hostile dwellers of the borderlands (the Egyptians, perhaps), in a cloud-enveloped wasteland. This passage resembles Beowulf's approach to Grendel's mere. The same eerie language is used: *enge anpaðas, uncuð gelad*. The word *ān-pæþ* (single-file path) appears only twice in extant Old English literature, in these two instances. Was this particular phrasing common, or is its repetition in these two poems merely a coincidence?

The 'mark-dwellings' of the *Exodus* poem sound as though they are temporary structures, an encampment on the way through the desert. A more general word for a temporary structure is ***ge-teld*** (tent). Old English *ge-teld* is used as a translation for Latin *tabernaculum* (tabernacle) in bilingual psalters, where you may also find alternative forms like *ge-teldung* and *teldung*, as well as ***eardung*** (habitation, dwelling). A tabernacle is a tent or portable dwelling place. Following the divine instructions of God, Moses builds a tabernacle in the wilderness, so God could live among men. When the Israelites settled in the land of Canaan, the tabernacle became a more permanent fixture at the ancient Samarian city of Shiloh (modern-day West Bank). Supposedly God abandoned the tabernacle when its most precious treasure, the Ark of the Covenant, was taken. Along with *ge-teld* and *eardung*, the tabernacle at Shiloh has another name, one that appears only once in Old English: ***snytro-hūs***, or 'wisdom-house'.

Snytro-hūs appears in a poetic translation of the Psalms, in a manuscript that's known (somewhat confusingly) as the Paris Psalter. The Paris Psalter was made in eleventh-century England and is written in Latin and Old English; there is nothing Parisian about it. But manuscripts are often named for their present home, not their provenance, and the Paris Psalter currently resides at the Bibliothèque Nationale de France. The psalter may have been made for a pious layperson, possibly a woman, whose primary language was Old English, not Latin. The first fifty psalms are written in prose, with the Latin on the left, the Old English on the right, and the remainder are written as Old English poetry. Psalm 77 tells how God 'rejected the wisdom-house' (*wiðsoc snytruhuse*): 'It was his own house, where he had taken a home among men and had power.' Why did the poet use the compound *snytro-hūs?* Were they inspired by the etymology of the biblical city name 'Shiloh', which derives from the Hebrew for 'peace-place' or 'tranquillity-town'? A 'wisdom-house' is certainly more poetic than a mere tent.

Hof, hūs, ge-teld and *eardung* are all words for dwellings, built structures. A more general word is **stōw** (place), and it appears in numerous place names across Britain. It can stand alone (Stowe or Stow) or in combination with other words (Walthamstow, Stow-on-the-Wold, Padstow). The Welsh town of Chepstow takes its name from Old English **cēap-stōw** (market-place). Old English **cēap**, from which we get modern English 'cheap', means 'purchase', 'sale', 'price' or 'payment'.

I've yet to come across a Costnungstow, although I can think of places that fit that description. The verb **costnian** means 'to tempt', so **costnung-stōw** is a 'temptation-place'. This hapax appears in an Old English translation of Deuteronomy:

You shall not tempt your God, as you did in the <u>place of temptation</u> (*costnungstowe*).

Costnung-stōw is a translation of the Latin *loco tentationis* (place of temptation). More modern translations of the Bible call this place 'Massah', which means 'test' or 'proving' in Hebrew. The *costnung-stōw* is where the Israelites tested God to see if he would provide for them in the desert. (The test was passed in flying colours when Moses struck a rock and drinking water sprang out.)

I'd like to think that although *costnung-stōw* is a hapax for a specific place in biblical history, we could repurpose the word for our own places of temptation, wherever those may be.

Beware the false island

How many modern English words can you think of for the vast expanses of saltwater that cover 71 per cent of the earth's surface? There's 'ocean', 'sea' and 'open water' – 'the deep', perhaps. When translating Old English into modern English, one of the greatest difficulties you face is coming up with a sufficient variety of 'sea' words.

In Old English there's **sǣ**, of course, from which we get 'sea', but there are also the words **holm**, **brim**, **secg**, **mere**, **wæter-scipe** (like 'friendship' but with water), and *lagu* (the L-rune ᚱ, see Chapter 5). **Faroþ** refers specifically to the shallow water along the coast, the edge of the sea. 'Holm' is now an old-fashioned word for a small island in a lake or estuary or near the mainland; in Swedish and Danish it's a dockyard or shipyard (like Stockholm). *Brim* became obsolete in Middle English. A modern English 'water ship' used to be a ferry or tugboat, and now it's a boat that carries fresh water. While Old English *mere* referred to any body of water, most often the sea, modern English 'mere' is merely a pool or marshy area. (We still have 'mermaid', though, a compound formed in the fourteenth century from the Middle English words for 'sea' and 'woman': 'meremayde'.)

Compound words for the sea include **ȳþ-lād** (wave-path), **brim-lād** (sea-path), **mere-strǣt** (sea-street) and **lagu-fæðm** (sea-embrace). And we haven't even begun to consider all the 'sea' kennings: **hwæl-weg** (whale-way), **hwæles ēðel** (whale's home), and **segl-rād** (sail-road). There's the mysterious but fairly common compound **gār-secg**, which means 'ocean', although no one has been able to suitably explain its etymology. *Gār* means spear (see *gār-lēac*, Chapter 8), while *secg* can mean a number of different things, including 'sedge' (a kind of plant), 'man', 'warrior', 'sea' and 'sword'. 'Spear-sedge' and 'spear-sword' make little sense. If it's meant to be 'spear-warrior' or 'spear-man', *gār-secg* could perhaps be identified with Triton (a.k.a. Poseidon or

Neptune), the vengeful god of the sea. Maybe 'spear-sea' refers to the violence of the tossing waves.

Clearly there was a far richer vocabulary for the ocean in Old English, but then travel by boat was much more significant in early medieval England than it is now. The English then (as now) lived on an island, but, unlike today, boats were the fastest way to get around. The historian John Blair says that the eleventh century was England's first 'canal age', and ships were key for maintaining connections, both with local villages and towns as well as with the rest of the North Sea world. The sea coast was more of a highway than a barrier, and rivers allowed for travel far inland. Although trade and politics necessitated ocean voyages on larger ships, most people (even those living on the coasts) would have been most familiar with the smaller vessels used for inland travel.

A vessel either large or small, for travel at sea or by river, could be called a ***bāt*** (boat). Most boats were made from timber, usually wood from the strong, curvy oak tree, although ash wood made for a lighter and faster vessel. An ***æsc*** – in addition to an ash tree and the Æ-rune ᚫ (Chapter 1) – was a light, swift ship made of ash-wood, a Scandinavian design. In addition to *bāt* and *æsc*, the English travelled the ocean expanses by ***scip*** (ship) and ***sǣ-bāt*** (sea-boat). ***Cēol*** (ship, pronounced CHAY-oll), ***naca*** (boat) and ***ȳþ-lida*** (wave-traverser) are more poetic words. A ***snacc*** is not something light to eat but a type of swift-sailing boat, a small warship. A ***wunden-stefna*** is a ship with a curved prow, such as the Vikings had. And then there are the 'ship' kennings, of course: ***flōd-wudu*** (flood-wood) and ***faroþ-hengest*** (sea-horse), the latter being quite different from what we call a seahorse today. Either ship or seafarer could be a ***sǣ-genga*** (sea-goer). Another word for 'sea-farer' is the hapax ***brim-gyst*** (sea-guest), which emphasises the fact that sailors can only ever be guests of the sea; they don't belong there.

A guest of the sea must remember that their host can turn

inhospitable at any moment. There are plenty of dangers for a *brim-gyst* to face, the deadliest of which is **Fastitocalon**. This creature appears in an Old English poem and is described as 'a kind of fish, a great whale'; but *Fastitocalon* is far more menacing than a whale. The poem says:

> Seafarers often meet him by accident. Everyone gives him the name *Fastitocalon*, he who floats in the ancient streams. His appearance is like a rough stone, the greatest sea-bank that crumbles near the water's edge. He is clothed in sand dunes so sailors think they are seeing an island. Men moor their tall ships with anchoring ropes to the false land, settling their sea-steeds at the water's end. Boldly, they go upon that isle. Encircled by the current, the ships stay secure near the shore. The weary seafarers – with no thought of danger – make camp on the island. They light a flame and kindle a great fire. They are tired but happy, ready for bed. When the wily, deceitful one senses that the travellers are secure upon him, keeping camp and hoping for fair weather, he plunges down all of a sudden beneath the salty waves. The demon of the ocean seeks the sea-floor, delivering his plunder to death's hall, ships with drowned men.

Fastitocalon has another name in medieval bestiaries: *Aspidochelone*. This name comes from Greek *aspis* (asp, viper) + *chelone* (turtle), so he's also known as the Asp-Turtle, but this creature resembles neither an asp nor a turtle. Medieval manuscripts generally portray him as a giant fish with a ship perched on his back, although in one illustration he has legs and feet. No matter what form his body takes, *Fastitocalon* always appears as a false island to sailors, and anyone who makes camp on his back will soon be at the bottom of the sea.

When did this legend come to be? In the first century CE, the Roman author and philosopher Pliny the Elder writes about fish and whales of monstrous proportions, but these do not kill seafarers by

A whale tricks some hapless sailors in an English bestiary from the late twelfth or early thirteenth century

pretending to be islands. In the seventh century, the scholar Isidore of
Seville writes that whales can be as big as mountains; after all, in the
Bible Jonah is swallowed by a whale with a belly so immense it resem-
bles hell. The Old English poem that features *Fastitocalon*, known as
The Whale, is recorded in the tenth-century Exeter Book and is prob-
ably derived from the Latin *Physiologus* (introduced in Chapter 6).
Allegorically, the creature represents Satan, who deceives you with the
promise of security before dragging you down to hell.

It seems that 'false-island' creatures have long plagued sailors around the world, through all the wīd-wegas: Jasconius (Irish),
Lyngbakr and Hafgufa (Icelandic), Zaratan (Middle Eastern), Cuero
(Chilean), Imap Umassoursa (Inuit) and many others. Cuero, a flat
aquatic creature resembling a cowhide, stretches out upon the surface
of the water, engulfing and sucking the blood of anything that comes
too close. Imap Umassoursa actually does the opposite of *Fastitocalon*:
rather than dragging a ship to the ocean floor, it lurks just out of sight
below the water's surface and, when it senses a boat above it, rises to
capsize the vessel.

The mythology of these creatures lives on in modern fiction, film
and games. Tolkien wrote a poem about *Fastitocalon*, based on the
Old English poem, that appears in his collection *The Adventures of
Tom Bombadil* (1962). In the 1984 film *The NeverEnding Story*, Morla, a
giant, swamp-dwelling turtle, is mistaken for a mountain. The col-
lectable card game *Magic: The Gathering* features a card in its 1995
Fourth Edition set called 'Island Fish Jasconius', with an illustration
of a craggy-looking, partially submerged fish with trees growing on
its back. The video game *Final Fantasy VIII* (1999) includes an enemy
called 'Fastitocalon', a fish that swims in the earth; a twist on the idea
of a fish disguising itself as land, this creature appears as a fin sticking
out of the ground.

Another mysterious creature of the Old English deep is the **nicor**, defined by *Bosworth-Toller* as either a 'hippopotamus' or 'water-monster'. Possible cognates include Icelandic *nykr* (sea-goblin, hippopotamus) and Old High German *nichus* (crocodile). The *nicor* appears in Alexander the Great's letter to Aristotle, when Alexander's men attempt to cross a river in India. When they try to swim, they are attacked by a great number of *nicoras*, 'greater and more savage in appearance than elephants'. The creatures pull the men beneath the waves, tear them apart with their mouths, and leave behind only blood and gore. A homily that describes St Paul's vision of hell says that beneath the dark mists and under stone is the dwelling place of *nicoras*. The souls of the damned hang above this place, a dark lake beneath a cliff, and devils with the appearance of *nicoras* seize them when the branches break. *Beowulf* has to fight off nine *nicoras* during his famed swimming contest, and Grendel and his mother dwell in the *mere* of *nicoras*, a place greatly resembling St Paul's hell.

Modern English 'nicker' is now archaic, but these creatures have certainly not disappeared from Northern European lore. Iceland has the *nykur*, or water-horse, and Germany the *Nickel*, an underground-dwelling mine goblin. The Cornish 'knocker' also lives in mines but is a friendlier sort than the *Nickel*. There is a 'knucker hole' near Lyminster in Sussex, allegedly the home of a water-dragon. While some say that bottomless knucker holes are entrances to hell, they are probably etymologically unrelated to 'Old Nick', a name for the Devil dating back to the seventeenth century. (It has been suggested that this 'Nick' is a shortened form of Iniquity, a term used for Vice in Early Modern English morality plays.)

The Nuckelavee, a sea-monster of Scotland, may also be related to the *nicor*. The Nuckelavee can travel on land by horse, and some people mistook him on his horse for a single creature. W. Traill Dennison, a nineteenth-century Scottish farmer and folklorist, collected local tales from around his native Orkney. In his 1891 article for *The Scottish Antiquary*,

Dennison included a witness description from an old man called Tammas. Tammas, or Tammie, encountered the Nuckelavee one moonless night:

> The lower part of this terrible monster, as seen by Tammie, was like a great horse with flappers like fins about his legs, with a mouth as wide as a whale's, from whence came breath like steam from a brewing-kettle. He had but one eye, and that as red as fire . . . But what to Tammie appeared most horrible of all, was that the monster was skinless.

The surface of the creature's body is 'only red raw flesh', in which you can see 'blood, black as tar, running through yellow veins, and great white sinews, thick as horse tethers, twisting, stretching, and contracting as the monster moved'. Although Nuckelavee lives in the sea, he avoids fresh water at all costs and keeps away when it rains – which may explain why he is rarely seen. (This is Scotland, after all.)

Another incarnation of the *nicor* lives in London. *Portals of London*, a blog that describes itself as 'a catalogue of London's inter-dimensional gateways', explores the mythology behind a 'folkloric entity' known as the Deptford Creek Necker. Deptford Creek, about half a mile in length, flows north into the Thames just opposite the Isle of Dogs. In 2019 *Portals of London* interviewed a mudlarker who got a funny, unpleasant feeling whenever he approached a certain part of the creek. Local wildlife seems to avoid this particular area, which makes it even more mysterious that there are occasionally large piles of animal bones washed up on the bank.

But if the watery depths are home to frightening creatures like *Fastitocalon* and the *nicor*, they are also a treasure trove where valuable sea-grit can be found. Old English **mere-grota**, literally 'sea-grit' or 'sea-particle', is a pearl, a gem of the ocean. The word 'pearl' is very similar in different languages across Europe: *perla* (Czech, Icelandic, Italian, Polish, Spanish), *perle* (Danish, German, French,

Norwegian), *perlog* (Welsh), *pärla* (Swedish) and *parel* (Dutch). Often words in Old English are quite similar to words in modern German, Icelandic and Dutch, but Old English *mere-grota* comes from the Latin *margarita* (pearl), which has cognates in Greek (*margaritári*) and Albanian (*margaritar*). In general, *mere-grota*'s cognates are less common than those of modern English 'pearl'.

Mere-grota appears in the Old English *Wonders of the East*, a text featuring griffins, two-headed snakes, gold-gathering ants and many other marvellous creatures. On an unnamed island, a temple in a golden vineyard faces the direction of the rising sun. The grapes of this vineyard are 150 feet tall, and as if that weren't impressive enough, the grapes produce pearls (*meregrota*). But are these pearls the seeds of the grape? Are they giant pearls, or is there one regular-sized pearl hidden in the middle of each oversized grape? Only those who dare travel the *hwæl-weg*, braving creatures like *Fastitocalon* and the *nicor*, can know such things for sure.

Tenth *wordhord*

ān-pæþ, noun (AHN-PATH / 'aːn-ˌpæθ): Single-file path, narrow path.
æppel-hūs, noun (AP-pell-HOOS / 'æp-pɛl-ˌhuːs): Storehouse for fruit.
æsc, noun (ASH / 'æʃ): Light swift ship.
bāt, noun (BAWT / 'baːt): Boat.
bæþ-hūs, noun (BATH-HOOS / 'bæθ-ˌhuːs): Bathhouse.
bēd, noun (BAID / 'beːd): Prayer.
bēd-hūs, noun (BAID-HOOS / 'beːd-ˌhuːs): Prayer house, oratory.
bell-hūs, noun (BELL-HOOS / 'bɛl-ˌhuːs): Bell tower, belfry.
bōc-hūs, noun (BOAK-HOOS / 'boːk-ˌhuːs): Library (book-house).
brim, noun (BRIM / 'brɪm): Sea, ocean.
brim-gyst, noun (BRIM-YUEST / 'brɪm-ˌjyst): Sailor (sea-guest).

brim-lād, noun (BRIM-LAWD / ˈbrɪm-ˌlaːd): Ocean (sea-path).

cēap, noun (CHAY-op / ˈtʃeːap): Purchase, sale, business transaction; possessions; price, payment.

cēap-stōw, noun (CHAY-op-STOH / ˈtʃeːap-ˌstoːw): Market-place.

cēol, noun (CHAY-oll / ˈtʃeːɔl): Ship, sea-going vessel.

costnian, verb (KOST-ni-yahn / ˈkɔst-nɪ-an): To tempt.

costnung-stōw, noun (KOST-nung-STOH / ˈkɔst-nʌŋ-ˌstoːw): Place of temptation.

cræt, noun (KRAT / ˈkræt): Cart.

drenc-hūs, noun (DRENCH-HOOS / ˈdrɛntʃ-ˌhuːs): Drinking house.

eardung, noun (EH-ar-dung / ˈɛar-dʌŋ): Dwelling, habitation.

faroþ, noun (FAH-roth / ˈfa-rɔθ): Sea edge, shallow water along the coast.

faroþ-hengest, noun (FAH-roth-HENG-gest / ˈfa-rɔθ-ˌhɛŋ-gɛst): Ship (sea-horse).

fastitocalon, noun (FAH-stit-oh-KAH-lon / ˈfa-stɪ-tɔ-ˌka-lɔn): Large whale that pretends to be an island.

fisc-hūs, noun (FISH-HOOS / ˈfɪʃ-ˌhuːs): 'Fish-house', place or building for storing and perhaps selling fish.

flōd-wudu, noun (FLOAD-WUH-duh / ˈfloːd-ˌwʌ-dʌ): Ship (water-wood).

gamen-wāþ, noun (GAH-men-WAHTH / ˈga-mɛn-ˌwaːθ): Joyful path, joyous journey.

gār-secg, noun (GAR-SEDGE / ˈgar-ˌsɛdʒ): Ocean.

ge-teld, noun (yeh-TELD / jɛ-ˈtɛld): Tent, tabernacle, pavilion.

grorn-hof, noun (GRORN-HOFF / ˈgrɔrn-ˌhɔf): House of sadness.

heolstor-hof, noun (HEH-ol-stor-HOFF / ˈhɛɔl-stɔr-ˌhɔf): Dark dwelling, hell.

hlāf-hūs, noun (HLAHV-HOOS / ˈhlaːv-ˌhuːs): Bethlehem (bread-house).

hof, noun (HOFF / ˈhɔf): House, hall, dwelling, building.

holm, noun (HOLM / ˈhɔlm): Ocean, sea, water.

hūs, noun (HOOS / ˈhuːs): Building, house; temporary shelter; room.

hūs-bōnda, noun (HOOZ-BOAN-dah / ˈhuːz-ˌboːn-da): Master of a house.

hwæles ēðel, compound (H'WAL-uz-AY-thell / ˈhwæ-ləz-ˌeː-ˌθɛl): 'Whale's home', the ocean.

hwæl-weg, noun (H'WAL-WAY / ˈhwæl-ˌwɛj): 'Whale-path', the ocean.

hwēol, noun (H'WAY-oll / ˈhweːɔl): Wheel.

lagu-fæðm, noun (LA-guh-FATH-um / ˈla-gʌ-ˌfæ-θəm): Sea's embrace, water's embrace.

mearc-hof, noun (MEH-ark-HOFF / ˈmɛark-ˌhɔf): 'Mark-dwelling', dwelling in the borderlands.

mere, noun (MEH-ruh / ˈmɛ-rə): Sea; mere, lake; artificial pool.

mere-grota, noun (MEH-ruh-GROT-ah / ˈmɛ-rə-ˌgrɔ-ta): Pearl.

mere-stræt, noun (MEH-ruh-STRAT / ˈmɛ-rə-ˌstræːt): Sea (sea-street).

morþor-hof, noun (MOR-thor-HOFF / ˈmɔr-θɔr-ˌhɔf): 'Murder-hall', place of torment, hell.

morþor-hūs, noun (MOR-thor-HOOS / ˈmɔr-θɔr-ˌhuːs): 'Murder-house', house of torment, hell.

naca, noun (NAH-ka / ˈna-ka): Boat, ship.

nicor, noun (NICK-or / ˈnɪ-kɔr): Water-monster.

nīw-fara, noun (NEE-ew-VAH-ra / ˈniːw-ˌva-ra): Newcomer, stranger.

ranc, adjective (RAHNK / ˈrank): Proud, haughty, arrogant; showy (in dress); bold, valiant.

ranc-stræt, noun (RAHNK-STRAT / ˈrank-ˌstræt): 'Bold-road', 'proud-road' (definition uncertain).

sand-hof, noun (SAHND-HOFF / ˈsand-ˌhɔf): Grave (sand-house).

sǣ, noun (SAE / ˈsæː): Sea.

sǣ-bāt, noun (SAE-BAHT / ˈsæː-ˌbaːt): Sea boat.

sǣ-genga, noun (SAE-YENG-ga / ˈsæː-ˌjɛŋ-ga): Sea-goer, mariner; ship.

scip, noun (SHIP / ˈʃɪp): Ship.

secg, noun (SEDG / 'sɛd͡ʒ): Man, warrior; the sea; sword.

segl-rād, noun (SAIL-RAWD / 'sɛjl-ˌraːd): Sea (sail-road).

snacc, noun (SNAWK / 'snak): Swift-sailing vessel.

snytro-hūs, noun (SNUE-troh-HOOS / 'sny-trɔ-ˌhuːs): House of wisdom.

stōw, noun (STOH / 'stoːw): Place, location.

strǣt, noun (STRAT / 'strætˌ): Street, road.

sūsl-hof, noun (SOO-zull-HOFF / 'suː-zəl-ˌhɔf): Place of torment, hell.

wāþ, noun (WAHTH / 'waːθ): Wandering, roving.

wǣgn, noun (WAEYN / 'wæjn): Wagon.

wǣter-scipe, noun (WAT-er-SHIP-uh / 'wæ-tɛr-ˌʃɪ-pə): Water, body of water.

weg-fērend, noun (WEY-FAY-rend / 'wɛj-ˌfeː-rɛnd): Wayfarer, traveller.

wīd-wegas, plural noun (WEED-WEH-gahs / 'wiːd-ˌwɛ-gas): 'Wide-ways', distant regions, regions far and wide.

wunden-stefna, noun (WUN-den-STEV-na / 'wʌn-dɛn-ˌstɛv-na): Ship with a curved prow.

ȳþ-lād, noun (UETH-LAWD / 'yːθ-ˌlaːd): Ocean (wave-path).

ȳþ-lida, noun (UETH-LI-da / 'yːθ-ˌlɪ-da): Ship (wave-traverser).

II

Beyond Human

The stories of speech-bearers

A WHALE THAT PRETENDS to be an island, giant grapes that produce pearls – these marvels survive due to our passion for storytelling. Indeed, our need for stories is part of what makes us human.

Although the most common word for a human being in Old English is *mann* (Chapter 5), it's certainly not the most beautiful. I prefer a word for 'human' that is only used in poetry: **reord-berend** (speech-bearer). **Reord** means 'speech', 'voice' or 'language'. Today 'reird' means 'shout' in Scots, but the word hasn't been used in English since the end of the medieval period. *Reord-berend* appears only a handful of times, two of which are in the poem *The Dream of the Rood* (introduced in Chapter 9). The wooden cross speaks to the anonymous (presumably human) narrator, but even so it is not a *reord-berend*. Only humans have the privilege of bearing speech.

In *Beowulf* Grendel's inability to speak separates him from humanity and seems to torment him. Joyful singing and storytelling come from the mead-hall, while Grendel waits in the darkness. He hears the sound of the harp and the poem of the *scop* (poet, Chapter 4), but he can only participate in human life through wordless violence.

But in 1971 this voiceless creature found his *reord*. In John Gardner's novel *Grendel*, the titular character describes the first moment he heard human speech: 'The sounds were foreign at first, but when I calmed myself, concentrating, I found I understood them: it was my own language, but spoken in a strange way.' The poem *Beowulf* does not in any way indicate that Grendel can communicate with or even understand speech, but in Gardner's novel we see him recognising his own language among strangers. Grendel's mother, according to the novel, had 'forgotten all language long ago, or maybe had never known any' – but is her child becoming more human? And yet later in the novel, Grendel is angry about the wilful destruction wrought by humans and is filled with 'a wordless, obscurely murderous unrest'. And he doesn't even have words to use for swearing! Unable to put his anger into words, he can only respond with '*AAARGH!*' In the novel *Grendel*, the *scop* shapes history and truth 'by the power of his songs' and 'with casual words'. To Grendel, it seems as though the *scop*'s story-telling has turned him into a monster, for the stories split the world into two sides, darkness and light – 'And I, Grendel, was the dark side.' According to the *scop*, Grendel's race is cursed, and Grendel, hearing his powerful words, believes him.

Whether we're talking about a modern *scop* like Gardner or a *scop* in King Hrothgar's hall, the teller of stories is also the maker of monsters, the one who decides which side is darkness and which is light.

A particularly skilled *reord-berend* might be called **word-wīs** or **word-snotor**, words that mean 'wise in speech', literally 'word-wise'. As unpleasant as **snotor** may sound in modern English (and even though Old English **snot** means exactly what it does today), *word-snotor* does not mean someone who sneezes snotty words. *Snotor* is related to Old High German *snottar* and Old Norse *snotr*, both of which mean 'wise'. *Snot*, however, is related to Old English **snȳtan** (to blow the nose), from which modern English 'snout' most likely derives. While we've kept 'snot' and 'snout', and indeed developed 'snooty', *snotor* fell out of use in Middle English. Perhaps the *word-wīs* speech-bearers had grown weary of snotty *snotor* jokes. Whatever the reason, the power of a *reord-berend*'s words, wise or otherwise, cannot be stressed enough. Words give us stories, and stories give us meaning, ways of understanding both the mundane and the mysterious. These stories are of humans and non-humans, as well as creatures of indeterminate humanity – the ones who, like Grendel, are somewhere in between.

Secret-crafty mystery-men

Some stories aren't meant to be overheard. *Rūn* (Chapter 1) means 'whisper', or 'secret speech', a definition that persisted throughout the Middle Ages. It has cognates in a number of Germanic languages; in modern-day Switzerland, *Raune* is a regional German word that refers to voting by whispering your choice into the magistrate's ear. *Rūn* may also have referred to consultations or counsels – not secret per se, but probably limited to the ears of certain privileged individuals. One of the most likely locations for the negotiations between King John and his rebellious barons in 1215, and the signing of the Magna Carta, is Runnymede, a place name that may derive from *rūn* (counsel) + *īg* (island) + *mǣd* (meadow). Runnymede – the riverside water-meadow of consultations.

Related to *rūn*, the word *rȳne* means 'mystery' or 'mysterious saying'. A person who is skilled in explaining mysteries is a *rȳne-mann* (mystery-man), what we might refer to as a Sherlock Holmes. A *rȳne-mann* is *rūn-cræftig* (secret-crafty), able to explain the most impenetrable of secrets. In an Old English poem based on the Book of Daniel, King Belshazzar calls in *rūn-cræftig* men to interpret a mysterious message that appears on the wall at his feast. An angel of God makes a disembodied hand materialise to the people there, and it writes on the wall a warning to the king. But not even the most *rūn-cræftig* can explain it. Only the prophet Daniel is *rūn-cræftig* enough to make sense of the wordplay, a message that warns Belshazzar that God has judged him and his days as king are numbered. The king fails to heed the warning, even after the *rȳne-mann*'s explanation. He is killed that same night. Nowadays when people fail to 'read the writing on the wall', it means they have ignored the signs of impending disaster or misfortune.

A *rūn* or secret can take many forms, including the shape of a monster. In *Beowulf* we encounter the word **hell-rūne**, which literally translates to 'hell-secret':

> The hostile fighter (Grendel), a dark shadow of death, continued persecuting retainers old and young, lurking and plotting, and ruling the misty moors in perpetual darkness. Men cannot know where the *helrunan* wander along those paths.

The word *helrunan* has been translated a number of different ways: 'hell-demons', 'those in conspiracy with hell', 'reavers from hell', 'hell's intimates' (which sounds rather like a devilish line of lingerie), and so on. Michael Swanton's translation, 'those who share hell's secrets', is wordy but probably the most accurate. But I particularly like Kevin Crossley-Holland's evocative yet very literal 'hell-whisperers', since 'whisper' is another meaning of *rūn*.

Another *rūn-cræftig* person, who may or may not be a *hell-rūne*, is a **drȳ**, a magician, sorcerer or soothsayer. Unlike the 'rune-craft' of a *rȳne-mann*, the esoteric knowledge of a *drȳ* is usually portrayed as wicked and dangerous. For instance, in Mermedonia, a city of cannibals located somewhere in Greece or the Black Sea region, *drȳas* brew a toxic drink that makes people lose their minds.

Sorcerers (*dryas*) bitterly mixed together through magic-craft a deadly drink that turned the mind, the thoughts of men, the heart in the breast. The minds of these men were changed.

Those who are forced to partake of the *drȳ*'s drink forget how to be human, and hunger for hay and grass.

This *drȳ* is indirectly related to modern English 'druid', which entered English in the sixteenth century. 'Druid' was a borrowing from French *druide*, not a word that came from Old English *drȳ*. *Drȳ* itself derives from Old Irish *druí*. But ultimately, all these words go back to Latin *druidae*. *Druidae* appears as early as the first century BCE, in Julius Caesar's account of the war against the Germanic and Celtic peoples of Gaul. According to Caesar, the *druidae* were in charge of religion among their people. The historian Barry Cunliffe describes them as 'a caste of intellectuals', since they had a variety of functions: philosopher, teacher, judge, mystic, mediator between humans and gods. We have no written records by the people known as *druidae*, and no writers who describe them actually encountered them in person (with the exception of Caesar). In the first century CE, Pliny writes that the name for the Druids comes from Greek *drûs* (tree, oak). Scholars have theorised that the druids were thus 'those with the knowledge of the oak'. From this Greek word we also get modern English 'dryad', a nymph that inhabits trees in classical mythology. In Latin one of these wood nymphs was a *dryas* (plural: *dryades*).

So druids, dryads and *drȳ* all share a distant ancestor. They are linguistically similar, and all three are mysterious, magical beings. Whatever the origin of each of these words, these beings all wield a mysterious, supernatural power that can be neither understood nor trusted.

Elf-shot or elf-shining?

If you're in the habit of reading about mysterious, supernatural creatures, where might you find a book about elves? The fantasy section of a bookshop? The mythology aisle?

If the shop specialises in Old English literature you should head straight for the books on health, because elves mostly appear in medical remedies. They are a well-known cause of illnesses, and sometimes a disease can be traced back to the evil-doings of an *ælf* (elf). Today elves are usually portrayed as attractive, pointy-eared, flowing-haired people, but Old English *ælf* is not as specific as that. An *ælf* is a kind of spirit, one who could be good or bad, helpful or harmful. Various *ælf-cynn* (elf-kind) appear in the Old English translations for supernatural beings in classical literature. A *sæ-ælfen* (sea-elf) was a naiad, a water spirit who presided over fountains, wells, springs, streams and other bodies of freshwater. (This makes the *sæ* element rather puzzling, since the word usually refers specifically to seawater.) A *munt-ælfen* (mountain-elf) was a mountain-dwelling spirit, and a *wudu-ælfen* (wood-elf) was a dryad, a tree nymph. *Wilde* (wild) elves were hamadryads, wood nymphs so integrally tied to their trees that they were said to live and die with them.

The *ælf* may have been an amoral troublemaker in early medieval folklore, but under the influence of Christianity it became unambiguously evil, no better than a demon from hell. An illness's external symptoms might indicate demonic possession or injury by invisible, evil spirits, and because of this leechbooks include treatments for elf-related ailments.

Here is a recipe for a topical solution that treats not only fever but *ælcre feondes costunga* (all temptations of the Devil) as well as something called *ælf-siden* (elf-enchantment):

1   Pound together nine different kinds of plants and herbs.

2   Boil them in good-quality butter and wring them through a cloth.

3   Place these herbs beneath a church altar before singing nine Masses or prayers over them. (The numbers three and nine appear in several of these remedies and charms; three is a significant number throughout religion, myth and folklore, and nine is three threes.)

4   Smear the salve on your temples, above your eyes, over your head and breast, and on your sides beneath the arms.

Another salve works specifically against night spirits, *ælf-cynn*, and 'those with whom the Devil has had sex'. A third recipe instructs you to write in Latin on a dish (specifically a ciborium, a receptacle for a consecrated Eucharistic wafer). After that you need to ask a virgin to bring you running water from a stream, which she must collect without making a sound. Unfortunately, none of these remedies bothers to explain what the symptoms of *ælf-siden* actually are. The leech must already know how to diagnose 'elf-enchantment' and only require guidance for the cure.

The symptoms of **ælf-ādl** (elf-disease) are almost as unclear as those of *ælf-siden*. The *Dictionary of Old English* suggests that it is a kind of skin disease but admits uncertainty. Whatever *ælf-ādl* is, there are a number of possible remedies. For example:

1   Wrap several different types of plants in a cloth, including lichen that grew on a holy cross. Dip in baptismal water three times, and sing three Masses over them.

2   Place the plants on hot coals, letting the patient bathe in the smoke. Do this at *undern* (Chapter 2) or during the night. Sing

some prayers and make the sign of the cross on the patient's arms and legs.

3 Boil some more of the same plants in milk, and add three drops of holy water. The patient should consume this drink before eating.

Or:

1 On a Wednesday evening after sunset, find where there grows a plant called elecampane (or elfdock, from the sunflower family). Sing some prayers and then stab the plant with a dagger. Go away, leaving the dagger stuck in the plant.

2 Go to church before daybreak. Cross yourself and pray.

3 Return to the plant, keeping completely silent. Don't say a word, even if you come across someone or something terrifying! Sing some prayers and dig up the plant, but leave the dagger stuck in it.

4 Return to the church quickly with the plant and put it (with the dagger) beneath the altar. Leave it there until the sun is up.

5 Wash the plant and make it into a drink (with some other plants). Add three drops of holy water.

6 Sing prayers over the patient, and, using a sword, make the sign of the cross on each of their four sides. Give the drink to the patient to consume.

These complex procedures to cure *ælf-ādl* seem to have more to do with the performing of rituals than the properties of the herbs themselves.

The treatment for **ælf-sogeþa** (elf-ailment) actually indicates one of the symptoms. The leechbook says that if a person suffers from *ælf-sogeþa*, 'their eyes are yellow where they should be red'. We know from modern medicine that if the blood vessels in the eye turn yellow, it could indicate jaundice. Jaundice is a sign of anaemia, so could that be what *ælf-sogeþa* is? The leechbook also says that the remedy works against *ælcre feondes costunge* (every temptation of the Devil), so it's a very effective multipurpose cure!

As if there weren't enough of their diseases to worry about, you also have to worry about elves shooting you. A charm for a sudden stitch or pain goes like this:

> If you were shot in the skin, or in the flesh, or in the blood, or in the limb, may your life never be wounded! If it was the shot of gods, or the shot of elves (*ylfa gescot*), or the shot of witches, now I will help you.

Did people in the Middle Ages actually think witches and elves with bows and arrows shot painful darts into unsuspecting humans? Or is this charm merely a way to talk about an inexplicable shooting pain, a complaint that can only be explained by supernatural circumstances? No one is doing any shooting in the first three lines. You are shot in the skin ... by whom? The lack of a subject might indicate that the charm is referring to the *sensation* of being shot, not actual physical projectiles. The concept of being shot by elves is by no means limited to the medieval period. The first attested use of the word 'elf-schot' in English was during the Scottish witchcraft trials of the seventeenth century. Livestock allegedly became ill when struck by some kind of supernatural projectile.

Even if we can't say definitively what 'elf-disease' or 'elf-enchantment' are, one thing remains certain: elves cause lots of trouble in Old English. They shoot you with disease and pain; any encounter with them might make you very ill and require complex charms, potions and medical procedures; and to top it off, their wicked doings are associated with the Devil himself.

Why, then, are elf names so popular in early medieval England? Old English names beginning with the word *ælf* include Ælfric (Elf-power) and Ælfsige (Elf-victory) for men, while women are called Ælfflæd (Elf-beauty) and Ælfgifu (Elf-gift). Ælfgifu is particularly bizarre, since an elf's 'gifts' seem to consist of pain, disease and confusion. Ælfred (Elf-counsel) is still a popular name today, spelled Alfred. It seems strange to name your child after a creature that causes harm and is aligned with the forces of evil.

But perhaps an answer can be found in another elf word: ***ælf-scȳne*** (elf-shining), meaning something along the lines of 'radiant like an elf'. Surely such a lovely word is complimentary? *Ælf-scȳne* is used to describe two women from the Bible: Judith, who beheaded Holofernes, and Sarah, the wife of Abraham. According to her Old English poem, Judith is 'wise in thought, an <u>elf-shining</u> (*ælfscinu*) woman', while in a retelling of Genesis 20 Sarah is described as 'elf-shining'. In the Book of Genesis, the closest parallel word in Latin is *pulcher* (beautiful). Abraham anxiously tells his wife that when they enter Egypt, all the men will look lustfully at her and think 'that you, <u>elf-shining</u> (*ælfscieno*) woman, are my radiant bed-companion' (which, incidentally, is the truth).

Abraham's brilliant plan – pretending that Sarah is his sister – has already been explained in Chapter 5, but what was the result? Abraham's ruse makes King Abimelech assume that Sarah is single, and he decides to marry her. But to prevent unintended adultery, God reveals Sarah's secret to the king. The king assures Sarah that her husband shouldn't be angry at her, since no adultery took place:

> Your lord Abraham has no need to blame you, <u>elf-shining</u> (*ælfscieno*) woman, for walking my hall-paths.

Never mind that it was Abraham who got Sarah into this awkward situation in the first place.

In neither the description of Judith nor that of Sarah is *ælf-scȳne* a straightforward compliment. Some scholars have suggested that the *ælf* here might have a more malign connotation. Judith and Sarah are admirable women, to be sure, but they are still examples of women who – in the words of philologist Alaric Hall – are 'beautiful, but perilously so'. Judith uses her beauty to seduce and assassinate her people's foe. Although Sarah doesn't *try* to cause any harm, her beauty is the reason for Abraham's physical and King Abimelech's moral endangerment.

So perhaps elves are not always bad, but they are always associated with a power that is seemingly supernatural in its strength. And maybe it's that power that inspired parents to choose *ælf*-related names for their children. After all, if you want your child to be strong, wise or beautiful, they may as well be supernaturally so.

Pucks and shucks

The **pūcel** (goblin) is ubiquitous. This malevolent spirit has its own hole (Putshole, Devon), field (Pock Field, Cambridgeshire), ridge (Puckeridge, Hertfordshire), town (Puxton, Somerset) and even church (Pucklechurch, Gloucestershire).

Pūcel also pops up in mildly demonic Middle English surnames: Ricardus Puchel, Nicholas Pokel, John le Pochel, Thome Pouk and the unfortunate Galfridus Puke. It's possible these men associated the *pūcel* with other qualities. After all, one text translates Latin *priapos* with *pūcel*, Priapus being a Greek and Roman fertility god, protector of livestock, gardens and male genitalia. The god Priapus is easily recognisable due to his oversized, permanent erection, and it's from this that we get the modern medical term 'priapism'. So, who knows what qualities – demonic or divine – Mr Puke and Mr Puchel associated with their surnames?

Long after the Middle Ages, the *pūcel* is still around. In modern English it appears as 'puckle' or 'puck'. Reginald Scot, a Member of Parliament, wrote *The Discoverie of Witchcraft* in 1584 in an attempt to counter superstitious beliefs about witches and other magical beings. In a time when pretty much everyone else believed in witchcraft, Scot writes:

> [I]n our childhood our mothers maids [. . .] have so fraied us with bull beggers, spirits, witches, urchens, elves, hags, fairies, satyrs, pans, faunes, sylens, kit with the cansticke, tritons, centaurs, dwarfes, giants, imps, calcars, conjurors, nymphes, changlings, Incubus, Robin good-fellowe, the spoorne, the mare, the man in the oke, the hell waine, the fierdrake, <u>the puckle</u>, Tom thombe, hob gobblin, Tom tumbler, boneles, and such other bugs, that we are afraid of our owne shadowes.

So the puckle is in good company, and sometimes he is equated with other malevolent creatures. It was around the same time that Shakespeare's *A Midsummer Night's Dream* was first performed, featuring a mischievous sprite called Puck or Robin Goodfellow. This Puck is known for such antics as scaring maidens and misleading travellers at night, as well as getting in the way of doing basic household chores, like grinding the mill or churning the milk.

The puck or *pūcel* may amuse with his playful antics, but another demonic sort, the **scucca** (devil), is far more frightening. *Scucca* may even derive from the Germanic root *skuh-* (to terrify) (and modern English 'shy' may actually derive from this same root). Before the hero's arrival at Heorot in *Beowulf*, King Hrothgar despairs of protecting his hall against *scuccum ond scinnum*, the wonderfully alliterative 'shucks' (devils) and 'shinings' (evil spirits).

The *scucca* or 'shuck' continues to be a devil or demon throughout the Old English and Middle English periods, but that particular meaning eventually became obsolete. From the nineteenth century, 'shuck' came to refer to a spectre hound, a ghostly black dog portending death. In his *Highways and Byways of East Anglia* (1901) William Dutt reports that the Black Shuck can be found on the Norfolk coast. (The author does say at the start of the book that his aim is 'to follow the lead of the monkish chroniclers and relate both fact and myth, leaving it to others to judge where the line should be drawn between them', so scepticism is by no means discouraged.) Of the Black Shuck, Dutt writes:

> He takes the form of a huge black dog, and prowls along dark lanes and lonesome field footpaths, where, although his howling makes the hearer's blood run cold, his footfalls make no sound. You may know him at once, should you see him, by his fiery eye; he has but one, and that, like the Cyclops', is in the middle of his head. But such an encounter might bring you the worst of luck: it is even said that to meet him is to be warned that your death will occur before the end of the year.

There is, however, a substantial gap of several centuries between the recorded usages of 'shuck' for a devil and 'shuck' for a ghost-hound, so their connection is unclear.

But what about that very American expression 'aw shucks!' – could there be a connection there? The expression 'shucks' (an interjection of contempt or indifference) – is included in the *Oxford English Dictionary*'s entry for a different kind of shuck, the 'shuck' that is 'a husk, pod, or shell'. The etymology for this 'shuck' is unknown, but the noun was used as early as the seventeenth century to mean the husk, pod or shell on corn or nuts. In the nineteenth century, 'shuck' meant something worthless (like a corn husk), as in 'not worth shucks' (good for nothing). So 'aw shucks!' comes from corn, not the Devil.

The *pūcel* and the *scucca* are both demonic and definitively non-human, but another frightening being, the **wearg**, is different. When *wearg* refers to humans, it means 'villain', 'scoundrel' or 'criminal'. An Old English maxim says, 'The <u>criminal</u> (*wearh*) must hang and pay a fair price for what wickedness he has done to mankind.' But a *wearg* can also refer to a malignant creature or evil spirit, even something akin to an animal, such as those that appear in St Paul's vision of the damned:

> As St Paul was looking at the northern region of the earth, where all the waters flow down, he saw a grey stone there over the water. North of the stone the woods had grown very frosty, and there were dark mists. And under the stone was the dwelling place of <u>water monsters</u> (*niccra*: see *nicor*, Chapter 10) and <u>evil spirits</u> (*wearga*).

St Paul sees dark souls hanging from a cliff, the monstrous creatures below waiting to seize them 'like a greedy wolf'. In *Beowulf* Grendel and his mother live in a similar location:

> ... a secret land, wolf slopes, windy headlands, perilous fen-paths, where the mountain stream goes down under the dark of the headlands, water under earth. It is not that far from here, measured in miles, that the mere stands; frost-covered groves hang over it, a well-rooted wood overshadows the water.

Wolves characterise both of these ominous locations. Old Norse *vargr*, a cognate of Old English *wearg*, means both 'wolf' and 'outlaw' (see *wulf-hēafod-trēow*, Chapter 8). A *wearg* may not have been a wolf in Old English but, like a wolf, a *wearg* was inherently untrustworthy. Remember the *wine-lēas* man of Chapter 6, who has only treacherous wolves for companions – 'very often that companion will rip him apart'.

Modern fantasy has borrowed the word *wearg* for its frightening, untrustworthy creatures. In *The Hobbit* Tolkien says the Wargs are 'evil wolves over the edge of the Wild' who collude with the goblins in wicked deeds. In a response to some fan mail, Tolkien explained Wargs to an aptly named Mr Wolfe, saying: 'Warg is simple. It is an old word for wolf, which also had the sense of an outlaw or hunted criminal ... I adopted the word, which had a good sound for the meaning, as a name for this particular brand of demonic wolf in the story.' In Tolkien's *The Lord of the Rings*, the wizard Gandalf includes Wargs in his list of evil creatures that are best avoided (along with trolls, werewolves and orcs). More recently, wargs featured in George R. R. Martin's series *A Song of Ice and Fire* and the TV show *Game of Thrones*. In the words of Mance Rayder, King-Beyond-the-Wall, wargs are people who can 'enter the minds of animals and see through their eyes'.

Grund-wyrgen, related to the *wearg*, is still more difficult to translate. **Grund**, from which we get the modern English noun 'ground', is the lowest part of anything: the depths of the earth or sea, an abyss or chasm, even hell. The hapax *grund-wyrgen* appears in *Beowulf* when the hero enters the mere to fight Grendel's mother: 'Then the brave one perceived the <u>wolf of the deep</u> (*grundwyrgenne*).' Bosworth-Toller defines *grund-wyrgen* as 'wolf of the deep', while the Toronto *Dictionary of Old English* has 'accursed (female) creature of the deep'. Some modern translations of *Beowulf* emphasise Grendel's mother's lupine nature: 'she-wolf of the abyss' (John Earle), 'wolf-of-the-deep' (Francis Gummere), 'were-wolf of the deep' (Ian Serraillier). R. D. Fulk's translation, 'outcast of the deep', captures the twin meanings of Old Norse *vargr*, since both wolves and outlaws are outcasts in Old English. Many translations unambiguously align *grund-wyrgen* with malevolent, even demonic forces: 'the abyss's curse' (Edwin Morgan), 'sea-monster' (Kevin Crossley-Holland), 'witch of the sea-floor' (Howell

D. Chickering, Jr), 'accursed creature of the depths' (Michael Swanton), 'damned creature of the deep' (S. A. J. Bradley), 'water-witch' (Roy M. Liuzza), and the evocative 'swamp-thing from hell' (Seamus Heaney). Personally, I prefer 'wolf of the deep'. 'Wolf' evokes the dangerous, potentially non-human nature of Grendel's mother's without calling her a criminal. 'The deep' allows a bit of ambiguity about whether she is in the depths of hell or simply at the bottom of a lake.

The loathly-fingered lake-woman

Grendel's mother is nameless. In some modern illustrations she is an ogre-like swamp troll, although she is cast as a sensuous succubus in the Zemeckis film of 2007. The medieval *Beowulf* poem has no illustrations, so we can only imagine her based on the poet's words. But many modern readers experience *Beowulf* in translation, not in the original Old English, and so, as we have seen already, the choices of the modern translator can greatly affect how we perceive the (non-)human-ness of this mysterious character.

Depending on the translation, Grendel's mother might have 'loathsome fingers' or 'horrible fingers', 'savage talons' or 'hostile claws'. The words in Old English are *laþum fingrum*. Why do some translators turn Grendel's mother's human fingers into the talons or claws of an animal or monstrous hybrid?

Grendel's mother is called a *grund-wyrgen* (wolf of the deep) in the same passage in which she is referred to as *merewif mihtig*. A **mere-wīf** is a woman of the *mere*, a 'sea-woman' or 'lake-woman'. A **mihtig** (mighty) lake-woman, Grendel's mother is also an *ides* and an *aglæcwif*. An **ides** is a woman, although it has more specific meanings, never with negative connotations, like 'young woman', 'virgin', 'wife' and 'noblewoman'. Wealhtheow (Hrothgar's queen in *Beowulf*), Empress

Helena (the saintly mother of Emperor Constantine), Eve and the Virgin Mary have all been called *ides* in Old English. **Aglæcwīf** is a compound that refers to a **wīf** (woman) who is hostile, threatening, generally formidable. Yet Seamus Heaney translates *ides aglæcwif* as 'monstrous hell-bride'. How would our perception of this character change with a less poetic but more accurate translation – woman, formidable female-fighter?

Aglæcwīf is the female form of **āglæca,** one of my favourite words because it's so difficult to translate. *Bosworth-Toller* defines *āglæca* as 'a miserable being, wretch, monster', while the *Dictionary of Old English* goes with 'awesome opponent, ferocious fighter'. I think 'badass warrior' comes close. Many translators use 'monster', but there is no word in Old English that simply means 'monster'. 'Monster' didn't enter the English language until the influence of French in the late fourteenth century, with Middle English 'monstre' defined as 'a deformed human being or animal' but also 'a wonder'.

Āglæca refers to human heroes as well as antagonists of questionable human-ness. Grendel is an *āglæca*, but so too is Beowulf, and the fact that the same word is used for both adds depth and complexity to their characters. How were they meant to be perceived? Jennifer Neville argues that it is not Grendel's physique that makes him a monster, for though he is enormous and supernaturally strong, so is Beowulf. It is the fact that Grendel is a **mearc-stapa** (boundary-stepper) that makes him monstrous; he is someone who moves outside the limits of civil society. Neville says, 'He is a monster, not simply because he has glowing eyes, but because he breaks those boundaries, intrudes into human society, performs acts forbidden by society, and thus threatens society's very existence.'

How easily those we perceive as outsiders inevitably become our monsters.

The oath-breaking warlock

A story needs an opponent, a threat if not a monster, someone for the hero or heroine to defeat. Every protagonist needs a *wiþer-wengel*.

Wiþer-wengel (adversary) comes from **wiþer** (against, in opposition) and . . . *wengel*? *Wengel* doesn't appear on its own in the surviving Old English texts, so it's hard to say what it means (if anything). *Wiþer* is unrelated to modern English 'wither', to become dried up or shrivelled up – that comes from the verb 'weather'. A piece of outdoor furniture can be 'weathered' from the sun and rain. You can 'weather' a storm or even a serious illness. It is from this weather-'wither' that we get withering stares and glances, pointed looks meant to make someone feel ashamed. The 'wither' that comes from Old English, meaning 'hostile' or 'against', became obsolete after the Middle Ages, although it still appears as a prefix in Scots: a 'witherweight' is a counterbalancing weight, and 'withershins' (or 'widdershins') is the wrong way, anti-clockwise.

A particularly shameful *wiþer-wengel* is the **wǣr-loga**. Old English *wǣr-loga* is an oath-breaker, someone who is false to their covenant, a faithless, perfidious traitor. This definition became obsolete after the Middle Ages, and now a 'warlock' is usually someone in league with the Devil, such as a wizard or sorcerer. In the role-playing game *Dungeons & Dragons*, a character of the Warlock class gains power from 'a bargain with an extraplanar entity'. The desire for knowledge and power is what drives the charismatic *D&D* Warlock. While the *D&D* Warlock is defined by their faithfulness to an oath or pact, the *wǣr-loga* is defined by just the opposite, their breaking of oaths.

'Warlock' looks like it has to do with warfare, but the **wǣr** in *wǣr-loga* means 'pledge', 'covenant' or 'agreement'. *Wǣr* is a cognate of Old Norse *vár* (pledge, promise, vow), from which the Varangian Guard derived its name. (The Varangian Guard, an elite unit of mercenaries in the Middle Ages, were pledged to protect the emperors of Byzantium.) It's unclear where the *-loga* comes from, possibly **lygen**, which means 'lying' or 'false'. *Loga* also appears in **trēow-loga** (one who fails to keep faith or fails in loyalty), **āþ-loga** (perjurer), **word-loga** (one who is false to their word) and **wed-loga** (one who is false to a pledge or engagement). That last example, *wed-loga*, is not related to modern English 'wedlock', which actually derives from **wed-lāc** (pledge), which eventually came to mean 'marriage'.

The oath-breakers of Old English are usually people who break with God's covenant. That happens when someone (typically Christian) gets aligned with or tempted by the Devil. (That's what all those remedies against the temptations of the Devil are for.) The fate of the *wǣr-loga* on Judgement Day isn't pretty:

> Then the dark sinner will stand at judgement, frightened before God, and marked by death, cursed with stains, the oath-breaker (*wærloga*) will be filled with fire.

In the poem *Andreas*, the oath-breakers consist of some cannibalistic heathens, as well as the Devil himself. Angels in the poem *Genesis A* use the term *wǣr-loga* for the sinners of Sodom and Gomorrah. Another poem soberly warns Christians not to choose the 'home of the oath-breaker' as their permanent dwelling. That home is hell.

Another name for the *wǣr-loga*'s home is **orc**. Tolkien's orcs in *The Lord of the Rings* are creatures who have been tortured and corrupted by the Dark Powers until they became monstrous. In the same letter to Mr Wolfe about Wargs, Tolkien writes that 'orc' was a word derived from an Old English word for 'demon'. This is not technically true. Old English *orc* is not a creature (a demon) but a place (the infernal regions). *Orcus* is Latin for 'hell'. Modern English 'ogre' may also derive from Latin *orcus*, via French *ogre*. *Orc* vanished from English for a time, then resurfaced in the sixteenth century, but it is unlikely that this post-medieval 'orc' derives from Old English. It's more likely to come from the Italian *orco*, a man-eating giant.

Ogre, hell-dweller, oath-breaker – in a hero's story, the humanity of each *wiþer-wengel* is called into question. But is the least human of them all an ***un-mann***, an 'un-human'?

Un-human

If a *mann* is a man or gender-non-specific human, what exactly is an *un-mann*? The primary meaning of *un-mann*, the negative form of *mann*, is 'a bad or inhuman person'. Its Icelandic cognate *ú-mannan* means 'a person fit for nothing'.

Ælfric of Eynsham describes Judas's betrayal of Jesus in one of his homilies. When the soldiers arrive to arrest Jesus, one has his ear sliced off by the sword of Peter, one of Jesus's loyal disciples. Jesus reproves Peter and heals the soldier's ear, saying that he could have twelve legions of angels from heaven to defend him if he wished. Those twelve legions – 72,000 angels in total – could easily have defended Jesus against the *unmannum*, Ælfric explains, but Jesus chose to suffer for our salvation. The soldiers, who are referred to as 'impious persecutors', abuse Jesus during his Passion, but even as they dehumanise the Son of God they are dehumanised by Ælfric's word *unmannum*. *Un-mann* also appears in Archbishop Wulfstan's warning about the corruption and evil-doings of bishops who eagerly flatter *unmannum* (bad people) with praise.

Un-mann in these contexts is undoubtedly negative, but another instance, in the *Life of St Guthlac*, is less clear. The saint's life describes Guthlac's boyhood and coming of age, during which he becomes strong, serious and intelligent, notably uninterested in things that occupy the thoughts of other boys (including lies, flattery and the study of birdsong; such are the sources of entertainment for a seventh-century Mercian boy). As Guthlac grows into a man, he thinks more and more frequently about 'the strong deeds of *unmanna* and earthly rulers'. If spending your time learning about birdsong is frowned upon, surely time spent pondering over the deeds of bad men is worse. So is 'bad men' really what *unmanna* means?

Some scholars write off this strange usage as an error of the scribe who, they say, meant to write the word *iumanna* instead. *Iumanna* appears nowhere else in Old English, but *iū* means 'formerly' or 'of old'. So *iumanna* could mean something like 'former peoples' or 'men of old', more appropriate people as the subject of the young Guthlac's contemplation. But there is no question that *unmanna* is what is written; the word *iū* appears on the reverse (verso) side of the page, written by the same hand, and there is no confusing them.

Unmanna appears on the front (recto) side of the page

The words *iu wæron* (formerly were) are on the reverse (verso) side of the page

Bosworth-Toller suggests a rather surprising secondary definition for *un-mann* that better fits this context: 'hero'. The logic there is that a hero is an 'un-human' because they are *more* than a mere human being, kind of like a superhero. And yet this is the only example of this kind of usage. Although I love the idea of an ambiguous word that could mean either 'bad man' or 'hero', it's more likely that Guthlac isn't thinking about heroes at all. The text continues to describe a major change in Guthlac's personality; when the once sober-minded child hits his teens, he gathers warriors and weapons and marches off to burn, ravage and slaughter. It's another nine years before God's divine inspiration stops him from being an ass-hole. So chances are that the *unmanna* he thinks about in his younger years are powerful conquerors and rulers of the world, corrupt rather than heroic role models.

Perhaps an *un-mann* is simply a powerful and corrupt human being. After all, Wulfstan's evil bishops would have no reason to flatter *unmanna* unless those 'un-humans' were men of high social and economic status. Perhaps the un-human-ness of the *un-mann* has more to do with one's moral character than physical disposition.

'Doubt-man' (who sounds like one of Marvel's less successful super-heroes, perhaps one who fights the world's confidence men) is quite different from the *un-mann*. **Twēo-mann**, which translates literally as 'doubt-person' or 'uncertainty-person', is a creature of doubtful humanity. Usage of the word *twēo-mann* is itself rather dubious, as it appears only once in Old English. This single occurrence is in *Wonders of the East*, a text that describes a number of fascinating peoples and creatures, including some who are given the Latin name *Homodubii*. There are only two extant copies of this text, both housed at the British Library. Manuscripts are often collections or miscellanies of various texts, and one copy of *Wonders of the East* is part of MS (manuscript) Vitellius A XV, the same late-tenth-century manuscript as *Beowulf*. The other copy is in the eleventh-century MS Tiberius B V/1. These two versions of the text are similar, but they differ in the section about the *Homodubii*:

MS Tiberius B V/1:

Homodubii hi sindon hatene, þæt bioð <u>twylice</u>, ond be hreawan fisceon hi libbað ond þa etað.

They are called *Homodubii*, that is <u>doubtfully</u>, and they live on raw fish and eat them.

MS Vitellius A XV:

Homodubii hy syndon hatene, þæt beoð <u>twi-men</u>, ond be hreawum fixum hy lifiað ond þa etaþ.

They are called *Homodubii*, that is <u>doubt-men</u>, and they live on raw fish and eat them.

Why does the eleventh-century manuscript use the adverb **twēolīce** (or *twylice*: doubtfully), while the earlier manuscript uses the *twēo-mann* (or *twi-men*) compound? It makes sense that the words of each passage have different spellings (*sindon* and *syndon*, *fisceon* and *fixum*), since this is long before standardisation. Spellings could differ based on manuscripts' place and time of origin. But changing *twi-men* to *twylice* – that's going from a noun to an adverb, and the adverb doesn't even make sense contextually. Did 'doubt-man' fall out of use over time? Was it only ever used by one scribe, who coined the word to create a direct translation for *Homodubii*? Did the later scribe misunderstand the text or think the adverb could be used as a noun? Alas, the truth remains in doubt.

Regardless of whether this name was used by anyone other than a single inventive scribe, the *twēo-mann* is a fascinating creature. It is six feet tall, with a beard down to its knees and hair to its heels. But the strangest characteristics of the *twēo-mann* appear in a later passage of *Wonders of the East*, which sounds like a description of a completely different creature: 'They are in the shape of a human to the navel and then the shape of an ass. They have long legs like birds and a gentle voice.' These descriptions aren't mutually exclusive, but

Homodubii

it seems strange that the donkey-shaped lower half and bird legs weren't worth mentioning from the start. Surely those are more important traits for identifying a *twēo-mann* than being hairy and six feet tall. Are these passages actually describing two different creatures of doubtful human-ness, not necessarily the same species? The illustration in MS Tiberius B V/1 depicts the creature in the first description quite well, but it certainly doesn't work for the latter.

Perhaps there is only one sure thing about the *twēo-mann*: its nature and its human-ness will forever be in doubt.

Eleventh *wordhord*

āglǣca, noun (AH-GLACK-ah / ˈaː-ˌglæː-ka): Hostile fighter, fierce combatant, great opponent.

aglǣcwīf, noun (AH-GLACK-weef / ˈa-ˌglæːk-wiːf): Hostile female fighter, fierce female combatant.

āþ-loga, noun (ATH-LOG-ah / ˈaːθ-ˌlɔ-ga): Perjurer.

ælf, noun (ALF / ˈælf): Elf.

ælf-ādl, noun (ALF-AH-dull / ˈælf-ˌaː-dəl): Elf disease (unknown illness, perhaps a skin disease).

ælf-cynn, noun (ALF-KUEN / ˈælf-ˌkyn): 'Elf-kind', the race of elves.

ælf-scȳne, adjective (ALF-SHUE-nuh / ˈælf-ˌʃyː-nə): 'Elf-shining', radiant or beautiful like an elf.

ælf-siden, noun (ALF-SID-en / ˈælf-ˌsɪ-dɛn): 'Elf-enchantment' (unknown affliction accompanied by fever).

ælf-sogeþa, noun (ALF-SO-yeh-tha / ˈælf-ˌsɔ-jɛ-θa): Elf ailment (unknown illness, perhaps anaemia).

drȳ, noun (DRUE / ˈdryː): Magician, sorcerer, soothsayer.

grund, noun (GRUND / ˈɡrʌnd): Bottom, lowest part of anything; ground, earth; abyss, hell.

grund-wyrgen, noun (GRUND-WUER-yen / ˈɡrʌnd-ˌwyr-jɛn): Wolf of the deep.

hell-rūne, noun (HELL-ROON-uh / ˈhɛl-ˌruː-nə): Demon, one who knows hell's mysteries.

ides, noun (IH-dess / ˈɪ-dɛs): Woman; young woman, virgin; wife; woman of high standing, noblewoman.

īg, noun (EE / ˈiːj): Island.

lygen, adjective (LUE-yen / ˈly-jɛn): Lying, false.

mǣd, noun (MAD / ˈmæːd): Meadow.

mearc-stapa, noun (MEH-ark-STAH-pa / ˈmɛark-ˌsta-pa): 'Boundary-stepper', one who wanders the desolate borderland.

mere-wīf, noun (MEH-ruh-WEEF / ˈmɛ-rə-ˌwiːf): 'Mere-woman', 'water-woman'.

mihtig, adjective (MI'H-tih / ˈmɪx-tɪj): Mighty, powerful.

munt-ælfen, noun (MUNT-AL-ven / ˈmʌnt-ˌæl-vɛn): Mountain elf, mountain nymph.

orc, noun (ORK / ˈɔrk): Hell, the infernal regions.

pūcel, noun (POO-chell / ˈpuː-t͡ʃɛl): Goblin, demon.

reord, noun (REH-ord / ˈrɛɔrd): Speech, language, voice.

reord-berend, noun (REH-ord-BEH-rend / ˈrɛɔrd-ˌbɛ-rɛnd): 'Speech-bearer', human.

rūn-cræftig, adjective (ROON-KRAF-tih / ˈruːn-ˌkræf-tɪj): Skilled in explaining mysteries.

rȳne, noun (RUE-nuh / ˈryː-nə): Mystery, mysterious saying.

rȳne-mann, noun (RUE-nuh-MAHN / ˈryː-nə-ˌman): One skilled in explaining mysteries.

sǣ-ælfen, noun (SAE-AL-ven / ˈsæː-ˌæl-vɛn): Sea elf, sea nymph.

scucca, noun (SHUCK-ah / ˈʃʌ-ka): Devil, demon; Satan.

snot, noun (SNOT / ˈsnɔt): Mucus from the nose, snot.

snotor, adjective (SNOT-or / ˈsnɔ-tɔr): Prudent, wise.

snȳtan, verb (SNUE-tahn / ˈsnyː-tan): To clear the nose.

trēow-loga, noun (TRAY-oh-LOG-ah / ˈtreːɔw-ˌlɔ-ga): One who fails to keep faith; one who fails in loyalty to their leader.

twēolīce, adverb (TWAY-oh-LEE-chuh / ˈtweːɔ-ˌliː-t͡ʃə): Doubtfully, uncertainly.

twēo-mann, noun (TWAY-oh-MAHN / ˈtweːɔ-ˌman): 'Doubt-person', creature whose humanity is uncertain.

un-mann, noun (UN-MAHN / ˈʌn-ˌman): Bad person, inhuman person; hero, one who is more than an average person.

wǣr, noun (WAER / 'wæːr): Covenant, agreement, pledge.

wǣr-loga, noun (WAER-LOG-ah / 'wæːr-ˌlɔ-ga): One who is false to their covenant; faithless and deceitful person.

wearg, noun (WEH-arg / 'wɛarg): (For humans) villain, felon, scoundrel, criminal; (for non-humans) malignant creature, evil spirit.

wed-lāc, noun (WED-LAHK / 'wɛd-ˌlaːk): Pledge; wedlock.

wed-loga, noun (WED-LOG-ah / 'wɛd-ˌlɔ-ga): One who is false to a pledge or engagement.

wīf, noun (WEEF / 'wiːf): Woman, female; married woman, wife.

wilde, adjective (WILL-duh / 'wɪl-də): Wild.

wiþer, preposition/adverb (WITH-er / 'wɪ-θɛr): Against; in opposition.

wiþer-wengel, noun (WITH-er-WENG-gell / 'wɪ-θɛr-ˌwɛŋ-gɛl): Adversary.

word-loga, noun (WORD-LOG-ah / 'wɔrd-ˌlɔ-ga): One who is false to their word.

word-snotor, adjective (WORD-SNOT-or / 'wɔrd-ˌsnɔ-tɔr): 'Word-wise', wise in speech.

word-wīs, adjective (WORD-WEES / 'wɔrd-ˌwiːs): 'Word-wise', wise in speech.

wudu-ælfen, noun (WUH-duh-AL-ven / 'wʌ-dʌ-ˌæl-vɛn): Wood elf, wood nymph.

12

Searching for Meaning

Who received that load?

ANOTHER THING THAT remains shrouded in mystery and doubt is what happens after we die.

A ship waits in the harbour, icy and sea-ready. At the mast, in the ship's bosom, lies a beloved king, a renowned treasure-giver. Alongside him are many precious things, brought there from distant lands. Never was there a ship more splendidly equipped with weapons and armour, swords and coats of mail. The king's people have laid treasures upon his breast, and a golden standard rises high above his head. His people, sorrowful in mind, with hearts in mourning, give their king to the ocean, letting the sea take him. Not even the wisest men, counsellors of the hall and warriors under heaven, can say truly *hwa þæm hlæste onfeng* (who received that load).

In this opening scene of *Beowulf*, the *hlæst* is the ship's burden – in this case the body (and soul?) of the late King Scyld. **Hlæst** means 'load', 'cargo', 'freight' or 'burden'. It's a rare word that appears primarily in poetry. (We do not have, for example, prosaic items like Old English inventories listing the contents of a ship's *hlæst*.) The Old English hapax **brim-hlæst**, literally 'sea-cargo', is a lovely kenning for fish. *Hlæst* lasted through the Middle Ages, losing the h in Middle English 'last'. From the fourteenth century we see 'last' used as a unit of measure for fish (a nice echo of *brim-hlæst*), as well as for beer, wine, grain and other commodities that were shipped. In the sixteenth century 'last' takes on other meanings: 'a unit for the carrying capacity of a ship (typically two tonnes)', as well as 'a Shetland unit of land with an annual rentable value of twelve shillings'. But these definitions are far more precise and specific than the poetic burden of Old English *hlæst*.

But *hwa þæm hlæste onfeng*, who received that load? Is it God? *Beowulf* is a Christian poem about a pagan world, and already the poet faces a conflict in faith. How can a pagan king – even one who is otherwise admirable in every way – go to **heofon** (heaven)? King Scyld's subjects honour him with gold and give him a send-off worthy of his stature, but where is that funeral ship going? If not the Christian *heofon*, then where? As the *scop* says, no one can truly say.

Cristen-dōm (Christianity) had arrived in Roman Britain as early as the third century, but the conversion period didn't begin in earnest till the end of the sixth century, when Pope Gregory the Great sent Augustine, a prior of a monastery in Rome, on a mission. After gathering information and translators in Francia, the missionaries proceeded to the court of Æthelberht of Kent, the most powerful king in southern Britain at the time. Although Æthelberht was a pagan, Bertha, his queen, the daughter of a Frankish king, was Christian. In fact, the agreement of her marriage to Æthelberht was on condition that she could maintain her Christian faith, and Bertha founded a Christian church at Canterbury. As Æthelberht had not only been exposed to the faith but had demonstrated a tolerance of it, the King of Kent was a logical starting point for mass conversion. Converting the British kingdoms to *cristen-dōm* depended on converting its kings, a small but powerful minority, who would sometimes find the new faith advantageous to promoting their own political ambitions.

Although Old English literature has plentiful tales of early Christian martyrs (*þrōwendas*, Chapter 9), their holy sacrifices generally take place in other parts of the world. In Britain relatively few people were killed for their faith. Missionaries presented *cristen-dōm* as a political advantage to British rulers, who then adopted the new faith with relatively little opposition. Conversion began in Kent, but by the end of the seventh century the Kings of Northumbria, Mercia, East Anglia, Wessex and Sussex were all at least nominally Christian. The earliest Old English literature we have dates to the seventh century, and most of it is from much later, the tenth or eleventh centuries. Thus, essentially all extant texts written in Old English are from a Christian England, where paganism was for the most part a thing of the past.

So what is a Christian poet to do with a pagan protagonist?

While some Christians – like King Alfred in the late ninth century – saw the appeal and intellectual value of Germanic legends about pagan heroes, others were decidedly less receptive of such tales. In the year 797 (a century before King Alfred's reign), the scholar and clergyman Alcuin of York wrote a letter to the head of another religious community, in which he bemoaned the fact that his clerics preferred the entertainment of pagan stories to the enlightenment of Christian sermons. Alcuin writes in Latin:

> *Quid Hinieldus cum Christo? Augusta est domus; utrosque tenere non poterit.*
> (What has Ingeld to do with Christ? The house is narrow; it cannot contain them both.)

Ingeld is a pagan hero from Germanic legend; in fact, Beowulf mentions him in the report to King Hygelac. One might ask, then, what has Beowulf to do with Christ? Is there room for this hero's story in a Christian scriptorium?

So it would seem.

Heaven swallowed the smoke

Beowulf takes place in pre-Christian Scandinavia, and the Geats and the Danes are pagans. Yet throughout the poem there are references to the Christian God. When Beowulf brings him Grendel's bloody head, King Hrothgar says, 'Thanks be to the Creator, the eternal Lord', seeming to forget momentarily that he has not yet received knowledge of that eternal Lord. King Hrethel of the Geats chooses 'God's light' (*godes leoht*) when he dies. When Beowulf dies, his soul departs 'to seek the <u>judgement</u> (*dom*, Chapter 1) of the righteous'. It is ambiguous whether Beowulf is the righteous man to be judged, or if he is to be judged *by* the righteous. Does Beowulf go to *heofon* or **hell**?

Today we would call this anachronistic. How could a pre-Christian society have Christian faith? As the editors of *Klaeber's Beowulf* point out, modern readers who are used to consuming historical novels may expect a depiction of 'a past culture as it is really supposed to have been', but such anachronisms are far from unusual. Medieval manuscripts often show individuals from the ancient world wearing medieval clothing. Characters in a play that takes place before the birth of Jesus swear by Christ and his saints.

There is no doubt that Beowulf and friends are **hǣþen** (heathen, pagan). There are three instances of burning the dead, a practice that went against Christian doctrine. In fact, the poem is bookended by *hǣþen* rituals: Scyld's body floating out to sea in a funerary ship, and Beowulf's body engulfed in a funeral pyre's flames. The poem does not say whether these people entered *heofon*, but neither does it say they were banished to *hell*.

But must pagans always go to *hell*? Is that where the poet meant to send his heroes? Perhaps these are 'noble pagans', people who *would* have been Christian if they had been given the chance. (There have to be some of these, otherwise everyone in the Old Testament would be banished to *hell* – Abraham, Moses . . . the lot.)

At Beowulf's funeral, the poem says, '<u>Heaven</u> (*heofon*) swallowed the smoke'. *Heofon* is not mentioned frequently in the poem: only five times in over 3,000 lines of verse. Yet the final occurrence of the word is here, in the midst of a pagan funerary ritual. Does *heofon* receive Beowulf's soul or merely the residue of his 'flesh-covering' (*flǣsc-hama*, Chapter 7)?

The arrival of *cristen-dōm* in Britain did not make heroes of the ancient world any less compelling. Not only were such heroes inspiring, they were ancestors important to the ancient bloodlines of kings. Is it any surprise that these kings would rather not see their heathen forebears damned? The historian Patrick Wormald points out that a king in the eighth century would have preferred 'feasting with his forebears in hell to dining alone in heaven'.

Beowulf and Christ are very different heroes indeed, but it seems they both have a place in the books and imaginations of medieval Christians. And regardless of where his soul was meant to go, Beowulf's story has stayed with us.

Go ahead and do your worst!

The English word **god** (god) has remained unchanged for well over 1,000 years. The word's origin is unknown, although it has cognates in German, Norse, Danish and other Germanic languages. Even though Old English *god* (god, pronounced GOD) and *gōd* (good, pronounced GOAD) look very similar, they are pronounced differently and are etymologically unrelated. Godly names were common in early medieval England, both for men and women. A man might be called Godrīc (God-power) or Godwine (God-friend), while a woman might have the name Godgifu (God-gift).

Some words for the Christian God may have once been used in a pagan context. The word *metod*, for instance, means measurer. While the Christian *metod* (God) certainly could be said to measure out life, in pagan belief *metod* might have been a personification of fate, destiny or death. Other words for God also appear in secular contexts to describe men of wealth, status and power. A *healdend* (guardian) could be a secular ruler or protector, while a *hyrde* (keeper, guardian) could refer to a mortal herdsman or shepherd. Rulers on earth as well as the one in heaven go by titles like *dryhten* (lord, prince), *wealdend* (wielder of power), *frēa* (lord) and *þēoden* (prince, king, chief). (In his *Lord of the Rings*, Tolkien uses *þēoden* for the name of the King of Rohan: Théoden.) Sometimes a word that is normally secular is combined with another, like 'sky' or 'spirit', to form a divine compound. God is not just a king but a *swegel-cyning* (sky-king), *gāst-cyning* (spirit-king), *hēah-cyning* (high-king), and *wuldor-cyning* (glory-king).

Prayers can be directed to God (under any of his many aliases), but if he's not answering, your next-best bet is a *hālga* (saint). *Hālga* is derived from *hālig* (holy); a saint is someone who is holy, and a *hālga* is someone who is *hālig*. In Old English you also come across the word *sanct* (saint), from Latin *sanctus* (saint). At the end of the twelfth century, during the Middle English period, we start seeing 'seint' or 'sainte', adopted from the Old French of the Normans.

A *hālga* or *sanct* is an icon – religious and cultural. With their looks, power and fame, saints are the superheroes of the Middle Ages. The word 'icon' derives from Greek *eikōn* (likeness, image). In a religious context, an icon can be a representation of Christ, the Virgin Mary or a saint, like those you might see painted with oil on a wood panel. But more generally, an icon is a person or thing symbolising a belief, nation, people or culture. Captain America, for instance, was a popular icon of the United States during the 1940s, a patriotic supersoldier who fought against the Axis powers of World War II. His shield identified him as a protector or guardian. Superheroes like Captain America are often more recognisable from their insignia, costumes or weaponry than by unique facial features. You recognise Thor because of his hammer. You know Batman by his bat insignia.

And you know the *hālga* George by his *draca* (dragon, Chapter 9). In the time of the Roman Empire, St George was executed for refusing to worship the pagan gods. St George didn't worry about his death sentence. He distributed his wealth to the poor beforehand, and when the time came he was lacerated on a wheel of swords (during which he was resuscitated three times) and finally decapitated. These details, while moving and rather graphic, are not the *iconic* moment of his life. Today St George is the patron saint of England (as well as Ethiopia, Portugal, Palestine, Georgia, Lithuania, Greece, Germany and many other places), and he's pretty recognisable as saints go in the twenty-first century. But is this recognition due to imagery of him giving money to the poor or refusing to worship pagan gods? No – his iconic moment is slaying a *draca*!

A *hālga* also uses moments of vulnerability to exhibit their special **miht** (power). The iconic image of the *hālga* Sebastian has him bound to a stake or tree and shot through with arrows. Although the arrows make St Sebastian resemble an **igil** (hedgehog or porcupine), he is strong, fierce and undefeatable. He even survives this particular form of torture, although he is eventually beaten to death. But even in death he is victorious, his **sāwel** (soul) having gone straight to God.

A depiction of the *hālga* shot through with arrows thus reminds the viewer of this hero's extraordinary *miht*.

The *hālga* Guthlac is not as well known as the saints George and Sebastian are today, but he was certainly more relevant in early medieval England. Unlike England's patron saint (George, a Cappadocian Greek), Guthlac was born in England, or more accurately Mercia, one of the kingdoms in England before it was England. Guthlac, who was of noble birth, served in the Mercian army as a teenager in the late seventh century. At first it seemed Guthlac was more cut out for depravity than divinity. Young Guthlac formed a gang with other youths, and they attacked, raided and robbed neighbouring settlements. But one night an **engel** (angel) and a **dēofol** (devil) had a fight over his *sāwel*. The *engel* won, and Guthlac immediately committed himself to a life of asceticism and prayer. He became a *munuc* (monk, Chapter 4) at the age of twenty-four, but two years later he left his monastery, where the other monks resented him for being so provokingly penitent. (The guy wouldn't even drink alcohol!)

Guthlac became an **ān-būend** (hermit, 'one-dweller'), moving to a marshy island, a truly undesirable piece of real estate. It was here in Croyland (now Crowland) that he planned to live out a holy and ascetic life. He made a home for himself in an old barrow, a grave-mound that had been partially excavated by treasure-hunters. The devils who haunted the barrow attempted unsuccessfully to distract him from God. Guthlac responded by inviting the devils to torture him, saying, 'Go ahead and do your worst, if Christ allows you to lead his **wer-genga** to such a fate!' A *wer-genga* is a stranger who seeks protection in a strange land. Guthlac has entered a frightening land of devils, and he needs his *healdend* (guardian) to protect him from harm.

Guthlac's protection is not an army, not even a god, but an ever-growing host of 'spirit-mysteries'. A **gāst-gerȳne** (spirit-mystery)

Guthlac overcomes the demons on the 'Guthlac Roll' (so-called because it's
a roll of parchment, not a book)

is secret knowledge of God. To the devils who threaten him, Guthlac
says:

> Standing before you, I am not as destitute as I appear, without a host
> of men, for a greater contingent dwells and grows within me, sacred,
> <u>spiritual mysteries</u> (*gæstgerynum*) which guard me fiercely ... The
> doctrine within me comes from the heavens.

Many years later on his deathbed, Guthlac tells his disciple there is no reason to be concerned. He has pleased God with spiritual mysteries (*gæstgerynum*) for his entire life (well, perhaps not his teenage years), so he need not worry about meeting his maker. What exactly are these 'spirit-mysteries'? They give life meaning and get you into heaven, protecting you from devils along the way.

St Guthlac died in 714, after several days of conversing with angels. When his *sāwel* was ferried to heaven by angels, a mysterious glow, brighter than the sun, rose from his little hut up into the sky. A melody was in the air, the victory song of angels, as all of *heofon* rejoiced. A year after his death, his body was uncovered in pristine condition, perfectly preserved without a hint of decay. His saintliness was thus confirmed.

Born to be corn-wealthy

In the search for meaning in life, we might yearn to achieve something, whether that's a place in heaven or fame and fortune. We might be **georn** (pronounced YEH-orn) – eager to obtain or achieve something. A *feoh-georn* person is covetous and greedy. The word literally means 'cattle-eager' or 'money-eager'. (Remember from Chapter 2 that the primary definition of *feoh* is livestock or cattle, but it's also used to mean wealth or property.) *Feoh-georn* appears in the Old English version of the *Distichs of Cato*, a collection of proverbs from third- or fourth-century Rome:

> Woe to the nation that has a foreign king – immoderate, <u>eager for money</u> (*feohgeorne*), and merciless – because his greed will be on the people and his mind's discontent on his land.

A tenth-century homily warns against becoming *feoh-georn*, and bishops are similarly cautioned not to be *feoh-georn* and acquire wealth unjustly. If someone is eager to get going, they are ***fēþe-georn*** (walking-eager). If, on the other hand, they are eager to sit around doing nothing, they are ***īdel-georn*** (idle-eager). An *īdel-georn* individual should heed this proverb:

> Be neither too addicted to sleep nor too <u>idle-eager</u> (*idelgeorn*), because sleep and idleness bring bad habits and infirmity of the body.

A philanthropic sort of person might be described as ***ælmes-georn*** (alms-eager), diligent in giving alms or charity to those in need. Someone who is ***fyrwit-georn*** (knowledge-eager) wants to learn all they can. The ***friþ-georn*** (peace-eager) make good diplomats. In spite of the suffering that awaits the wicked in hell, the world still has people who are ***firen-georn*** (sin-eager). A poem about Judgement Day warns that hell will be open and visible, 'so that <u>sin-eager</u> (*firengeorne*) men must fill it with their dark souls'.

Those who yearn (who are *georn*, YEH-orn) for renown and prestige are either ***dōm-georn*** (fame-eager) or ***gylp-georn*** (glory-eager). The *dōm-georn* crave fame that they deserve, something that is less important to the *gylp-georn*. The *gylp-georn* are vainglorious, living for the opportunity to boast. The ***lof-georn*** (love-eager) desire praise above all else, whether it is in a *dōm-georn* or *gylp-georn* way. *Beowulf* ends with these final words of tribute to the hero:

> So the Geat people, <u>hearth-companions</u> (*heorðgeneatas*: see *heorþ-genēat*, Chapter 6), lamented the fall of their lord. They said that of all the kings of the world, he was the mildest of men and the most gracious, the kindest to his people and the <u>most eager for praise</u> (*lofgeornost*).

Beowulf is admired not only for his brave deeds but for his desire to be loved and praised. Perhaps he sounds needy, but in the world of the poem this quality is indicative of a good leader.

The eagerness for fame, glory and praise was a heroic ideal of the pagan world which did not fit as well into the Christian one. Ælfric of Eynsham lists the 'eight chief sins that assail us greatly'. Better known today as the Seven Deadly Sins, Ælfric's *eahta heafodleahtras* (eight head-sins) are based on earlier classifications. (In the fourth century, the Christian monk Evagrius Ponticus allegedly came up with the Eight Evil Thoughts or Eight Terrible Temptations.) Ælfric's Eight Chief Sins are **gīfernes** (gluttony), **for-legnes** (fornication), **gītsung** (greed), **wēamōdness** (anger), **un-rōtness** (sorrow), **slǣwþ** (sloth), **īdel-gylp** (vainglory) and **mōdig-ness** (pride). *Īdel-gylp* describes someone who is *lofgeorn*, 'praise-eager' and hypocritical, who only performs good deeds for the sake of their own glory. 'Fame', Ælfric warns, 'is the reward for his deeds, and his punishment awaits in the future world.'

Whatever you yearn for in life, the one thing everyone wishes for is to be **ge-sǣlig** (pronounced yeh-SAE-lih). *Ge-sǣlig* has a range of pleasant meanings: cheerful, prosperous, blessed, fortunate. The word vanished from English but happily survived in Scots as 'seil' or 'sele'. William Alexander, a Scottish novelist, uses it in *Sketches of Life Among My Ain Folk* (1875), when a bellman remarks of a married couple, 'Seil, upo' them, they're a winsome pair' (good luck to them, they're a lovely couple). A **weorold-gesǣlig** person prospers in worldly goods; they are 'world-blessed' or 'world-wealthy'.

Corn-gesǣlig also means prosperous, but more literally it's 'corn-wealthy', fortunate to have plenty of corn (which used to be grain, not what we think of today as 'corn'). *Corn-gesǣlig* appears in a prognostic text, another lunarium like those in Chapter 8. A boy born on the ninth day of the lunar cycle would supposedly be *corn-gesǣlig*, as well as calm, clever and strong. True, he will suffer (non-specific) troubles until his seventh year of age, but if he makes it to thirty he will be a *ge-sælig* man indeed!

Contemplating the dust

No matter what we strive for in life, mortality awaits the poor and the *corn-gesælig* alike. From dust we come and to dust we shall return.

Old English **dūst** can refer to dust, ashes or powder; the remains of a disintegrating or decaying substance; or the material from which the human body is made, to which it returns and from which it will rise again. As we saw in Chapter 7, the poets of early medieval England had a real knack for evoking the physicality of a mortal existence. In *Soul and Body II*, the fierce *wyrmas* have a field day chewing up a decaying corpse, while the body is unable to speak or act. The mortal body can only suffer, while the immortal soul is destined for hell. The poem ends with a solemn warning that the body will eventually be worms' food, sustenance in the earth. In the end, the damned soul will revile its useless, rotting body: 'To everyone wise of mind', the poem says, 'may this be a reminder.'

Reading such a poem is one way to practise **dūst-scēawung** (dust-viewing). The hapax *dūst-scēawung* appears in an anonymous homily, in which a man visits his friend's grave. Longing for his old companion, he realises that in the end the body turns to dust. The dry bones of his dead friend, who was once a wealthy man, speak to him:

> <u>Oh</u> (*Eala*), my <u>friend</u> (*freond*) and kinsman! Be mindful of this. See for yourself that what you are now is what I was formerly. And after a time, you will be what I am now.

When the living man hears these words, he departs from his *dūst-scēawung*, sorrowful and grief-stricken. But after seeing himself as *dūst* he is able to turn away from all transient, worldly affairs. While you may not have had a conversation with the bones of a dead friend, you have probably seen a gravestone with a skull or hourglass. These symbols are part of our own *dūst-scēawung*, which is the same idea as *memento mori* (Latin for 'remember death'). *Memento mori*, a phrase that refers to a warning or reminder of death's inevitability, entered English in the sixteenth century, after the Middle Ages, but the concept goes back to classical antiquity.

Although death's shadow is never far away, the word **dēaþ-scūa** (death-shadow) appears only twice in Old English. Once is in *Beowulf*, when Grendel is described as a *deorc deaþscua* (dark death-shadow), a suitable epithet for a creature that lurks, plotting murderous attacks, ruling the misty moors at night. The second occurrence is in a psalm, although *not* the more familiar Psalm 22: 'For though I should walk in the midst of the shadow of death, I will fear no evils, for thou art with me.' In the Old English translation of this psalm, 'shadow of death' is a direct translation of the Latin (*umbrae mortis*), written as two separate words (*sceadue deaþes*), not as a compound word. The compound word *dēaþ-scūa* actually appears in Psalm 6. The Latin says:

> *Quoniam non est in morte qui memor sit tui*
> (For there is no one in death who is mindful of you).

The Old English is slightly different:

> *Forþan þe nis on deaþe ł on deaðscufan þe gemyndig sy þin*
> (For there is no one in death or death-shadow who is mindful of you).

The ł is shorthand for Latin *vel* (or). For whatever reason, the scribe decided 'death' on its own was not enough and further emphasised the word with 'death-shadow'. Or perhaps *dēaþ-scūa* could mean something like 'not-quite-death', with only death's shadow falling upon the dying person.

Death, whether or not it has a shadow, is inevitable, out of human control. This is **wyrd**, often translated as 'destiny' or 'fate' but really meaning something more prosaic like 'what happens'. A **wyrd-writere** (*wyrd*-writer) is a historian, someone who writes an account of things that happen. In King Alfred's translation of Boethius's *Consolation of Philosophy*, *wyrd* is defined as 'God's work that he does every day, both what we see and what is invisible to us'. *Wyrd* is different from a divine plan: God the craftsman may think about and plan his work before undertaking the work itself. Forethought or providence is the divine plan, while *wyrd* is what happens when God's plan is carried out.

Wyrd may or may not have originally been a pagan term. Hardly anything is known about the religious beliefs of pagans in early medieval England. Scholars who argue in favour of *wyrd*'s pagan origin point out the word's etymological relation to Old Norse *Urðr*, one of the Norns, the three women who govern fate in Scandinavian mythology. By the Old English period, however, *wyrd* would primarily have been an abstract concept, not a deity. Some scholars argue that *wyrd* is strictly Christian, but that is not necessarily the case either. Whether Christian or pagan, *wyrd* is etymologically connected to **weorþan** (to become, to happen). *Wyrd* is inevitable; as Beowulf says, '*Wyrd* always goes as it must.' *Wyrd* is decreed to humans by the *metod*, the 'measurer' of life.

Another name for the Norns was the 'thre werd systeris', for by the end of the medieval period, the adjective 'weird' had come to mean 'having the power to control the fate or destiny of human beings'. These 'Weird Sisters' appear in Shakespeare's *Macbeth*, first performed in 1606. But now in modern English 'weird' is an adjective meaning 'strange' or 'unusual'.

Wyrd cannot be altered by a person who is doomed to die. Such a person is **fǣge** (fated to die), usually in battle or combat or by the judgement of God. *Fǣge* eventually became modern English 'fey'. During the nineteenth century, the word 'fey' acquired a new meaning – possessing or displaying magical, fairylike or unearthly qualities – which is generally how it's defined today. According to the heroine of Marie Corelli's *The Secret Power*, a 1920s sci-fi romance, 'fey' people are magic: 'they see what no one else sees, – they hear voices that no one else hears – voices that whisper secrets and tell of wonders as yet undiscovered'. But a *fǣge* person in early medieval England wasn't magical, only doomed.

Before his battle with Grendel, Beowulf says, 'Wyrd often saves an *unfǣgne* man when his bravery avails', the adjective **un-fǣge** being the opposite of *fǣge*. The causality here is a bit ambiguous: is the man saved by *wyrd* because he is *un-fǣge*, or is he *un-fǣge* because *wyrd* saved him? Is the warrior simply *un-fǣge* until he happens to die one day, or was the curse of being *fǣge* undone on the battlefield by *wyrd*? Beowulf's words could be interpreted in different ways, their exact meaning uncertain. Either way, whether Christian or pagan, immediate or delayed, *wyrd* is neither good nor bad in nature. It's simply what happens.

Even the strongest, bravest hero of Old English literature is helpless against *wyrd*. Beowulf speaks these final words as he lies dying from a mortal wound: 'Wyrd swept away all my relations, decreed death to men of valour. And I must follow them.'

Twelfth *wordhord*

ān-būend, noun (AHN-BOO-end / ˈaːn-ˌbuːɛnd): Hermit (one-dweller).
ælmes-georn, adjective (AL-mez-YEH-orn / ˈælmɛz-ˌjɛɔrn): Diligent in giving alms, benevolent.
brim-hlæst, noun (BRIM-H'LAST / ˈbrɪm-ˌhlæst): Fish (sea-cargo).
corn-gesælig, adjective (KORN-yeh-SAE-lih / ˈkɔrn-jɛ-ˌsæː-lɪj): Wealthy in corn or grain.

cristen-dōm, noun (KRIS-ten-DOAM / ˈkrɪs-tɛn-ˌdoːm): Christianity, the Christian faith.

dēaþ-scūa, noun (DAY-ath-SHOO-ah / ˈdeːaθ-ˌʃuːa): Shadow of death, death.

dēofol, noun (DAY-oh-voll / ˈdeːɔ-vɔl): Devil, demon; Satan, the Devil.

dōm-georn, adjective (DOAM-YEH-orn / ˈdoːm-ˌjɛɔrn): Eager for (deserved) renown.

dryhten, noun (DRUE-h'ten / ˈdryx-tɛn): Ruler, lord, prince; the Lord (God or Christ).

dūst, noun (DOOST / ˈduːst): Dust (of the earth); dust or ashes; what anything is reduced to by disintegration or decay; material out of which the human body is made (to which it returns and from which it will arise again).

dūst-scēawung, noun (DOOST-SHAY-ah-wung / ˈduːst-ˌʃeːa-wʌŋ): 'Dust-viewing', observation or contemplation of dust (visiting a grave or considering one's mortality).

engel, noun (ENG-gell / ˈɛŋ-gɛl): Angel.

fǣge, adjective (FAE-yuh / ˈfæː-jə): About to die; doomed.

feoh-georn, adjective (FEH-oh-YEH-orn / ˈfeːɔx-ˌjɛɔrn): Covetous, avaricious, desirous of money.

fēðe-georn, adjective (FAY-thuh-YEH-orn / ˈfeː-θə-ˌjɛɔrn): Desirous of going.

firen-georn, adjective (FI-ren-YEH-orn / ˈfɪ-rɛn-ˌjɛɔrn): Sinful, wicked (sin-eager).

for-legnes, noun (for-LEY-ness / fɔr-ˈlɛj-nɛs): Fornication, adultery.

frēa, noun (FRAY-ah / ˈfreːa): Lord, master, the Lord.

friþ-georn, adjective (FRITH-YEH-orn / ˈfrɪθ-ˌjɛɔrn): Eager for peace; peaceable, peace-making.

fyrwit-georn, adjective (FUER-wit-YEH-orn / ˈfyr-wɪt-ˌjɛɔrn): Curious, inquisitive, eager for knowledge.

gāst-cyning, noun (GAHST-KUE-ning / ˈgaːst-ˌky-niŋ): Spirit-king, God.

gāst-gerȳne, noun (GAHST-yeh-RUE-nuh / ˈɡaːst-jɛ-ˌryː-nə): Spiritual mystery.

georn, adjective (YEH-orn / ˈjɛɔrn): Eager, desirous; eager for, desirous of; diligent, zealous.

ge-sǣlig, adjective (yeh-SAE-lih / jɛ-ˈsæː-lɪj): Happy, prosperous, blessed, fortunate.

gīfernes, noun (YEE-ver-ness / ˈjiː-vɛr-nɛs): Gluttony.

gītsung, noun (YEET-zung / ˈjiːt-zʌŋ): Greed, covetousness.

god, noun (GOD / ˈɡɔd): God, a god.

gōd, adjective (GOAD / ˈɡoːd): Good.

gylp-georn, adjective (YUELP-YEH-orn / ˈjylp-ˌjɛɔrn): Vainglorious, arrogant, proud; eager for glory.

hālga, noun (HALL-ga / ˈhaːl-ga): Saint, holy person.

hālig, adjective (HALL-ih / ˈhaː-lɪj): Holy.

hǣþen, adjective (HATH-en / ˈhæː-θɛn): Heathen, pagan, not Christian.

hēah-cyning, noun (HAY-ah-KUE-ning / ˈheːax-ˌky-nɪŋ): High-king, God.

healdend, noun (HEH-all-dend / ˈhɛal-dɛnd): Protector, guardian, ruler.

hell, noun (HELL / ˈhɛl): Hell.

heofon, noun (HEH-oh-von / ˈhɛɔ-vɔn): Heaven.

hlæst, noun (H'LAST / ˈhlæst): Load, cargo, freight, burden.

hyrde, noun (HUER-duh / ˈhyr-də): Herdsman; keeper, guardian.

īdel-georn, adjective (EE-dell-YEH-orn / ˈiː-dɛl-ˌjɛɔrn): Gladly at leisure, keen to be idle.

īdel-gylp, noun (EE-dell-YUELP / ˈiː-dɛl-ˌjylp): Vainglory, vain pride, idle boasting.

igil, noun (IH-yill / ˈɪ-jɪl): Hedgehog or porcupine.

lof-georn, adjective (LOV-YEH-orn / ˈlɔv-ˌjɛɔrn): Desirous of praise; (in a good sense) eager to deserve praise; (in a bad sense) ostentatious, boastful.

metod, noun (MEH-tod / ˈmɛ-tɔd): Measurer, Lord; (in pagan context) fate, destiny.

miht, noun (MIʼHT / ˈmɪxt): Power, might.

mōdig-ness, noun (MO-di-ness / ˈmoː-dɪj-nɛs): Pride.

sanct, noun (SAHNKT / ˈsankt): Saint.

sāwel, noun (SAH-well / ˈsaː-wɛl): Soul.

slǣwþ, noun (SLAEWTH / ˈslæːwθ): Sloth, laziness.

swegel-cyning, noun (SWEH-yell-KUE-ning / ˈswɛ-jɛl-ˌky-niŋ): Sky-king, heaven-king, God.

þēoden, noun (THAY-oh-den / ˈθeːɔ-dɛn): Prince, king, chief, lord; God, Christ.

un-fǣge, adjective (UN-FAE-yuh / ˈʌn-ˌfæː-jə): Not doomed or fated to die.

un-rōtness, noun (UN-ROAT-ness / ˈʌn-ˌroːt-nɛs): Sorrow.

wealdend, noun (WEH-all-dend / ˈwɛal-dɛnd): Ruler, sovereign, lord; Lord, God.

wēamōdness, noun (WAY-ah-MOAD-ness / ˈweːa-ˌmoːd-nɛs): Anger.

weorold-gesǣlig, adjective (WEH-oh-rold-yeh-SAE-lih / ˈwɛɔ-rɔld-jɛ-ˌsæː-lɪj): Blessed with worldly goods, prosperous.

weorþan, verb (WEH-or-than / ˈwɛɔr-θan): To become, happen, befall, come to pass.

wer-genga, noun (WER-YENG-ga / ˈwɛr-ˌjɛŋ-ga): Stranger who seeks protection in the land to which they have come.

wuldor-cyning, noun (WUL-dor-KUE-ning / ˈwʌl-dɔr-ˌky-niŋ): Glory-king, God.

wyrd, noun (WUERD / ˈwyrd): Fate, fortune, chance; event, occurrence, circumstance; what happens (to a person), lot, condition.

wyrd-writere, noun (WUERD-WRI-teh-ruh / ˈwyrd-ˌwrɪ-tɛ-rə): One who writes an account of events, historian, historiographer.

13

Hoarding Words

In the beginning was the word

ON FRYMÐE WÆS WORD, begins the Gospel of John: 'In the beginning was the Word.' Much has changed in the centuries since the medieval scribe wrote this sentence in Old English – from our relationship to religion to our tools for writing and the language we use – but one thing has remained the same: the word 'word'. A love of words themselves is, of course, where this book began, and now also where it ends.

'Word' may be first in the Bible, but it comes second in life. A word names that which already exists, and even in the Old English sentence above, *word* is standing in for something else. The scribe is translating the Latin word *verbum*, which is itself a translation of Greek *logos*. Although this is a conventional translation, if we look closer we find that *logos* doesn't really mean 'word' in the grammatical sense. Instead, it is 'the word or that by which the inward thought is expressed' or 'the inward thought itself'. *Logos* is thought and reason.

So even though 'logophile' (first used in English in the 1950s) is defined as 'a lover of words', the term more accurately describes a lover of thought. Words and thoughts in this sense become interchangeable: after all, words are a human's means of under-standing the world, the thoughts of one *reord-berend* (speech-bearer, Chapter 11) shared with another. When a thought is locked away in the mind, unable to be communicated to others, it is beyond words. In Old English the sublime power of God is **un-āsecgendlīc** (ineffable). Something *un-āsecgendlīc* is so great that it's beyond the powers of lan-guage to describe – one cannot or should not speak of it. For people in the Middle Ages it was God's mysteries that were truly 'beyond words'.

Words in Old English are powerful and precious. A **word-samnere** (word-gatherer) amasses treasured words in their **word-loca** (word-locker). Why? Is it a need for a varied and evocative *wordhord*? Is a stockpile of fancy phrases more likely to be rewarded with a **word-lēan** (word-reward), compensation in money or mead? No. Words are valuable in and of themselves. Each word carries a story, an entire his-tory of thoughts. In fact, the Old English word *word* can mean 'story' as well as 'word' or 'speech' (so perhaps it's not a bad translation of Greek *logos* after all).

Words also have the power to conjure a story, to create worlds. Such worlds may have been created in oral poetry many centuries prior to their preservation in writing (if they made it into written record at all). Indeed, words don't need to be written down to be powerful. The earliest known Old English poem is from the seventh century, supposedly com-posed by an illiterate cowherd named Cædmon. In a divine vision, the young cowherd was commanded to sing, and sing he did, so impressively that Abbess Hild invited him to join her monastery at Whitby. Cædmon's spoken words have great power, and the purpose of his **glīw-word** (song-word: see *glīw*, Chapter 5) is to worship God with joyous music. So many words have the power to do positive things like this. A **here-word** (praise-word) praises those who have earned our admiration and esteem. A **frōfor-word** (comfort-word) consoles a troubled friend. A **þanc-word** (thank-word) shows gratitude to those who have helped and supported us.

But as with any powerful tool, a word can also be used to harm others. Along with the stories of the *scop*, words can conjure up powerful spells and dark magic. A sorcerer may commit evil deeds by uttering a **galdor-word** (incantation-word). Today 'cutting words' wound with the acerbity of a clever insult, but before the cutting word was Old English **heoru-word**: fierce or hostile speech. *Heoru-word*'s literal translation is 'sword-word', so it seems that harsh language has always been metaphorically sharp. Other words meant to cause harm are the **hosp-word** and **sceand-word** (SHEH-ond-WORD), both of which mean 'shame-word'. You might speak a 'shame-word' to your *un-wine* (un-friend, Chapter 6), an insult to demonstrate your contempt. Or perhaps you would use a **torn-word** (grief-word) on your mission to cause distress, sorrow or anger. **Torn** is passionate anger or grief, violent emotions that tear you apart. (It likely shares an ancestor with **teran**, 'to tear'.) When his virgin wife Mary becomes pregnant, Joseph moans that he is 'bereft of reputation', for many a *torn-word* has been directed his way, shameful insults from his community. (This is of course before he discovers that Mary will give birth to the Son of God.)

If words cause anger, shame or grief, emotions that tear you apart, they are also the means of expressing and sharing the pain of those feelings. A **sorh-word** (sorrow-word) conveys a potent mixture of anxiety and grief. Like shame-words and grief-words, sorrow-words aren't specific words that you say; rather, they are a way of describing a kind of speech. We might think that 'Alas!' or 'Oh no!' are modern-day sorrow-words, but really *sorh-word* describes the conversation you have at a loved one's funeral, or the report you hear about a tragic accident. In the poem *Genesis B*, Adam and Eve exchange a *sorh-word* after eating from the Tree of Knowledge, when they realise they have failed to obey God's command, God's word. The poet doesn't tell us precisely what words they speak, only that the emotion conveyed by those words is sorrow.

As powerful as words may be, they are only as good as the deeds that prove them. If you break your promises, after all, you are no better than a wretched *wǣr-loga* (oath-breaker, Chapter 11). The very first clause of the law code of King Alfred emphasises how important it is to be true to one's word: 'At first, we teach what is most necessary, that each man carefully keep his <u>oath</u> (*að*) and his <u>pledge</u> (*wed*).' (Remember *wed-lāc* from Chapter 11?) A boast is perfectly acceptable in Old English poetry, as long as you are true to your word. Beowulf speaks a ***gilp-word*** (boast-word) when he says he'll fight Grendel solo and unarmed. By this point in the poem, his audience knows that such speech is no empty promise: truly boast-worthy action has been seen. Later, at the end of the poem, Beowulf utters a ***bēot-word*** (boast-word or threat-word) at the start of his fight with the dragon, perhaps intending to egg the angry *wyrm* on. But as soon as his boast or threat is made, Beowulf must die to keep his ***āþ*** (oath) and his ***wed*** (pledge), at least if he wishes to be remembered as a hero.

One type of *āþ* in early medieval England was the ***wit-word*** – literally 'a word of ***wit*** (intelligence, understanding)' – but this is no clever remark or bon mot. A *wit-word* is actually a 'witness-word', a word that appears in Old English laws and charters, including the law code of King Æthelred. The Wantage Code, as it is called, was issued at the town of Wantage in Oxfordshire in 997, containing what is possibly the earliest description of a jury of presentment, when a jury of witnesses vouches for the innocence of the accused. The Wantage Code lists rights that must stand and 'not be perverted', including the rights to *wit-word* (testimony on the character of the accused) and ***ge-witnes*** (the testimony of witnesses who can confirm or deny the charge from personal observation).

If Old English *wit-word* was a way of resolving conflicts while alive, by the sixteenth century it had become a way of settling disputes once you were dead. In Shakespeare's time, modern English 'wytword' was still around, but by then it meant 'will' or 'testament'. (A will or testament in Old English, incidentally, is **irfe-gewrit**, literally 'inheritance-writing'.) So over the centuries an 'understanding-word' (word of *wit*) went from being a *wit-word* (the word of others) to a 'wytword' (the last words of one's life).

The last words of your life may be the prosaic, practical directions of an *irfe-gewrit*, but last words like these probably won't be famous. In the beginning was the word . . . but often the most important words of a story come at the very end. Last words can be memorable but also greatly formulaic. Today's fairy tales often end with the predictable and conclusive 'and they lived happily ever after'. The last words of Old English poetry are similar, though the medieval 'happily ever after' is not earthly life in a treasure-filled castle with Prince Charming. In Old English 'happily ever after' is eternal life in heaven with God and his angels. Like ever-afters, Old English's endings often refer to the *ēce* (eternal), with phrases like *a on ecnysse* (always in eternity), *sið and ær* (early and late, i.e. at all times), *ealne widan ferh* (for all of life's expanse) and *butan ende* (without end). These stories also end happily, with **bliss** (joy), *lufu* (love, Chapter 6), **wuldor** (glory) and **blǣd** (prosperity), all of which can be found *on heofona rice* (in the kingdom of heaven). But unlike the conclusions of most fairy tales, these Old English endings tend to move away from one specific story about an individual to stories that stretch across time and space: *ofer middangeard* (across the middle-world), or in *ealra worulda woruld* (the world of all worlds, i.e. world without end, forever and ever).

Last words and *lāst-word*

Today the word 'amen' is usually thought of as the last word of a prayer or blessing or maybe a sermon. **Āmen** came to English via Latin and Greek, from Hebrew *ā-mēn* meaning 'certainty' or 'truth'.

The image opposite from the Lindisfarne Gospels shows *amen* concluding the Gospel of Luke. The Latin text was written down during the eighth century, but the Old English glosses (translations in between the lines) were added in the tenth century.

> Latin: *et erant semper in templo laudantes et benedicentes deum <u>amen</u>*
> Old English: *ond woeron symble in tempel lofando ond gebloedsando god <u>soðlice</u>.*
> (And they were always in the temple, praising and blessing God, <u>amen</u>.)

Āmen eventually became an Old English word in its own right, not just a Latin word, so it's interesting to see how, even as late as the tenth century, a scribe felt the need to translate it using a word more familiar to *englisc* speakers: **sōþlīce** (truly). The word **sōþ** (truth) turned into modern English 'sooth', a word that became obsolete in the seventeenth century, although it survives today as the 'sooth' in 'soothsayer', a person who claims to be able to tell the future or the truth about the world. 'Forsooth' came to be a way of expressing derision or disbelief, but it literally means 'in truth' or 'truly'.

Although today 'amen' is a way of expressing agreement in non-religious contexts ('amen to that'), it is still used primarily as a response in church to prayers, sermons and confessions of faith. But in the Old Testament the word 'amen' actually appears in a curse, with the meaning 'may it be so' or 'so be it'. This happens in Old English curses as well. A document concerning a land dispute around the year 1000 concludes thus:

> If anyone thinks to turn from this and break from this agreement, God will turn his face from him at the great judgement, so that he will be cut off from the joy of the kingdom of heaven and be entrusted to all the devils in hell, <u>amen</u> (*amen*).

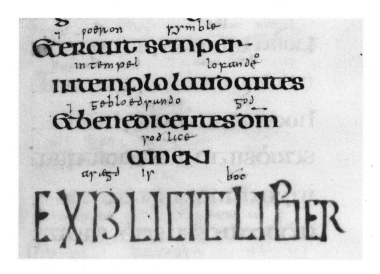

Ending of the Gospel of Luke in the Lindisfarne Gospels. Latin *amen* is
glossed with Old English *soðlice*.

This curse follows the document's list of witnesses and, in a sense, the
word *āmen* makes God a witness to the decision as well. In the New
Testament Christ is even referred to as the 'Amen', since he is the guar-
antee of God's promises. Today breaking a contract is merely met with
legal action – surely the threat of all the devils in hell on Judgement
Day is a far greater incentive to keep your promises!

In addition to prayers and legal agreements, Old English *āmen* can
also conclude leechbook remedies. One remedy instructs:

If a man is <u>month-sick</u> (a lunatic: see *mōnaþsēoc-ness*, Chapter 7): Take
the skin of a porpoise, work it like a whip, and beat the man with it.
Soon he will be well, <u>amen</u> (*amen*).

Āmen is not a common ending in this genre, and this is the only example of it in this particular leechbook. Why did the scribe use it here? Perhaps the porpoise-skin beating seemed a dubious remedy, and the scribe thought a confirmation of truth would give it more authority.

Āmen can also be a visual signal that you've reached the end of a piece of writing. Beginnings and endings are not always obvious in Old English texts. In the Lindisfarne Gospels example on the previous page, the manuscript has a page break before beginning the next text, but sometimes a new text will pick up right on the following line. As we saw in Chapter 1, Old English texts do not usually have titles, so they must use other ways to indicate where one's reading should start and finish. In the Gospel of Nicodemus example opposite, the scribe has made it easier for a *munuc* or *nunne* flipping through the pages to spot the ending: there is a large, capitalised *AMEN* before it picks up on the next line with a large letter H. Here *AMEN* works the same way the words 'THE END' do for us.

But if not with a confirmation of truth, an *āmen* or a *sōþlīce*, how else might a medieval writer conclude a text? Riddles sometimes end with a command: *Saga hwæt ic hatte* (say what I am called). The more optimistic of the leechbook remedies end with *Him bið sona sel* (he will be better soon). The poem *Deor* ends with a unique line of pragmatism: *Þæs ofereode, þisses swa mæg* (that passed, so may this). *Beowulf* concludes with an elegy to its hero that is packed with superlatives:

> They said that of all the kings of the world he was the <u>mildest</u> (*mildust*: most **milde**) and <u>gentlest</u> (*monðwærust*: most **mann-þwǣre**) of men, the <u>kindest</u> (*liðost*: most *līðe*, Chapter 3) to his people, and the <u>most eager for fame</u> (*lofgeornost*: most *lof-georn*, Chapter 12).

The poem *Precepts* ends with a father's warning to his child to stay out of trouble: 'So you, my child, remember the teaching of your

...wæs. hys þegn to hyre ... ge seten ...
wæron ... feower getog cempena þe ðone lichaman
healdan sceoldon. Ac he on ðam þriddan dæge
of deaðe aras. ⁊ þa hyrdas hyt eall asædon ⁊
hyt for helan ne mihton. Ac þa iudeas þa
hyg þæge hyrdon. hyg ðam hyrdon feohgea-
fon. ⁊ hyg þ secgan sceoldon þ hys cnihtas co-
mon ⁊ þone lichaman forstælon ⁊ þa hyrdas þa þ feoh on fengon ⁊ hyg swa þeh þa soð-
fæstnysse þe ðeah ge woldon þæs for supian
ne mihton. Nu leof cyning ic þe eac lære for-
ðig þ ðu næfre ðeam iudea leasunga ne ge-
lyfe. Sy drihtne lof ⁊ deoflum seoþh a to
worulde AMEN.

Her kið hu saturnus ⁊ salomon ferdde
ymbe heora wisdom. þa cwæt saturnus to
salomane.

age me hwæt god sette þa he ge worhte heo

Ending of the Old English Gospel of Nicodemus, with the beginning of the
prose *Solomon and Saturn*

wise old father, and keep yourself out of wickedness!' And who could fault the genuine admiration conveyed in final sentences like *Þæt is æðele cyning* (that is a noble king) or *Þæt is æþele stenc* (that is a noble fragrance). (The latter describes the breath of the Panther, who featured in Chapter 6.) So while there is some repetition, like the happily-ever-afters of today's fairy tales, not every Old English ending is formulaic.

If the language of a text wasn't always repetitive, the scribe's back-breaking labour certainly was. Some scribes even ended their texts with a gentle reminder to the reader of the work involved in copying out a text by hand. At the end of Ælfric of Eynsham's brief summary of scientific knowledge, a scribe bemoans his inevitable repetitive strain injury:

Ending of Ælfric's *De temporibus anni* in Old English

Sy þeos gesetnys þus her geendod. God helpe minum handum.
May this composition be ended here thus. God help my hands.

The weary scribes had at least three more centuries to go before the arrival of the printing press in England.

In a tenth-century manuscript from further afield, the Spanish scribe Florentius finished copying a commentary on the Old Testament's long-suffering Job. Perhaps identifying too much with his scriptural subject matter, Florentius complains bitterly about his clouded eyes, his hunched shoulders, even his pained kidneys, and then warns the reader to treat their work with appropriate care. A careless reader could ruin the precious parchment with their rough page-turning and spoil the vivid inks with their grubby fingers.

Sometimes a scribe signed off with a straightforward request for a prayer. A tenth-century English manuscript ends: 'Whoever may read this book, pray for the soul of Sigestan who wrote me. Amen.' Sigestan (whose name means 'victory-stone') had just finished copying out a lengthy treatise on the nature of the Eucharist, so a prayer seems a reasonable enough request.

Not all extant texts have endings. The poem *Waldere* survives on two sheets of vellum that had been used to pad the binding of a later printed book. The beginning and ending of the poem are lost, and even the proper sequence of the two pages is uncertain. Another poem, with the fitting modern title of *The Ruin*, is so badly damaged that its final words must be based more on conjecture than on substance. A poem about St Guthlac must have had an ending at one time, but at some point the single page it survives on was carelessly trimmed. Its last legible words are *hyge drusendne*, leaving the text to trail off with a 'languishing heart'. The manuscript that contained *The Battle of Maldon* burned in the Ashburnham House library fire of 1731 (the same fire that singed *Beowulf*). All that remains of the poem is a librarian's transcription from a few years prior to the fire, and even then it lacked a beginning and ending. With this poem, like so many Old English texts, we begin (to borrow the Latin) *in media res* and end with uncertainty, the rest of the narrative lost to history. But the lack of an ending doesn't diminish it – after all, these fragments and partial glimpses, torn manuscripts and burned books are the same texts which have taught modern scholars to read and understand Old English. Even if we don't always know their last words, the words they do offer enrich our understanding.

This book has been full of those words, and now it's time for one more which has barely changed since its first use – **ende** (end)

– although in Old English it has some different permutations. An **ende-mann** is a person who lives in this day and age, during the 'final age' of the world. Anyone who lives before the end of days is an *ende-mann*, and since we're not there yet, that includes modern readers too. The final day of your life is your **ende-dæg** (end-day) or **ende-tīma** (end-time). The **woruld-ende** is the end of the world, and an **ears-endu** (EH-arz-EN-duh) is the end of . . . well, it's obvious isn't it (and it's not the ears). The next time someone is being a pain in the arse, you could call them this or even **end-wærc** (end-pain). Although those last two sound like insults – and for all we know could have been – *ears-endu* appears only in Latin-English glossaries and *end-wærc* is a hapax in a leechbook.

The **ende-mest** (endmost) part of a book – and yes, you're almost there – is not the same as a **lāst-word**, though it is at this point that thoughts might turn to the latter. Rather than 'last' or 'final', Old English **lāst** means 'track' or 'step'. A *lāst-word* isn't a 'last word' but a 'track-word', the story a person leaves in their tracks. Today we might call such a story one's 'reputation' or 'legacy'. The poem *The Seafarer* describes the ideal *lāst-word*, the one to which we should all aspire:

> For each man, the <u>best of reputations</u> (*lastworda betst*) is the praise of the living, those who speak after his death. Before departing he should perform good deeds on earth, oppose the malice of enemies, and do brave deeds against the Devil. Children of men shall praise him afterwards, and his glory will endure forever and ever among hosts of angels, the joyous splendour of eternal life.

A text like *The Seafarer* encourages readers to consider what our 'track-words' might be: what will be the legacies we hand down, the impressions left by our words? Your *lāst-word* or reputation is made from the stories of others, the words people say about you. Whether a ruler

concerned with preserving the law, a physician having their remedies transcribed for wider transmission or a cheeky scribe making sure
their own name lives on, as *reord-berend*, speech-bearers, people have a
tendency to leave word-tracks. Indeed, along with archaeology, word-
tracks are the reason we know anything about early medieval England.

Old English words were left behind by a society where most people
were peasants, where kings held power, where monks hoarded literacy. These words tell a story about the English language, how the language of *Beowulf* morphed into the words and phrases we use today.
They also reveal piece by piece the history of the people who inhabited early medieval England, how they worked and played, imagined
and prayed – the history of their thoughts. This history is incomplete,
as histories inevitably are. The thoughts of most people were not
recorded in writing, or if they were, the books that held them have
been lost. Literacy was far from universal. All those unspoken words
leave gaps in our knowledge of this time and these people, no matter
how adamantly a scribe might insist that he or she writes truly, *sōþlīce*.

But the joy of words has its own kind of truth; it is personal and
immediate. For me, this joy comes from finding a word from another
place, and in this case another time, that captures your *logos*, your
thought, so perfectly. Perhaps when one language doesn't have a word
that conveys the thought you wish to express, another one does.

The thoughts I associate with a particular Old English word are
undoubtedly different from those of a tenth-century reader. At the
turn of the first millennium, a *morgen-drenc* (Chapter 2) might refer
to a specific medicinal potion concocted for a king, but today it is a
wonderful description of my morning coffee. The worries and anx-
ieties that keep me awake at three in the morning are not the same
ūht-cearu (Chapter 3) of the medieval woman's lament, but there is no
better word for them today. Perhaps if I see an *āglǣca* (hostile fighter,
Chapter 11) as neither friend nor foe, but as someone with the capacity

for both wickedness and heroism, I can understand an unfriendly 'other' more fully. The jubilation I feel upon nearing the end of this book, completing my labour of love, requires the double-joy of the word *wyn-drēam* (Chapter 5), for *wynn* (joy) is insufficient on its own. Perhaps you feel a little *wyn-drēam* too, having reached the end at last . . . and with a greatly expanded *wordhord*. And I'm certain there was a medieval scribe or two who felt *wyn-drēam* upon reaching the end of their own lengthy tomes. Truly.

Thirteenth *wordhord*

āmen, interjection (AH-men / ˈaː-mɛn): Amen.

āþ, noun (AWTH / ˈaːθ): Oath.

bēot-word, noun (BAY-ot-WORD / ˈbeːɔt-ˌwɔrd): Boast; threat.

blǣd, noun (BLAD / ˈblæːd): Glory, prosperity.

bliss, noun (BLISS / ˈblɪs): Bliss, joy.

ears-endu, noun (EH-arz-EN-duh / ˈɛarz-ˌɛn-dʌ): Buttocks.

ēce, adjective (AY-chuh / ˈeː-t͡ʃə): Perpetual, eternal.

ende, noun (EN-duh / ˈɛn-də): End.

ende-dæg, noun (EN-duh-DAIE / ˈɛn-də-ˌdæj): Last day, final day; day of death; Doomsday.

ende-mann, noun (EN-duh-MAHN / ˈɛn-də-ˌman): Person of this day, i.e. of the last age of the world (end-person).

ende-mest, adjective (EN-duh-MEST / ˈɛn-də-ˌmɛst): Endmost, last.

ende-tīma, noun (EN-duh-TEE-ma / ˈɛn-də-ˌtiː-ma): Final hour, the day of one's death.

end-wærc, noun (END-WAERK / ˈɛnd-ˌwærk): Pain in the buttocks or anus.

frōfor-word, noun (FRO-vor-WORD / ˈfroː-vɔr-ˌwɔrd): Word of consolation.

galdor-word, noun (GAL-dor-WORD / ˈgal-dɔr-ˌwɔrd): Word of incantation.

ge-witnes, noun (yeh-WIT-ness / jɛ-ˈwɪt-nɛs): Witness, testimony, knowledge; person who can provide testimony from personal observation; the practice of having witnesses present at a transaction.

gilp-word, noun (YILP-WORD / ˈjɪlp-ˌwɔrd): Boast.

glīw-word, noun (GLEE-ew-WORD / ˈgliːw-ˌwɔrd): Word of a song; song, poem.

heoru-word, noun (HEH-oh-ruh-WORD / ˈhɛɔ-rʌ-ˌwɔrd): Hostile or cutting word (sword-word).

here-word, noun (HEH-ruh-WORD / ˈhɛ-rə-ˌwɔrd): Praise, acclaim, approbation.

hosp-word, noun (HOSP-WORD / ˈhɔsp-ˌwɔrd): Word of contempt, insulting speech (shame-word).

irfe-gewrit, noun (IR-vuh-yeh-WRIT / ˈɪr-və-jɛ-ˌwrɪt): Will, testament, writing concerning an inheritance.

lāst, noun (LAHST / ˈlast): Step, track, trace.

lāst-word, noun (LAHST-WORD / ˈlast-ˌwɔrd): Reputation.

mann-þwǣre, adjective (MAHN-THWAE-ruh / ˈman-ˌθwæː-rə): Gentle, courteous.

milde, adjective (MILL-duh / ˈmɪl-də): Mild, gentle.

sceand-word, noun (SHEH-ond-WORD / ˈʃɛand-ˌwɔrd): Scornful or abusive speech (shame-word).

sorh-word, noun (SOR'H-WORD / ˈsɔrx-ˌwɔrd): Word of sorrow or anxiety.

sōþ, noun (SOATH / ˈsoːθ): Truth.

sōþlīce, adverb (SOATH-LEE-chuh / ˈsoːθ-ˌliː-t͡ʃə): Truly, really, certainly.

teran, verb (TEH-rahn / ˈtɛ-ran): To tear, rend, lacerate.

torn, noun (TORN / ˈtɔrn): Violent emotion of anger or grief.

torn-word, noun (TORN-WORD / ˈtɔrn-ˌwɔrd): Word that causes distress or grief; contemptuous or scornful word.

þanc-word, noun (THONK-WORD / ˈθank-ˌwɔrd): Word of thanks.

un-āsecgendlīc, adjective (UN-ah-SEDGE-end-leech / ˈʌn-aː-ˌsɛdʒ-ɛnd-liːtʃ): Beyond the powers of language to describe, unspeakable, ineffable; not proper to tell, not to be told.

wed, noun (WED / ˈwɛd): Pledge.

wit, noun (WIT / ˈwɪt): Wit, intelligence, understanding.

wit-word, noun (WIT-WORD / ˈwɪt-ˌwɔrd): Testament, covenant, statement that bears witness to something.

word-lēan, noun (WORD-LAY-ahn / ˈwɔrd-ˌleːan): Reward for words.

word-loca, noun (WORD-LOCK-ah / ˈwɔrd-ˌlɔ-ka): 'Word-locker', store of words.

word-samnere, noun (WORD-SAHM-neh-ruh / ˈwɔrd-ˌsam-nɛ-rə): Gatherer or collector of words.

woruld-ende, noun (WOR-uld-EN-duh / ˈwɔ-rʌld-ˌɛn-də): End of the world.

wuldor, noun (WUL-dor / ˈwʌl-dɔr): Glory.

Þanc-word (*thank-words*)

My first 'thank-words' are to the people to whom this book is dedicated. Thanks to my mum and dad for encouraging me to be a writer or, indeed, to be anything I wished to be. And thanks to Ryan for always believing in me, for providing thoughtful feedback and for making my *morgen-drenc* every morning.

I am indebted to many brilliant, thoughtful and generous people who provided information, advice, encouragement, critiques, feedback and inspiration on my book-writing and Old English-ing journeys.

Thanks to Louisa Dunnigan, my talented and *word-snotor* editor. Her suggestions, recommendations and critiques have vastly improved this book. Working with her has been a pleasure and a privilege. I am also grateful for the sharp eyes and careful editing of Linden Lawson. Thanks to Joanna Lisowiec for creating such a lovely cover.

I am grateful to my agent Charlie Campbell, who found the perfect home for this book at Profile. Thanks also to Andrew Furlow for his encouragement and advice early on in this book's creation.

Thanks to all my colleagues at King's College London who created a physical *wordhord* with me at Furtherfield Gallery in 2013: Fran Allfrey, Josh Davies, Rebecca Hardie, Carl Kears, Clare Lees, Kathryn Maude, James Paz and Victoria Walker. This event is what inspired @OEWordhord, and @OEWordhord is what ultimately inspired this book.

Thanks to Clare Lees, who supervised my doctoral dissertation and inspired me throughout my years at King's. If it weren't for her enthusiasm for public engagement and creative pedagogy, I would never have taken this path. I am grateful for her insistence that I step away from my work and play with Old English.

Thanks to the early readers of this book, the friends and family who so thoughtfully and generously provided feedback on early drafts and who supported me in the challenge of writing a book proposal: Teresa Crist, Ryan Lintott, Kathryn Maude, Fuad Musallam, Shirley Roseblade, Tara Roseblade, Susan Videen and Tom Videen.

Thanks to the Toronto *Dictionary of Old English*, especially Stephen Pelle, for sponsoring my access to library resources at the University of Toronto. I could not have completed this book without that access. I am indebted to the hard work of everyone who has contributed to *DOE* entries A to I, whether by researching, editing or coding. Thanks also to Hal Momma, who first introduced me to the *Dictionary* community by inviting me to 'cake day'.

Thanks to Craig Davis, the person who introduced me to Old English in the first place. I took his undergraduate class on a whim due to his infectious enthusiasm for history and dead languages. He was stuck with me in all his classes for the next four years.

Thanks to the members of the Old English Facebook group and the #medievaltwitter cohort. These scholars have answered my most random questions and have even provided copies of articles I couldn't access. Megan Cavell, Teresa Crist, Janel Fontaine and Jennifer Neville all helped me access resources that contributed to this book.

Thanks to all the writing studio regulars at Firefly Creative Writing.

I am grateful to the kind and generous people who have supported Old English Wordhord on Patreon over the years.

And I suppose I should also thank Crash and Knives, my furry assistants, who sit on my books, walk on my keyboard and purr in my face whenever distractions are needed.

Sources

General

Bosworth-Toller Anglo-Saxon Dictionary: bosworth.ff.cuni.cz
Douay-Rheims and Latin Vulgate Bible: drbo.org/drl/index.htm
Middle English Compendium: quod.lib.umich.edu/m/middle-english-dictionary
Oxford English Dictionary: oed-com
Toronto *Dictionary of Old English: A to I*: doe.utoronto.ca

1 The Language You Thought You Knew

LANGUAGE HISTORY

C. Breay and J. Story, *Anglo-Saxon Kingdoms: Art, Word, War* (2018);
D. Crystal, *The Cambridge Encyclopedia of the English Language* (1995);
M. Mohr, *Holy Sh*t: A Brief History of Swearing* (2016).

ROMAN BRITAIN

T. Charles-Edwards, *After Rome* (2003); D. Crystal, *The Cambridge Encyclopedia of the English Language* (1995); J. Ramirez, *Power, Passion and Politics in Anglo-Saxon England: The Private Lives of the Saints* (2015).

RUNES

D. Crystal, *The Cambridge Encyclopedia of the English Language* (1995);
M. Findell, *Runes* (2014); R. I. Page, 'Runes', in *The Blackwell Encyclopaedia of Anglo-Saxon England*, ed. by J. Blair et al. (1999), pp. 401–3.

2 Eating and Drinking

FOOD

D. Banham, *Food and Drink in Anglo-Saxon England* (2004); D. Banham and R. Faith, *Anglo-Saxon Farms and Farming* (2014); M. Bayless, *The Early English Bread Project* (2016–17), earlybread.wordpress.com; A. Gautier, 'Cooking and cuisine in late Anglo-Saxon England', *Anglo-Saxon England* 41 (2013), 373–406; C. Hough and C. Kay, *Learning with the Online Thesaurus of Old English* (2017), oldenglishteaching.arts.gla.ac.uk; C. Lee, 'Earth's treasures: Food and drink', in *The Material Culture of Daily Living in the Anglo-Saxon World*, ed. by M. C. Hyer and G. R. Owen-Crocker (2011), pp. 142–56.

ROYAL JELLY

E. Crane, *The World History of Beekeeping and Honey Hunting* (1999); V. R. Pasupuleti et al., 'Honey, propolis, and royal jelly: A comprehensive review of their biological actions and health benefits', *Oxidative Medicine and Cellular Longevity* (2017).

TOOTH DECAY

W. J. Moore and M. E. Corbett, 'The distribution of dental caries in ancient British populations: I. The Anglo-Saxon period', *Caries Res.* 5 (1971), 151–68.

SCOTS

Lallans: The Scots Language Society, lallans.co.uk/index.php.

MISSOURI LAW

S. F. Colb, 'Meat and marriage: The menace of changing definitions', *Verdict* (27 Feb. 2019), verdict.justia.com/2019/02/27/meat-and-marriage-the-menace-of-changing-definitions.

MONASTIC HOURS

C. H. Lawrence, *Medieval Monasticism: Forms of Religious Life in Western Europe in the Middle Ages* (2001).

CATTLE

S. Payne, 'Animal husbandry', in *The Blackwell Encyclopaedia of Anglo-Saxon England*, ed. by J. Blair et al. (1999), pp. 38–9.

COR-SNÆD

H. Foxhall Forbes, *Heaven and Earth in Anglo-Saxon England: Theology and Society in an Age of Faith* (2013); S. L. Keefer, 'Ut omnibus honorificetur Deus: The *Corsnæd* Ordeal in Anglo-Saxon England', in *The Community, the Family, and the Saint: Patterns of Power in Early Medieval Europe*, ed. by J. Hill and M. Swan (1998), pp. 237–64; J. D. Niles, 'Trial by ordeal in Anglo-Saxon England: What's the problem with barley?', in *Early Medieval Studies in Memory of Patrick Wormald*, ed. by S. Baxter et al. (2009), pp. 369–82.

GODWIN, EARL OF WESSEX

William of Malmesbury, *Chronicle of the Kings of England (Gesta regum anglorum)*, ed. by J. A. Giles (1847).

3 Passing the Time

NORSE DEITIES

Snorri Sturluson's *Edda*, trans. and ed. by A. Faulkes (1987).

THE MENOLOGIUM

K. Karasawa, *The Old English Metrical Calendar (Menologium)* (2015).

PAGANISM

S. D. Church, 'Paganism in conversion-age Anglo-Saxon England: The evidence of Bede's *Ecclesiastical History* reconsidered', *History* 93.2 (2008), 162–80.

CREATION IN MARCH

Bede, *The Reckoning of Time (De temporum ratione)*, ed. by F. Wallis (1999); H. Foxhall Forbes, *Heaven and Earth in Anglo-Saxon England: Theology and Society in an Age of Faith* (2016); M. MacCarron, *Bede and Time: Computus, Theology and History in the Early Medieval World* (2020).

4 Learning and Working

MAKING MANUSCRIPTS

K. Doyle and P. Lovett, 'How to make a medieval manuscript', *Medieval England and France, 700–1200* (British Library), bl.uk/medieval-english-french-manuscripts/articles/how-to-make-a-medieval-manuscript; R. Gameson, 'The archaeology of the Anglo-Saxon book', in *The Oxford Handbook of Anglo-Saxon Archaeology*, ed. by H. Hamerow et al. (2011), pp. 797–823; R. Gameson, 'The material fabric of early British books', in *The Cambridge History of the Book in Britain: Volume 1, c.400–1100*, ed. by R. Gameson (2011), pp. 13–63.

YORKSHIRE DIALECT

F. K. Robinson, *A Glossary of Yorkshire Words and Phrases* (1855).

SOCIETY AND OCCUPATIONS

D. Banham and R. Faith, *Anglo-Saxon Farms and Farming* (2014); R. Britnell, 'The economy of British towns 600–1300', in *The Cambridge Urban History of Britain: Volume 1, 600–1540*, ed. by D. M. Palliser (2000), pp. 105–26.

WOMEN

D. Banham, 'Did ladies originally make their own bread? Gender, status and food production in early medieval England', IHR Food History Seminar (1 Oct. 2020), https://youtu.be/0oPACsIz6WI; D. Banham and R. Faith, *Anglo-Saxon Farms and Farming* (2014); J. T. Schulenburg, 'Women's monastic communities, 500–1100: Patterns of expansion and decline', *Signs* 14.2 (1989), 261–92.

LAUGHTER

E. G. Stanley, 'Wonder-Smiths and Others: *smið* Compounds in Old English Poetry', *Neophilologus* 101.2 (2017), 277–304.

TAX

D. Banham and R. Faith, *Anglo-Saxon Farms and Farming* (2014); A. Gautier, 'Hospitality in pre-Viking Anglo-Saxon England', *Early Medieval Europe* 17.1 (2009), 23–44; C. Lee, 'Earth's treasures: Food and drink', in *The Material Culture of Daily Living in the Anglo-Saxon World*, ed. by M. C. Hyer and G. R.

Owen-Crocker (2011), pp. 142–56; P. A. Stafford, 'The "Farm of One Night" and the organization of King Edward's estates in Domesday', *Economic History Review* 33.4 (1980), 491–502.

5 Playing (and More Drinking)

HOSPITALITY
A. Gautier, 'Hospitality in pre-Viking Anglo-Saxon England', *Early Medieval Europe* 17.1 (2009), 23–44; J. Kerr, '"Welcome the Coming and Speed the Parting Guest": Hospitality in twelfth-century England', *Journal of Medieval History* 33 (2007), 130–46.

LAMENT OF THE ROHIRRIM
J. R. R. Tolkien, *The Lord of the Rings: The Two Towers* (1954).

GREAT HALLS
M. H. Austin, 'Anglo-Saxon "Great Hall Complexes": Elite Residences and Landscapes of Power in Early England, *c.*AD 550–700' (unpublished doctoral thesis, University of Reading, 2017); J. Blair, *Building Anglo-Saxon England* (2018); H. Hamerow, 'Anglo-Saxon timber buildings and their social context', in *The Oxford Handbook of Anglo-Saxon Archaeology*, ed. by H. Hamerow et al. (2011), pp. 128–55; S. James et al., 'An early medieval building tradition', *Archaeological Journal* 141.1 (1984), 182–215; J. Ramirez, *Power, Passion and Politics in Anglo-Saxon England: The Private Lives of the Saints* (2015).

GLEE CLUB
R. Clark, *The Words of the Most Favourite Pieces, Performed at the Glee Club, the Catch Club, and Other Public Societies* (1814).

GRENDEL
J. Gardner, *Grendel* (1971).

ALCOHOL
M. Bayless, 'Entertainment', in *The Blackwell Encyclopaedia of Anglo-Saxon England*, ed. by J. Blair et al. (1999), p. 172; C. Fell, 'Old English Beor', *Leeds*

Studies in English 8 (1975), 76–95; C. Hough and C. Kay, *Learning with the Online Thesaurus of Old English* (2017), oldenglishteaching.arts.gla.ac.uk.

6 Making Friends and Enemies

FRIEND WORDS
D. Clark, 'The semantic range of *wine* and *freond* in Old English', *Neuphilologische Mitteilungen* 114.1 (2013), 79–93.

NAMES
P. H. Reaney, *A Dictionary of British Surnames*, 2nd edn, with corrections and additions by R. M. Wilson (1976).

SHOULDER-COMPANIONS
V. I. Scherb, 'Shoulder-companions and shoulders in *Beowulf*', in *Masculinities and Femininities in the Middle Ages and Renaissance*, ed. by F. Kiefer (2010), pp. 31–44.

GIFTS
R. E. Bjork, 'Speech as gift in *Beowulf*', *Speculum* 69.4 (1994), 993–1022; J. M. Hill, 'Gifts and Social Tension in *Beowulf*', in *Teaching 'Beowulf' in the Twenty-First Century*, ed. by H. Chickering et al. (2014), pp. 139–46; M. Mauss, *The Gift: The Form and Reason for Exchange in Archaic Societies* (1990); S. Pollington, 'The mead-hall community', *Journal of Medieval History* 37.1 (2011), 19–33; A. L. J. Thieme, 'The gift in *Beowulf*: Forging the continuity of past and present', *Michigan Germanic Studies* 22.2 (1996), 126–43.

WOMEN
C. G. Clark, 'Women's rights in early England', *Brigham Young University Law Review* 1 (1995), 207–36; C. Fell, *Women in Anglo-Saxon England* (1984).

ALONE TIME
B. Crane, 'The virtues of isolation', *The Atlantic* (30 March 2017), theatlantic.com/health/archive/2017/03/the-virtues-of-isolation/521100; Google Ngram Viewer, 'alone time' (1950–2008), books.google.com/ngrams.

CHURCH OF ST MICHAEL THE ARCHANGEL

'The Blickling homilies', in *Longman Anthology of Old English, Old Icelandic and Anglo-Norman Literatures*, ed. by R. North et al. (2011), pp. 733–9.

PANTHER

A. Payne, *Medieval Beasts* (1990).

7 Caring for Body and Mind

MEDICAL LEECHES

B. Maetz et al., 'Infections following the application of leeches: Two case reports and review of the literature', *Journal of Medical Case Reports* 6.364 (2012); R. N. Mory et al., 'The leech and the physician: Biology, etymology, and medical practice with *Hirudinea medicinalis*', *World Journal of Surgery* 24.7 (2000), 878–83.

EARLY MEDIEVAL MEDICINE

W. Bonser, *The Medical Background of Anglo-Saxon England* (1963); M. L. Cameron, *Anglo-Saxon Medicine* (1993); K. L. Jolly, *Popular Religion in Late Saxon England: Elf Charms in Context* (1996).

PENALTY FOR EYE GOUGING

Early English Laws (2009–2020), Institute for Historical Research and King's College London, earlyenglishlaws.ac.uk/laws; M. Firth, 'Allegories of sight: Blinding and power in late Anglo-Saxon England', *Cerae* 3 (2016), 1–33.

RINGS

J. Y. Akerman, 'An account of excavations in an Anglo-Saxon burial ground', *Archaeologia* 35 (1854), 259–78; C. Edwards, *The History and Poetry of Finger-Rings* (1855); G. F. Kunz, *Rings for the Finger: From the Earliest Known Times to the Present* (1917); M. Searle and K. W. Stevenson, *Documents of the Marriage Liturgy* (1992); E. van Houts, *Married Life in the Middle Ages, 900–1300* (2019).

BLOOD

C. W. Bynum, *Wonderful Blood: Theology and Practice in Late Medieval Northern Germany and Beyond* (2007); H. Videen, '*Blōd, Swāt*, and *Drēor*: Material, Poetic, and Religious Discourses on Blood in Anglo-Saxon Literature' (unpublished doctoral thesis, King's College London, 2016).

DEVIL-SICKNESS

P. Dendle, 'Lupines, manganese, and devil-sickness: An Anglo-Saxon medical response to epilepsy', *Bulletin of the History of Medicine* 75.1 (2001), 91–101; A. L. Meaney, 'The Anglo-Saxon view of the causes of illness', in *Health, Disease and Healing in Medieval Culture*, ed. by S. Campbell et al. (1992), pp. 12–33.

EPILEPSY

'Symptoms of epilepsy and seizures', *WebMD*, reviewed by C. Melinosky on 23 July 2020, webmd.com/epilepsy/guide/epilepsy-seizure-symptoms; 'Tonic-clonic (grand mal) seizures', *Johns Hopkins Medicine* (2021), hopkinsmedicine.org/health/conditions-and-diseases/epilepsy/tonic-clonic-grand-mal-seizures.

BALD'S LEECHBOOK AND MRSA

E. Connelly, 'Medieval medical books could hold the recipe for new antibiotics', *The Conversation* (17 Apr. 2017), theconversation.com/medieval-medical-books-could-hold-the-recipe-for-new-antibiotics-74490; F. Harrison et al., 'A 1,000-year-old antimicrobial remedy with antistaphylococcal activity', *American Society for Microbiology* 6.4 (2015).

8 The World Outside

MEDIEVAL WARM PERIOD

D. Banham, '"In the Sweat of thy Brow Shalt thou eat Bread": Cereals and cereal production in the Anglo-Saxon landscape', in *The Landscape Archaeology of Anglo-Saxon England*, ed. by N. J. Higham and M. J. Ryan (2010), pp. 175–92; C. Lee, 'Body and soul: Disease and impairment', in *The Material Culture of Daily Living in the Anglo-Saxon World*, ed. by M. C. Hyer and G. R. Owen-Crocker (2011), pp. 293–309; P. McKenna, '"Medieval Warm

Period" wasn't global or even all that warm, study says', *Inside Climate News* (4 Dec. 2015), insideclimatenews.org/news/04122015/medieval.

NEORXNAWANG

J. W. Bright, *An Anglo-Saxon Reader* (1913); A. K. Brown, 'Neorxnawang', *Neuphilologische Mitteilungen* 74.4 (1973), 610–23; S. M. Hordis, 'Neorxnawang: Ælfric's flawed Anglo-Saxon paradise', *The Heroic Age* 16 (2015); G. Vigfússon, *Corpus Poeticum Boreale: The Poetry of the Old Northern Tongue from the Earliest Times to the Thirteenth Century* (1883).

PROGNOSTICS

R. M. Liuzza, *Anglo-Saxon Prognostics: An Edition and Translation of Texts from London, British Library, MS Cotton Tiberius A. iii* (2010).

TREE WATERED BY ABEL'S BLOOD

C. D. Wright, 'The blood of Abel and the branches of sin: *Genesis A, Maxims I* and Aldhelm's *Carmen de Uirginitate*', *Anglo-Saxon England* 25 (1996), 7–19.

RIDDLES

C. Fanger, 'A suggestion for a solution to Exeter Book Riddle 55', *Scintilla* 2–3 (1985–6), 19–28; K. P. Taylor, 'Mazers, mead, and the wolf's-head tree: A reconsideration of Old English Riddle 55', *Journal of English and Germanic Philology* 94.4 (1995), 497–512; F. Tupper Jr, *The Riddles of the Exeter Book* (1910).

BEES

F. Ruttner et al., *The Dark European Honey Bee: Apis mellifera mellifera Linnaeus 1758*, 2nd edn (2004).

9 Wildlife

NATURE

J. Neville, *Representations of the Natural World in Old English Poetry* (1999).

BESTIARIES

R. Barber (trans. and ed.), *Bestiary: Being an English Version of the Bodleian Library, Oxford MS Bodley 764* (1999); A. Payne, *Medieval Beasts* (1990).

ORIGIN OF 'ANIMAL'
J. Cresswell, *The Oxford Dictionary of Word Origins*, 2nd edn (2009).

BEES
L. Lentini, '20 things you didn't know about ... bees',
Discover Magazine (7 Mar. 2007), discovermagazine.com/
the-sciences/20-things-you-didnt-know-about-bees.

TRONDHEIM
G. Vigfússon, *An Icelandic-English dictionary, based on the ms. collections of the late Richard Cleasby* (1874).

BATS
M. J. A. Thompson, 'The Pipistrelle Bat (*Pipistrellus pipistrellus* Schreber) on the Vale of York', *The Naturalist*, 115.993 (1990), 41–56.

ALEXANDER'S LETTER TO ARISTOTLE
R. D. Fulk (trans. and ed.), *The 'Beowulf' Manuscript: Complete Texts and 'The Fight at Finnsburg'* (2010).

10 Travel

TRAVELLING ABROAD
C. Breay and J. Story, *Anglo-Saxon Kingdoms: Art, Word, War* (2018).

ST WILLIBRORD
Alcuin's *Life of St Willibrord*, in *The Anglo-Saxon Missionaries in Germany*, trans. and ed. by C. H. Talbot (1954); F. van der Pol, 'The Middle Ages to 1200', in *Handbook of Dutch Church History*, ed. by H. J. Selderhuis (2014), pp. 17–98.

LAWS
L. Oliver, *The Beginnings of English Law* (2012).

TRANSPORT AND ROADS
C. P. Biggam, 'The true staff of life: The multiple roles of plants', in *The Material Culture of Daily Living in the Anglo-Saxon World*, ed. by M. C. Hyer and G. R. Owen-Crocker (2011), pp. 23–48.

WINE-WHINE MERGER

A. M. Bruce, 'The development of orthographic *Wh-* in Early Middle English', *Journal of English Linguistics* 25.2 (1997), 97–101; J. Kruse, 'Accent variation reflected in the standard writing system of English', in *The Routledge Handbook of the English Writing System*, ed. by V. Cook and D. Ryan (2016), pp. 175–88.

BETHLEHEM

R. R. Losch, *The Uttermost Part of the Earth: A Guide to Places in the Bible* (2005).

PARIS PSALTER

R. Emms, 'The scribe of the Paris Psalter', *Anglo-Saxon England* 28 (1999), 179–83.

HOF

H. Lee, 'Follies of Konglish', *The Korea Times*, Seoul (4 June 2014), koreatimes.co.kr/www/news/opinon/2016/06/162_158502.html.

BOATS AND SEAFARING

C. P. Biggam, 'The true staff of life: The multiple roles of plants', in *The Material Culture of Daily Living in the Anglo-Saxon World*, ed. by M. C. Hyer and G. R. Owen-Crocker (2011), pp. 23–48; J. Blair, *Building Anglo-Saxon England* (2018); A. Lutz, 'Æthelweard's Chronicon and Old English poetry', *Anglo-Saxon England* 29 (2000), 177–214; K. Thier, 'Steep vessel, high horn-ship: Water transport', in *The Material Culture of Daily Living in the Anglo-Saxon World*, ed. by M. C. Hyer and G. R. Owen-Crocker (2011), pp. 49–72.

MONSTROUS WHALES

Isidore of Seville's *Etymologies*, Book 12, Chapter 6; Pliny's *Historia Naturalis*, Book 9, Chapter 4.

KNUCKER

'Dragons & serpents in Sussex', *Sussex Archaeology & Folklore*, sussexarch. org.uk/saaf/dragon.html.

NUCKELAVEE

W. T. Dennison, 'Orkney Folklore. Sea Myths', *Scottish Antiquary* 5.19 (1891), 130–33.

DEPTFORD CREEK NECKER

'Drowned lair: The Deptford Creek Necker', *Portals of London* (13 Jan. 2019), portalsoflondon.com/2019/01/13/drowned-lair-the-deptford-creek-necker.

11 Beyond Human

TRANSLATIONS OF *HELL-RŪNE* IN *BEOWULF*

'Hell-demons' (E. T. Donaldson); 'those in conspiracy with hell' (S. A. J. Bradley); 'reavers from hell' (S. Heaney); 'hell's intimates' (R. D. Fulk); 'those who share hell's secrets' (M. Swanton); 'hell-whisperers' (K. Crossley-Holland).

DRUIDS

B. Cunliffe, *Druids: A Very Short Introduction* (2010).

ELVES

A. Hall, *Elves in Anglo-Saxon England* (2007); A. Meaney, 'Folklore', in *The Blackwell Encyclopaedia of Anglo-Saxon England*, ed. by J. Blair et al. (1999), p. 189; R. C. A. Prior, *On the Popular Names of British Plants*, 2nd edn (1870); G. Storms, *Anglo-Saxon Magic* (1948).

WEARG

J. Neville, 'Monsters and criminals: Defining humanity in Old English poetry', in *Monsters and the Monstrous in Medieval Northwest Europe*, ed. by K. E. Olsen and L. A. J. R. Houwen (2001), pp. 103–22.

WARGS

H. Carpenter and C. Tolkien, *The Letters of J. R. R. Tolkien* (1981); J. R. R. Tolkien, *The Hobbit* (1937) and *The Fellowship of the Ring* (1954); HBO's *Game of Thrones*, Season 3, Episode 2 (2013).

WARLOCKS

Wizards RPG Team, *Dungeons & Dragons Player's Handbook* (2014).

ORCS

H. Carpenter and C. Tolkien, *The Letters of J. R. R. Tolkien* (1981).

TRANSLATIONS OF *LAÞUM FINGRUM* IN *BEOWULF*

'Loathsome fingers' (E. Morgan, S. A. J. Bradley); 'horrible fingers' (T. Meyer); 'savage talons' (S. Heaney); 'hostile claws' (R. M. Liuzza).

12 Searching for Meaning

CONVERSION TO CHRISTIANITY

C. Breay and J. Story, *Anglo-Saxon Kingdoms: Art, Word, War* (2018); M. P. Brown, 'Writing in the insular world', in *The Cambridge History of the Book in Britain: Volume 1, c.400–1100*, ed. by R. Gameson (2011), pp. 121–66; N. J. Higham, *The Convert Kings: Power and Religious Affiliation in Early Anglo-Saxon England* (1997).

RESPONSES TO PAGANISM

R. Frank, 'Germanic legend in Old English literature', in *The Cambridge Companion to Old English Literature*, 2nd edn, ed. by M. Godden and M. Lapidge (2013), pp. 88–106; P. Wormald, 'Anglo-Saxon society and its literature', in ibid., pp. 1–22.

RELIGION IN *BEOWULF*

Klaeber's Beowulf, 4th edn, ed. by R. D. Fulk et al. (2008); R. M. Liuzza, *Beowulf: A New Verse Translation* (2000).

LUNARIUMS

R. M. Liuzza, *Anglo-Saxon Prognostics: An Edition and Translation of Texts from London British Library, MS Cotton Tiberius A.III* (2010).

WYRD

M. Cavell, *Weaving Words and Binding Bodies* (2016).

13 Hoarding Words

GREEK *LOGOS*

H. G. Liddell and R. Scott, *An Intermediate Greek-English Lexicon* (1889).

LAW

T. J. McSweeney, 'Magna Carta and the right to trial by jury', in *Magna Carta: Muse and Mentor*, ed. by R. J. Holland (2014), pp. 139–57; P. Vinogradoff, *English Society in the Eleventh Century: Essays in Mediaeval History* (2005).

AMEN

A. Chupungco, 'Acclamations, liturgical', in *Encyclopedia of Ancient Christianity*, ed. by A. Di Berardino (2014), pp. 1:22–23; E. Ferguson, 'Amen', in *Encyclopedia of Early Christianity*, 2nd edn, ed. by E. Ferguson (1998), pp. 44–5.

SCRIBAL COMPLAINTS

S. J. Biggs, 'The burden of writing: Scribes in medieval manuscripts', *British Library Medieval Manuscripts Blog* (3 June 2014), https://blogs.bl.uk/digitisedmanuscripts/2014/06/the-burden-of-writing-scribes-in-medieval-manuscripts.html; T. Porck, 'Scribal complaints: Early medieval English copyists and their colophons', *ThijsPorck.com* (12 June 2017), https://thijsporck.com/2017/06/12/scribal-complaints.

MANUSCRIPT SURVIVAL

S. A. J. Bradley, *Anglo-Saxon Poetry* (1982).

Images

I am grateful to the British Library for making the images from their online Catalogue of Illuminated Manuscripts free to access, download and reuse. Catalogue information is made available under a Creative Commons CC0 1.0 Universal Public Domain Dedication.

page 6
Beginning of *Beowulf*. British Library, MS Cotton Vitellius A XV, folio 132r.

page 45
Christ's Harrowing of Hell. British Library, Cotton MS Nero C IV, folio 24r.

page 64
Animal skin is pretty sturdy, far more resilient than paper, but occasionally a repair is required. Here a hole in the *bōc-fell* has been stitched shut. British Library, Harley MS 55, folio 5r.

page 70
Latin: '*Quid dicit tu arator? Quomodo exerces opus tuum?*' Old English: '*Hwæt sægest þu yrþlingc? Hu begæst þu weorc þin?*' British Library, Cotton MS Tiberius A III, folio 60v.

page 123
A remedy from *Bald's Leechbook*. Many of the remedies start with *wiþ* (against): against headache, against mistiness of the eyes, against *smēga-wyrm* (Chapter 2), etc. Each *wiþ* here begins with a decorated W-rune ᚹ (*wynn*, Chapter 5). British Library, Royal MS 12 D XVII, folio 23v.

A Note from the Author

If you enjoyed this book and would like more Old English words in your life, you can follow me on Twitter at @OEWordhord, or download the Old English Wordhord app, for a new word every day.

oldenglishwordhord.com